DIGITAL CIRCUIT DESIGN

LABORATORY MANUAL
FIFTH EDITION

Akhan Almagambetov
J. Matt Pavlina
Yelena Mukhortova

Typeset using LaTeX in Times New Roman font. Headings set in Titling Gothic. Monotype text is set in M+1. Submitted to the publisher on 25 Apr 2020. Printed and bound in the United States by Automasis. Not for sale outside of the United States.

ISBN 978-1-71699-988-8 (paperback)

Keywords: 1. Electronic circuit design. 2. VHDL (Computer hardware description language). 3. System design.

Table of Contents

Laboratory Introduction

Complete all work in this notebook, as it will be evaluated for completeness at the end of the semester. **Screenshots and answers in the laboratory section must also be submitted on a separate submission page** (download link is available at the start of each laboratory section). A sample link is given in the margins.

GRADE SHEET DOWNLOAD
`https://sample.url`

Formatting Guidelines

A two-point penalty will be assessed for not adhering to the formatting guidelines below.

- **Complete ALL work in this notebook using a pen.** The only place when pencil should be used is for drawing breadboard circuit diagrams.
- **Do NOT scribble out any work or use correction fluid.** If corrections are made, use a single cross-out, initial, and date. Use scratch paper to avoid excessive corrections.
- Space will be provided to insert code and diagrams into the notebook: cut down the document and use tape around the edges. Prior to taping the right side, initial and date in the **bottom right** corner of the document, making sure that the date spans onto the notebook page (**Fig. 1**). **Do NOT sign across the tape!**

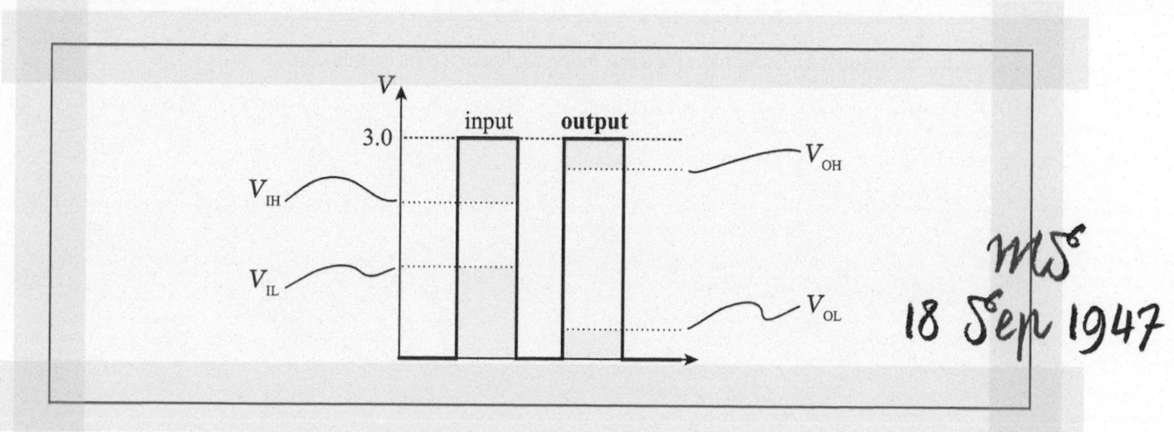

Figure 1: Example of adding deliverables to the lab notebook.

Make sure to have all code and schematics labeled as described in this section, prior to pasting them into the lab notebook. Block diagrams may need to be scaled by taking a screenshot and resizing it in a third-party image manipulation or word processing application.

VHDL Code Formatting Guidelines

All VHDL code must include a comments header, which contains the following (an example of a typical header is given below):

- Full name
- Sort number (if assigned)
- Course number and section
- Laboratory number
- Date created
- A brief description of the code

```
-- V. Shelkova (Sort No. 000)
-- CEC222.PC50 Lab #03
-- 14 Jun 2015
-- Description:
-- LAB03.VHD - VHDL implementation of 2-input AND gate logic circuit
```

Block Diagram Formatting Guidelines

Identifying information should be placed in the **lower right** corner of all block diagrams to ascertain that they are your own work (**Fig. 2**).

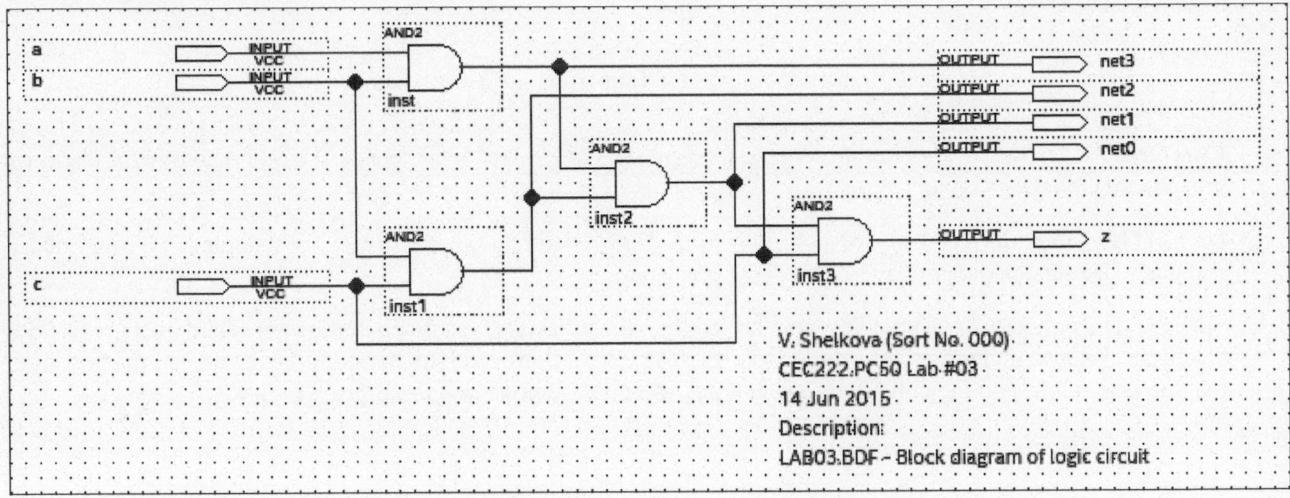

Figure 2: Example of adding deliverables to the lab notebook.

Pre-laboratory Grading

Pre-labs are due at the **start of the laboratory period** and must be completed in the laboratory notebook. A tardiness of 20 or more minutes without prior approval from the instructor constitutes a zero on the pre-laboratory portion. The pre-laboratory deliverables must be taped in to the notebook prior to lab and must adhere to the formatting guidelines.

It is the responsibility of the student to get the pre-lab tasks verified at the beginning of the lab period. If the pre-lab is not verified by the time most groups have started working on the lab, a zero grade will be assigned for the pre-lab portion.

Print the grading sheet, available as a downloadable PDF link on the first page of each laboratory, prior to coming to the laboratory (see example in the margin).

GRADE SHEET DOWNLOAD
https://sample.url

Task Completion

Initially, the pre-labs will be graded based on task completion. If the code was simply copied from an example (without addressing pre-lab assignment requirements), an "unsatisfactory" grade will be assigned. The same applies to incomplete circuit diagrams, tables, etc.

If the grader is using stamps to mark completion, stamps that fill the entire grade box will signify "satisfactory" (vertical), whereas horizontal stamps across the box will indicate "unsatisfactory". If no attempt has been made or the attempt was mostly incomplete, the verification box will be left empty.

If signatures are used, a line through the signature will signify an unsatisfactory mark.

Lab Submission

Lab tasks must be submitted (on a separate printable sheet of paper) to the instructor at the end of the laboratory period, regardless of the current state of completion. Required deliverables are listed on the printable grading sheet. Lab notebooks will be graded for completeness at the end of the semester—complete the laboratory tasks in the lab notebook.

In very rare circumstances, the instructor may grant an extension for lab notebook submission to the entire class. Individual exceptions will not be made.

Prior to leaving the lab (ideally, when the equipment is assigned to you), note down the two-digit inventory numbers for the FPGA development board and the Analog Discovery scope in the box shown on the right. Every "Laboratory" section has the box printed in the margins.

For laboratories that span multiple periods, note down the inventory numbers and date in the same boxes, directly below the previous entry.

Grading Criteria

Your work in the pre-lab and lab will be evaluated based on the rubric in **Table 1**.

The pre-lab will count for 25% (5 points) and the lab will count toward 75% (5 points $\times 3$) of the grade. The maximum grade for any laboratory is 20 points.

Table 1: Rubric for evaluating pre-laboratory and laboratory work.

Points	ABET Indicator	Pre-lab Criteria	Lab Criteria
5	*Exemplary*	All problem solutions are correct, with only minor errors present. In the case of VHDL code or wiring diagrams, they closely represent what will be completed in laboratory.	The lab has been fully demonstrated as working. All of the necessary figures, code, and screen captures are included in the laboratory notebook.
4	*Satisfactory*	General approach is correct, with minor conceptual errors in the solution(s).	A minor error is preventing the device from functioning correctly during the demonstration. Very minimal omissions from the deliverables.
3	*Developing*	Some knowledge of the approach is demonstrated, but there are major conceptual errors in the solution(s).	The device functions, however does not function correctly due to major problems in the implementation. Some deliverables are missing.
2	*Unsatisfactory*	Solution(s) attempted, but the methods used are critically flawed or do not represent the correct approach.	The student is unable to demonstrate a working device, however most of the deliverables are present and it is evident that a significant amount of effort was expended in completing the laboratory.
1	*(Poor)*	Minimal progress made toward solution (*i.e.*, code is simply copied from examples).	Minimal progress has been made toward a functioning device or completing the lab experiment. Most of the deliverables are missing or are incorrect.
0	*(Fail)*	No effort toward completing the problem, random (incorrect) solution is given, or pre-lab not turned in or verified prior to the start of the lab period.	Lab notebook not turned in or laboratory not completed / device not demonstrated.

Directory Structure and File Organization

The note below also appears in **Appendix D.5.1** and is **very important**!

Directory Structure

Make sure that all of the lab Quartus project files are stored in an accessible, easy-to-navigate directory structure.

The required directory structure is given in (**Fig. 3**).

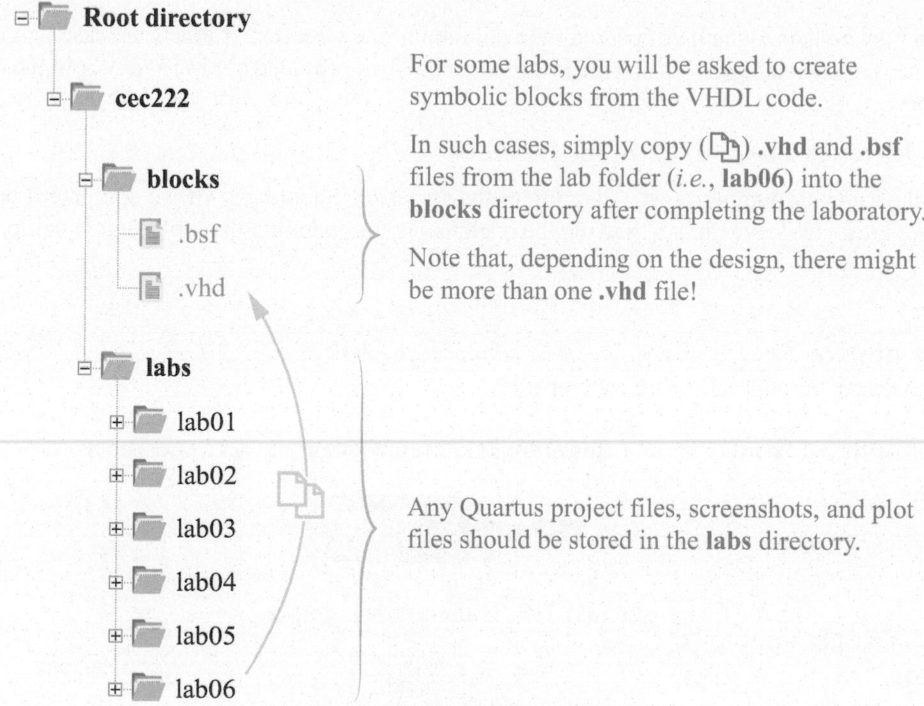

Root directory
cec222
blocks
.bsf
.vhd
labs
lab01
lab02
lab03
lab04
lab05
lab06
For some labs, you will be asked to create symbolic blocks from the VHDL code.
In such cases, simply copy ( ) .vhd and .bsf files from the lab folder (i.e., lab06) into the blocks directory after completing the laboratory.
Note that, depending on the design, there might be more than one .vhd file!
Any Quartus project files, screenshots, and plot files should be stored in the labs directory.

Figure 3: Required directory structure.

Note that not following these requirements will make later labs an absolute nightmare to complete and maintain. Most of the code after **Laboratory 6** will be re-used for subsequent laboratories.

It is strongly suggested that you create the directory structure ahead of time. Make sure that both partners have a complete copy of both the `labs` and `blocks` directories at the end of each laboratory (in case partners are shuffled around or the drive is lost or corrupted). Even campus network drives have been known to get corrupted!

If this advice is not followed and all laboratory work is lost midway through the lab sequence, all of the required code will need to be re-created.

None of the folders or files can have spaces! Spaces will cause weird errors, which do not represent the actual error and are extremely difficult to troubleshoot.

For example, `/Documents and Settings/almagama/cec222/labs/lab06` would most likely cause an error. Despite there not being spaces in most folder names, `Documents and Settings` has spaces and would prevent some files from being accessed by Quartus.

Lab Kit Contents

Ordering and Availability Information

If you are taking this class online, a kit of parts should be available for purchase through the link on the course page within your Learning Management System. In a traditional laboratory setting, the kit of parts should be available for purchase through the school bookstore, as well as online through the link within the course page.

Inventory Sheet (for loaner kits)

In some cases, you may be loaned the kit of parts for the duration of the semester. If this is the case, you **must** inventory the kit prior to the start of each lab period using the inventory sheet (link provided below) and submit the completed sheet with each laboratory.

Link to printable inventory sheet: **`https://git.io/JeY1x`**

Make sure to use the same kit number for the duration of the semester. Should any of the equipment or parts be found damaged or missing after you leave the lab, you will be responsible for obtaining the replacement equipment/parts.

Kit Contents

The kit of parts should contain the following components:

- Intel DE10-Lite FPGA board
- Analog Discovery 2 scope
- **(5x)** male-to-male pin headers

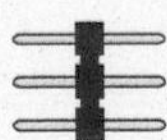

- **(6x)** male-female jumper wires

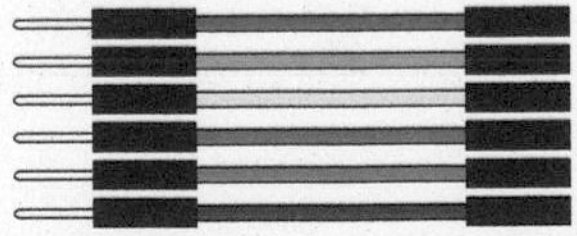

- **(5x)** LEDs

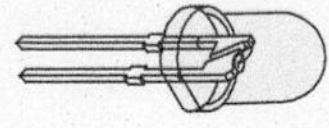

- TowerPro SG90 servo motor

- **(3x)** TIP122 power transistors

- DIP switch bank CTS 206-124

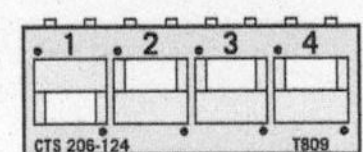

- seven-segment display 5166A

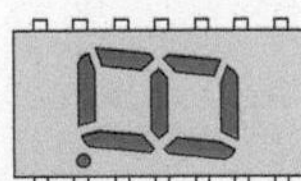

- SPDT switch

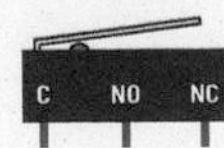

- resistors

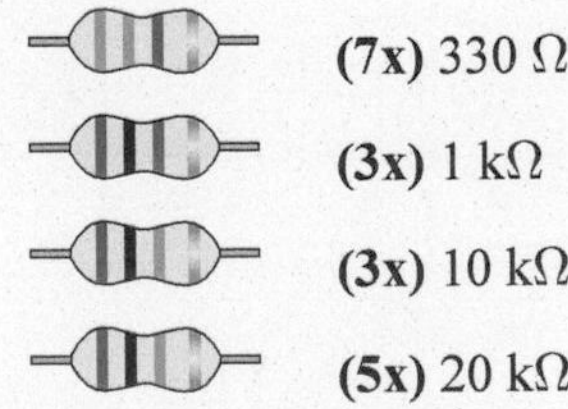

- integrated circuits (ICs)

  - **(2x)** 74HC00
  - **(2x)** 74HC02
  - **(2x)** 74HC04
  - **(2x)** 74HC08
  - **(2x)** 74HC32
  - **(2x)** 74HC86
  - 7447
  - 74590

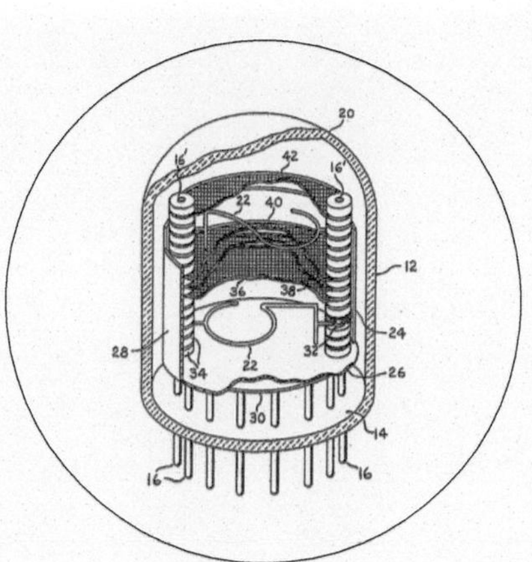

LABORATORIES

LABORATORY 1

Introduction to Digital Circuits Lab

1.1 Overview

This lab will cover the construction of a digital-to-analog converter (DAC) based on an R-2R resistor network. Four-bit digital values will be generated using a DIP switch module and converted to analog voltages using the DAC circuit. Calculated theoretical values will be compared to voltmeter measurements. At the conclusion of the lab, mystery signals will be measured using an oscilloscope to determine the frequency and magnitude of unknown digital signals.

GRADE SHEET DOWNLOAD
https://git.io/JeYME

1.2 Objectives

At the conclusion of this lab, the student should be able to:

1. Select resistors based on value / color code.
2. Identify basic components (*e.g.*, breadboard, switches, resistors).
3. Construct a resistor-based circuit using basic components.
4. Describe scenarios requiring test and measurement tools (*e.g.*, oscilloscope, voltmeter).
5. Outline steps required for using the oscilloscope to visualize time-variant signals.
6. Interpret results obtained from measurement equipment.
7. Distinguish between analog and digital signals, explain fundamental difference between the two signal types.

1.3 Background

Before starting the pre-laboratory exercise, read **Appendices A.1**, **A.3**, and **A.5**. This will provide a basic overview of the components used in this laboratory.

This lab will require the construction of a four-bit digital-to-analog converter (DAC) using an R-2R resistor network. The switch module will be used to generate a four-bit digital value, which will be converted into an analog voltage using the DAC circuit.

1.3.1 Theoretical Operation

An R-2R resistor network (**Fig. 1.1**) weights the contribution of each input to the final output voltage. This is the simplest and cheapest implementation of a DAC, since it uses only two resistor values (10 kΩ and 20 kΩ, for example).

One major drawback is that mismatched resistors in the upper bits can cause non-monotonic behavior, where the output is not linearly related to the binary input. Mismatches can even occur due to high tolerance values—the resistors are all within the manufacturer's specifications, however due to high variance, the DAC is not accurate.

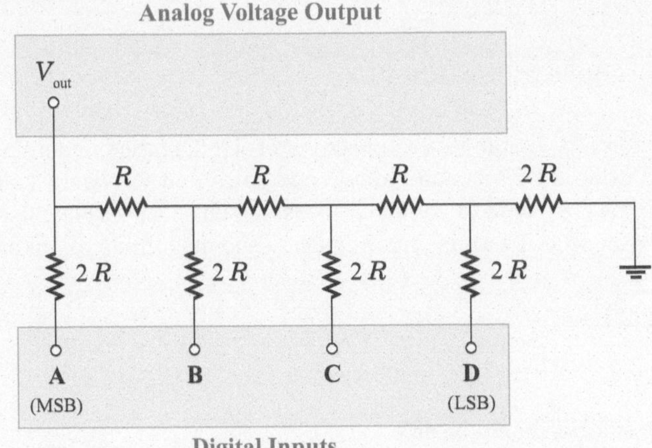

Figure 1.1: Theoretical four-bit R-2R resistor network.

The DAC in **Fig. 1.1** accepts a four-bit binary input (*ABCD*), where A is the most significant bit (MSB) and D is the least significant bit (LSB).

A general formula for deriving the output of an R-2R DAC is given in **Eq. (1.1)**.

$$V_{\text{out}} = V_{\text{supply}} \times \frac{\text{input}_{10}}{2^n - 1}, \tag{1.1}$$

where n denotes the number of bits in the input. The input is given as a base-10 decimal number.

For example, if the supply voltage is 5V DC and the binary number to be converted is 7 (*ABCD* switch settings are **0111**), the output will be equal to $V_{\text{out}} = 5 \times \left(7/\left[2^4 - 1\right]\right) = 2.333$ V.

1.4 Pre-laboratory

Complete this pre-laboratory exercise prior to the laboratory period. All work must be completed **in pen**. To allow for revisions, circuit diagrams may be completed in pencil. **Download and print** (single-sided) the grade sheet for this laboratory on the first page of this section.

1.4.1 Analog Discovery

Read **Appendices B.1** and **B.2** (Analog Discovery [AD]). Answer the following questions:

5E .. 1

1. Which leads of the AD are used for the oscilloscope/voltmeter? Which leads are used for the power supply? Specify colors and symbols on the pigtail connector of the AD.

2. What does the term *triggering* mean, in the context of capturing signals with a scope? Why do channels have to be triggered? How is triggering adjusted?

1.4.2 Wiring Basics

Using **Appendix A.1** of the lab manual, perform the following tasks:

5E .. 2

1. Complete **Table 1.1** with the appropriate resistor colors. Assume a 5% tolerance.

Table 1.1: Resistor value to color conversion.

Value (Ω)	1st band	2nd	3rd	4th
10 k				
20 k				
330				

2. Complete **Table 1.2** with the appropriate resistor values.

Table 1.2: Resistor color to value conversion.

Resistor				Value (Ω)	Tolerance (%)
red	yellow	green	silver		
brown	red	black	gold		
green	red	gold	gold		
yellow	violet	silver	gold		
orange	orange	brown	silver		

1.4.3 Digital-to-Analog Converter

5E ·· 3 Noting that the 4-bit binary pattern **0000** corresponds to a base-10 value of zero and **1111** corresponds to 15, use **eq. (1.1)** to fill out the *Base-10* and *Calculated* V_{out} *(V)* columns in **Table 1.3** on page 9. Assume a four-bit R-2R DAC with a supply voltage of 5.0 VDC.

1.4.4 Interpreting Oscilloscope Measurements

Given an oscilloscope plot of a single period of a square wave with a magnitude of 0 V to 3.3 V and frequency of $f = 1$ kHz, shown in **Fig. 1.2**, determine the *horizontal time scale*, in seconds per division (s/div) and the vertical magnitude scale in Volts per division (V/div) [*i.e.,* What does one box represent in the horizontal dimension? In the vertical dimension?].

Recall that $f = 1/T$.

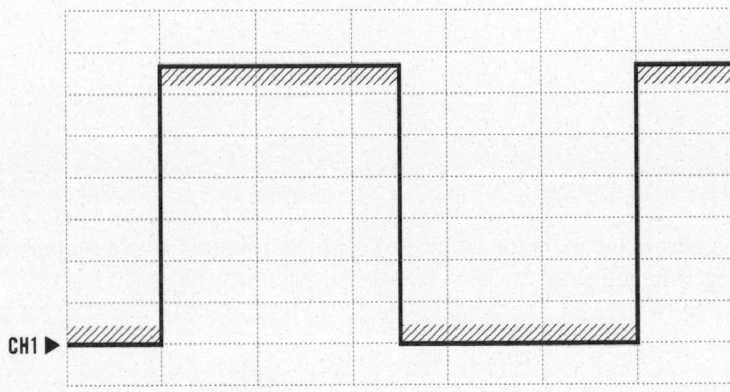

Figure 1.2: 1 kHz 0-3.3V square wave.

Magnitude (peak-to-peak voltage): ______________ Volts

5E ·· 4

Period: ______________ seconds

What does each division of the graph represent?

Horizontal magnitude scale: ______________ s/div

Vertical magnitude scale: ______________ V/div

1.5 Laboratory

1.5.1 Required Equipment and Parts

The following items are needed to complete this laboratory:

- breadboard
- resistors (5x 20 kΩ and 3x 10 kΩ)
- wires
- DIP switch bank (CTS 206-124)
- Analog Discovery scope
- FPGA board, USB cable

1.5.2 Circuit Wiring

Using the breadboard in **Fig. 1.4** with the switch bank already placed, draw resistors and all necessary wires to implement the DAC in **Fig. 1.3**. Draw the connections to the AD device and **have the TA check the wiring diagram upon completion.**

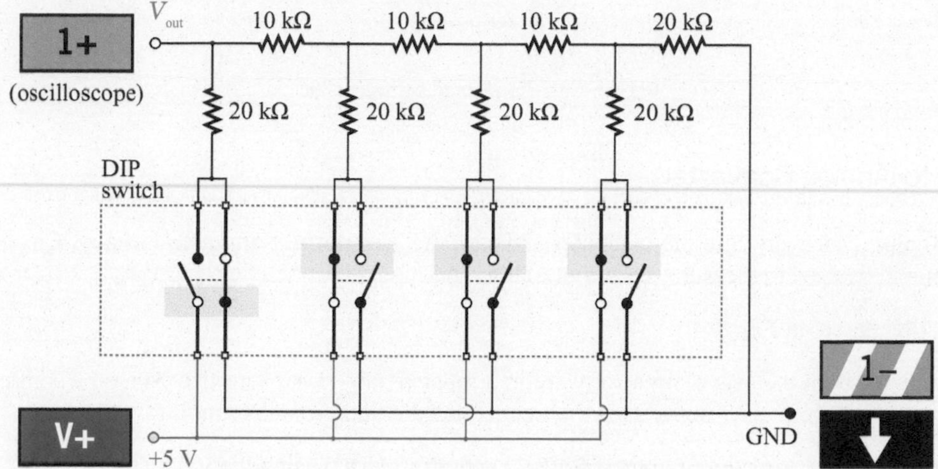

Figure 1.3: Switch and resistor connections for the DAC.

5E ·· 5

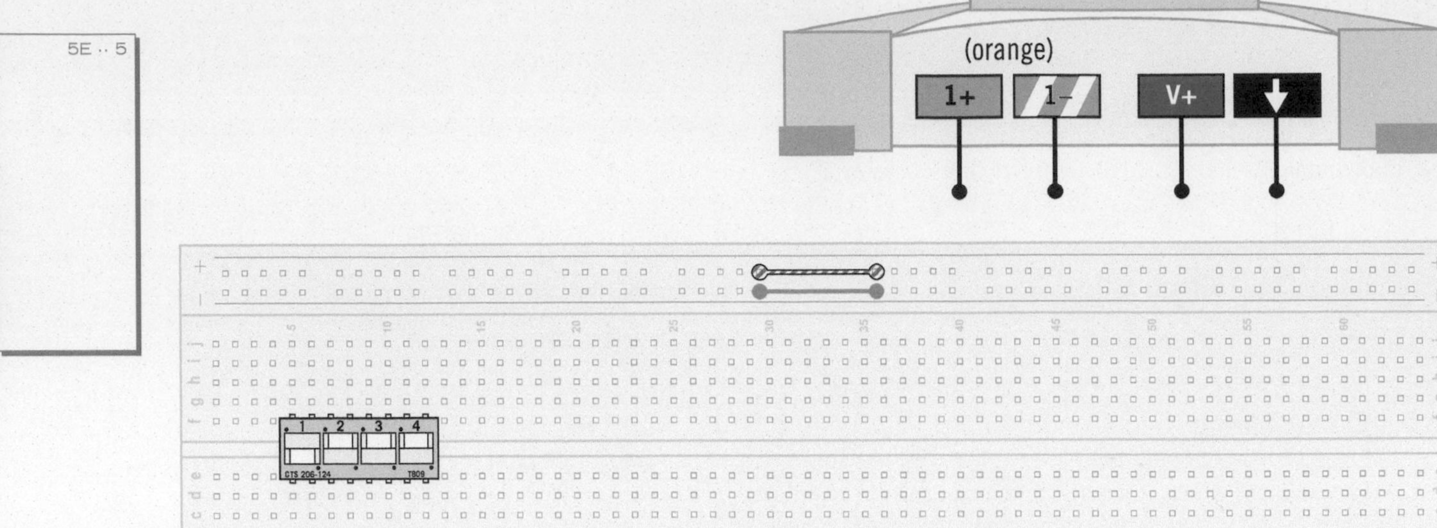

Figure 1.4: Breadboard configuration.

1.5.3 Digital-to-Analog Converter

1. Plug the Analog Discovery into the computer and start the Waveforms software. Initially, Ch. 1 of the **Logger** (voltmeter) will be used to measure the output of the DAC.
2. Build the DAC based on **Fig. 1.4**.
3. Turn on the **Supply** in the Waveforms software in a separate tab (make sure that **Master Enable** is on). Set the positive supply voltage to 5 V. Leave both the Logger and the Supplies tabs running.
4. Verify that each switch turns on (output of 5 VDC) and off (0 VDC) using the voltmeter.
5. Connect the voltmeter to the circuit. If all of the switches are flipped to the 'on' position, the output should be approximately 4.5-5 VDC; if all of the switches are off, the value should be close to zero (a couple of millivolts).

   Record V_{out} measurements of all 16 binary switch combinations in **Table 1.3**. **Demonstrate your set-up to a teaching assistant after you have filled out the table.**

   5E ·· 6 Explain the function of the DAC using results from **Table 1.3**:

1.5.4 Oscilloscope Measurements

The FPGA board has a pre-programmed mystery signal on pin 1 of the GPIO port (the 40-pin connector at the top of the board), which should be captured and characterized in this part of the experiment (everything else currently connected to the Analog Discovery can be safely disconnected).

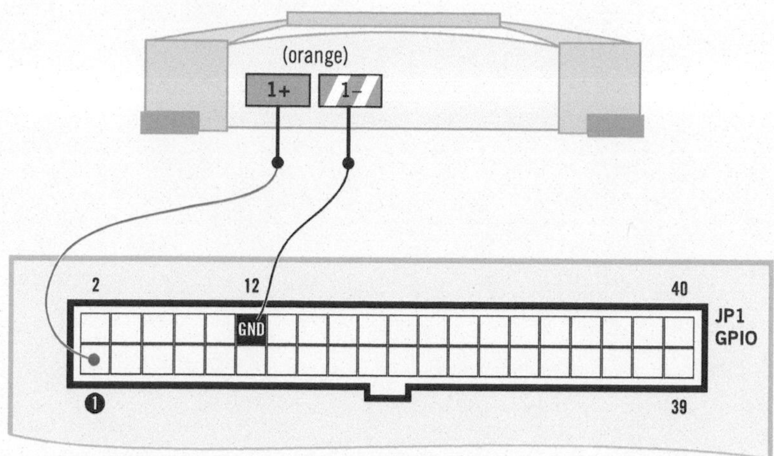

Figure 1.5: Connecting the oscilloscope to the FPGA board.

1. Connect Ch. 1+ to pin 1 of the GPIO port and Ch. 1− to the ground (GPIO pin 12), as indicated in **Fig. 1.5**. Plug the USB cable of the FPGA board into the computer.
2. Open the **Scope** screen of the Waveforms software. Trigger the oscilloscope. Once this step is completed, **demonstrate triggering to a teaching assistant.**
3. Determine the peak-to-peak magnitude (in Volts) and the frequency (in Hertz) of the captured waveform (either using automated measurement tools in the Waveforms software or by determining this information from the waveform).

Magnitude: ______________ V

Frequency: ______________ Hz

5E ·· 7

Table 1.3: Results of digital to analog conversion.

Base-2	Base-10	Calculated V_{out} (V)	Measured V_{out} (V)	$\lvert(\mathbf{M}-\mathbf{C})/\mathbf{C}*100\%\rvert$
0000	0	0		—
0001	1	0.333		
0010	2			
0011	3			
0100				
0101				
0110				
0111				
1000				
1001				
1010				
1011				
1100				
1101				
1110				
1111				

4. **Take a screen capture of the oscilloscope window**, while the oscilloscope is triggered and showing the waveform. Show more than one, but less that three periods of the waveform. You will likely need to further adjust the horizontal and vertical scales.

   Print out the capture and paste it below.

LABORATORY 2

FPGA Design Workflow

2.1 Overview

This laboratory will cover the workflow of programming an Intel FPGA development board using Intel Quartus software. The design of a digital-to-analog converter (DAC) from the previous laboratory will be used alongside an Intel FPGA board that will provide power and generate a four-bit digital value (input to the DAC circuit).

The second part of the laboratory will be using the DAC resistive network to drive a 7404 inverter integrated circuit (IC) with an analog voltage, monotonically increasing from 0 to 5 Volts. The behavior of the output will be observed and verified against the 7404 device data sheet.

GRADE SHEET DOWNLOAD
https://git.io/JeYMg

2.2 Objectives

At the conclusion of this laboratory, the student should be able to:

1. Follow the software workflow for new project development.
2. Target the appropriate FPGA part.
3. Assign pins on the field programmable gate array (FPGA) device, generate bitstream, and program the FPGA.
4. Interface circuits to the FPGA development board.
5. Interpret integrated circuit (IC) data sheets to determine gate characteristics.
6. Distinguish logic levels based on voltage readings.
7. Construct a circuit to test the functionality of ICs.
8. Outline the steps necessary for powering a gate IC and verifying its functionality.
9. Explain concepts relating to logic levels, Boolean values, binary values, and voltages.

2.3 Pre-laboratory

Complete this pre-laboratory exercise prior to the laboratory period. All work must be completed **in pen**. To allow for revisions, circuit diagrams may be completed in pencil.

2.3.1 Introduction to Intel Quartus

Review **Appendix C** on creating a new Intel Quartus project, implementing a logic circuit using VHDL, and programming an Intel FPGA development board. You may skip section **C.2** (*VHDL Primer*, we will cover this information in later labs). **Note that the code in the appendix is different than the code used in the laboratory!**

5E ·· 8

1. Which FPGA part no. will be targeted in the Intel DE10-Lite board?

2. Which characters are allowed in project and file names?

3. Five steps comprise the FPGA design workflow. In your own words, describe each one.

4. Briefly describe the steps for simulating *all input possibilities* of a digital circuit.

5. When using the Pin Planner tool, which values should I/O Standard, Current Strength, and Slew Rate be set to?

6. Which of the pin settings can be left at their *(default)* values?

2.3.2 Pin Assignments

Assign the pins in **Table 2.1** by referencing the FPGA development board pinout diagrams in **Appendix H**. As can be inferred from the port names, this design will use four switches, four LEDs, and four GPIO connector pins.

5E ·· 9

Table 2.1: Pin assignments table.

Port Name	Pin Location	Logic Level	Current Strength	Slew Rate
SW[3]	C12	3.3-V LVCMOS	2 mA	—
SW[2]				—
SW[1]				—
SW[0]				—
LEDR[3]	B10			2
LEDR[2]				
LEDR[1]				
LEDR[0]				
GPIO_1	V10			
GPIO_2				
GPIO_3				
GPIO_4				

2.3.3 Logic-HIGH/logic-LOW input and output

Review the data sheet of the 74HC04 inverter IC in **Appendix J**. Determine the meaning of (V_{IL}, V_{IH}) and (V_{OL}, V_{OH}) given in the data sheet. Some independent research may be necessary.

1. Describe the meanings of V_{IL}, V_{IH} and V_{OL}, V_{OH}, based on independent research and observations of the values in the datasheet.

2. What voltage ranges are guaranteed by the manufacturer to be interpreted as a logic-LOW/HIGH (assuming a supply voltage V_{CC} of 3.0 V and $t^{\circ} = 20°C$)? What is the range of output voltage that is guaranteed to indicate a logic-LOW/HIGH? Copy these values onto the diagram in **Fig. 2.1**.

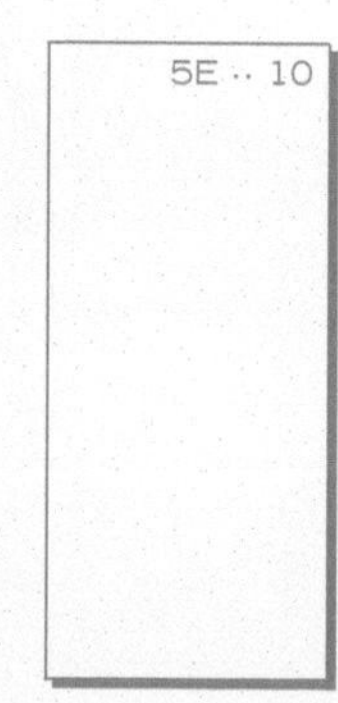

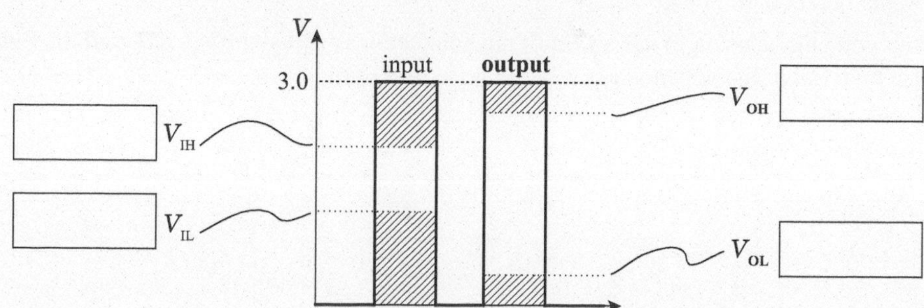

Figure 2.1: IC voltage ranges for logic-HIGH/LOW output.

2.3.4 Circuit schematic

IC data sheet pin listings will need to be translated into a breadboard setup to complete this laboratory. ICs have pin 1 marked by a deep notch in the middle of the chip or a small indentation near pin 1 of the chip (or both), see **Fig. 2.2**.

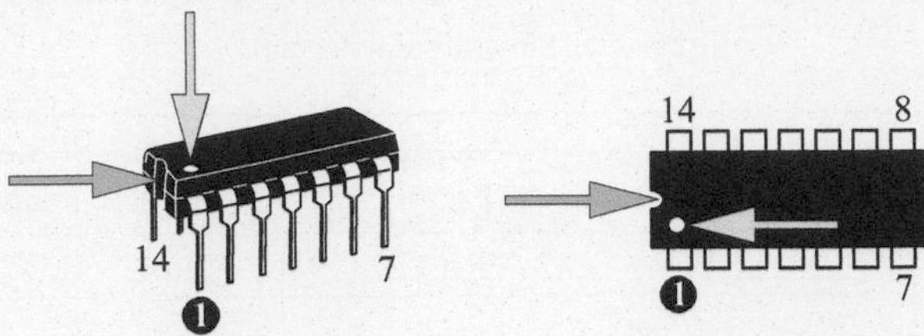

Figure 2.2: Pin 1 markings on standard IC DIP packages.

1. Determine the pins to be connected by referring to the 74HC04 data sheet in **Appendix J** and **Fig. 2.3**. Make sure to provide power and ground to the IC, in addition to using one of the input/output pairs on the 7404 IC (there are six inverters on the IC).

   Fill out the *IC Pin* column of **Table 2.2** with appropriate pin locations.

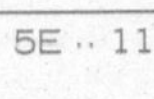

Table 2.2: Pin assignments for a single NOT gate.

Description	IC Pin	FPGA Board Pin	AD Pins
V_{CC}			NONE
GND			
input		NONE	
output		NONE	

2. The FPGA development board will supply the power to the IC and provide digital output from the switches. Using **Appendix H.2**, determine GPIO connector pins that provide 3.3 V and ground; add them to the *FPGA Board Pin* column of **Table 2.2**.

3. Both scope ports of the Analog Discovery will be used for this laboratory. Ch. 1 (**1+**) will capture the input voltage level to the IC, whereas Ch. 2 (**2+**) will capture the IC output voltage level. Ports **1-** and **2-** will be grounded. Complete the *AD Pins* column of **Table 2.2** with corresponding pin abbreviations.

   If you need to reference the Analog Discovery pin diagram, see **Appendix B**.

4. Draw the wiring diagram for the R-2R DAC, similar to the one from the previous laboratory. Be sure to use good technique allowing room to write in the values and easily observe the connections. The resistor network and chip are given in **Fig. 2.3**. Label the boxes near the pins in this figure with actual IC pin numbers, in order to make implementation easier.

   Using **Table 2.2**, draw wires from the IC, the GPIO connector of the development board, and the AD to the appropriate holes on the breadboard in **Fig. 2.4**.

   This is the setup you will be using in lab, so check pin connections against the IC, AD, and the FPGA development board reference material in the appendices.

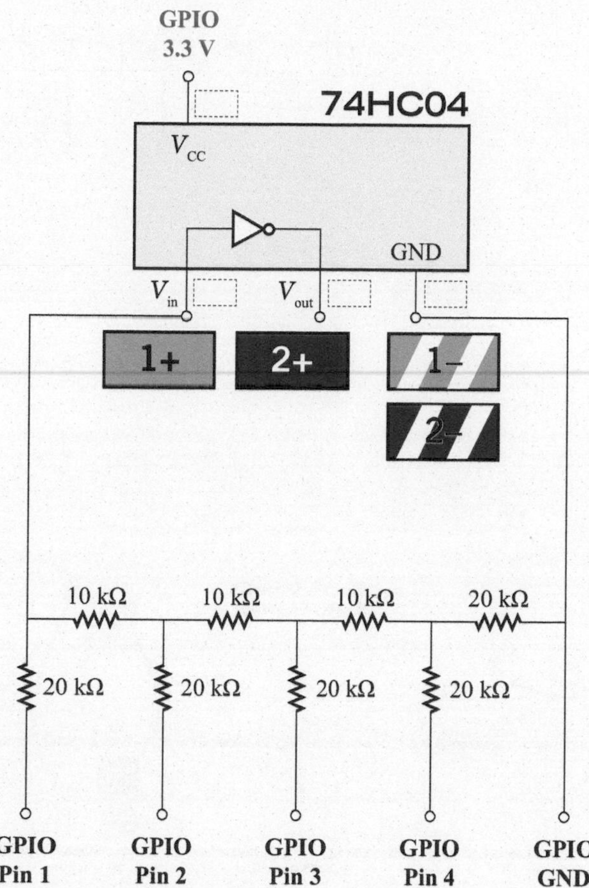

IC connection positions in the diagram do not represent the pin positions on the chip. Use the IC data sheet to determine pin locations and function.

Figure 2.3: Resistive DAC connected to a 74HC04 IC.

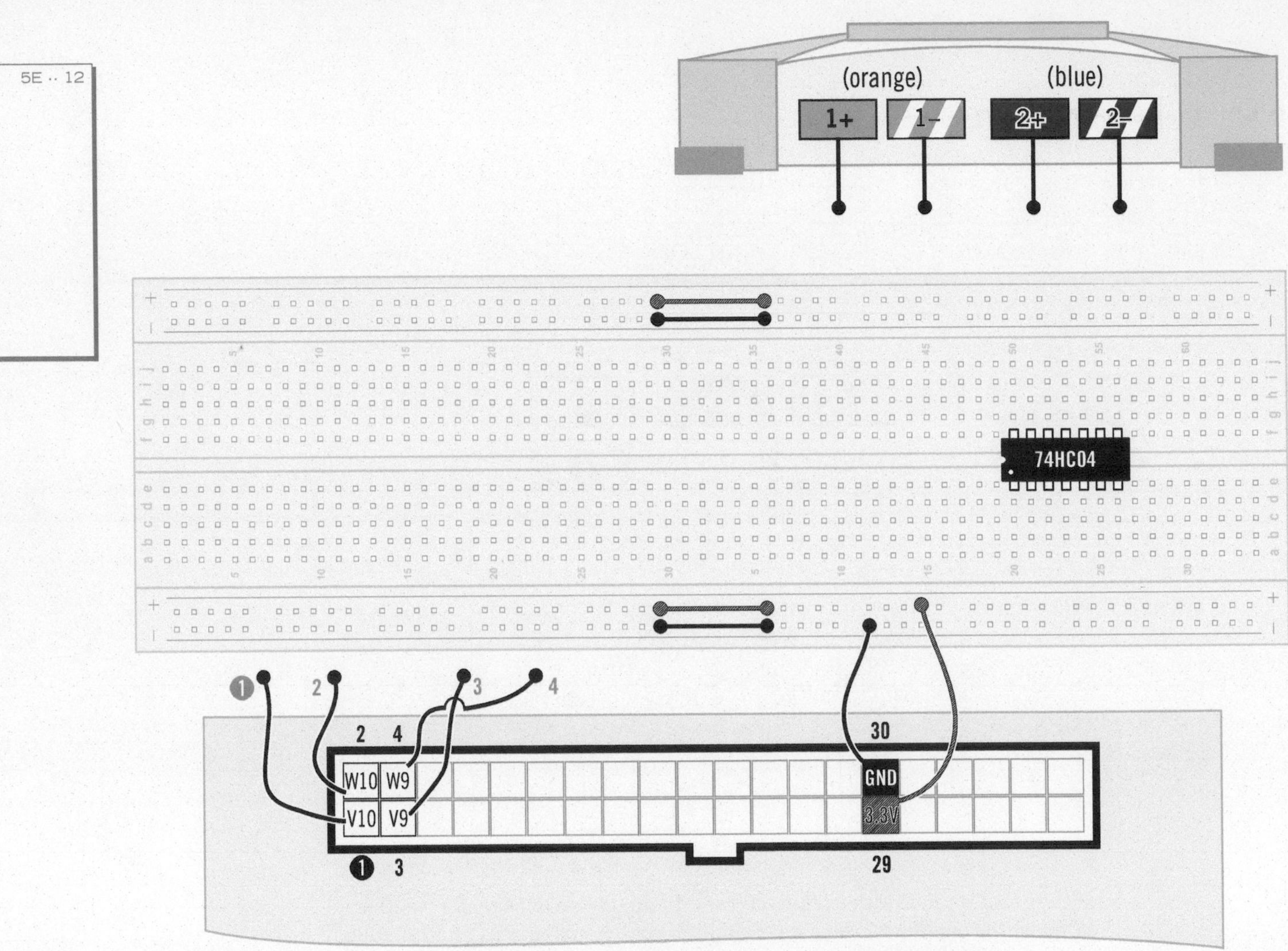

Run wires to the breadboard from the GPIO port (power and ground are already connected) and the Analog Discovery.

Figure 2.4: Connections between the breadboard, Analog Discovery, and FPGA development board GPIO.

2.4 Laboratory

2.4.1 Required Equipment and Parts

The following items are needed to complete this laboratory:

- breadboard
- wires
- 6x male-to-female jumpers
- resistors (5x 20 kΩ and 3x 10 kΩ)
- 2x male-male pin headers
- 74HC04 IC (**not LS!**)
- FPGA development board, USB cable
- Analog Discovery scope

2.4.2 Digital-to-Analog Converter

1. Program the FPGA development board by following the steps in **Appendix C** (required pre-lab reading). Use VHDL source code from **Appendix I.1** on page 166.

   A short link to the repository is provided in the appendix: the source code can simply be copied and pasted into a new project. The code from **Appendix C** is not the code that you will use in the laboratory!

   Make sure to use the laboratory directory structure given on page ix, otherwise completing future laboratories will become increasingly difficult!

   Verify the FPGA part being used. *Skip the simulation section of the appendix* for now (it will be covered in later laboratories). **The top-level entity name when creating the project must match the name of the VHDL file.**

2. Verify that the four LEDs directly above the four rightmost switches (**`LEDR3..0`**) turn on when their respective switches (**`SW3..0`**) are switched into the ON position.

3. Wire the D/A converter according to **Fig. 2.4**, completed in pre-lab. Using the Logger (Voltmeter), verify that when all four switches on the FPGA development board are ON, Ch. 1 voltage is approximately 3.3 VDC.

   If this is not the case, troubleshoot the circuit to determine the cause of the issue. No response from the circuit when switches are flipped may indicate that correct pins were not assigned in the Pin Planner, wrong GPIO pins are being used, or the board has not been programmed.

   Once you have verified the functionality of the switches, **demonstrate your set-up to a teaching assistant.**

4. Take the measurements of all 16 binary switch combinations in **Table 2.3**. 5E .. 13

   Explain what this table represents. Focus on the logic levels and why the readings make sense (or don't).

5. Using MATLAB (Excel is acceptable), plot measured voltages V_{in} and V_{out} against decimal values 0-15 (use * markers and connect individual points using a line; use two different line types for differentiation and include the plot title, axis labels, and a legend). A sample plot and MATLAB script for creating it are given in **Appendix I.1.2, Fig. I.1** on page 167. **Attach your plot on the following page.**

Table 2.3: Results of digital-to-analog conversion and IC levels.

Base 2	Base 10	Calculated V_{in} (V)	INPUT		OUTPUT	
			Measured V_{in} (V)	Level (low/high)*	Measured V_{out} (V)	Level (low/high)*
`0000`	0	0.000				
`0001`	1	0.220				
`0010`	2	0.440				
`0011`	3	0.660				
`0100`	4	0.880				
`0101`	5	1.100				
`0110`	6	1.320				
`0111`	7	1.540				
`1000`	8	1.760				
`1001`	9	1.980				
`1010`	10	2.200				
`1011`	11	2.420				
`1100`	12	2.640				
`1101`	13	2.860				
`1110`	14	3.080				
`1111`	15	3.300				

* Based on IC datasheet values of V_{IH}, V_{IL}, V_{OH}, and V_{OL}.

Attach your plot below. What can you observe from this plot?

LABORATORY 3

Combinational Logic Circuits

3.1 Overview

This laboratory will require the construction of a combinational logic circuit using two methods: discrete components (integrated circuits) and symbolic blocks within the Intel Quartus development environment. Quartus provides blocks for basic gates and devices. For more advanced designs in later labs, custom blocks can be created in Quartus.

The idea of the lab is to introduce both types of workflows: manual troubleshooting of wired circuits and troubleshooting of circuits that employ "virtual wiring".

In the computer portion of the lab, the circuit will be implemented as a block diagram, simulated using the *qsim* simulator within Quartus, and implemented on the FPGA development board.

In the laboratory portion, the circuit will be built using discrete components.

The output of both circuits will be compared at the end of the laboratory period.

GRADE SHEET DOWNLOAD
https://git.io/JeYM2

3.2 Objectives

At the conclusion of this lab, the student should be able to:

1. Interpret integrated circuit (IC) data sheets to determine gate input and output pins.
2. Wire standard 74xx series gate ICs based on a provided design.
3. Interface standard ICs to light-emitting diodes (LEDs) to test logic designs.
4. Use current-limiting resistors for proper operation of LEDs.
5. Interpret and explain experimental results, based on the behavior of a logic circuit.
6. Effectively use Intel Quartus for the creation of logic circuit block diagrams.
7. Develop basic troubleshooting skills for manually wired and "virtually-wired" circuits.

3.3 Pre-laboratory

Complete this pre-laboratory exercise prior to the laboratory period. All work must be completed **in pen**. To allow for revisions, circuit diagrams may be completed in pencil.

3.3.1 Combinational Logic

The relationship between the input(s) and the output(s) can be described by a logic circuit, a truth table, or a waveform. Considering the simple logic circuit presented in **Fig. 3.1**:

1. Label the output of all gates with a Boolean expression.

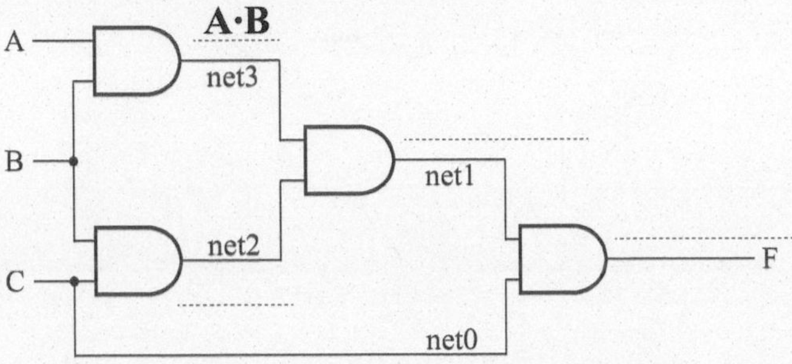

Figure 3.1: Combinational logic circuit.

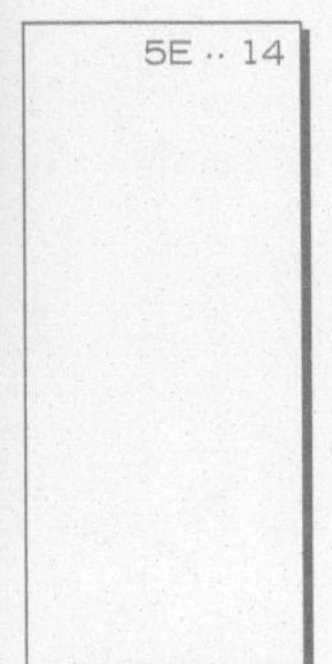

2. Fill in the intermediate results and outputs in the *Predicted* column of **Table 3.3** on page 24 (laboratory portion).
3. Draw the output waveform for *F*, given input values for *A*, *B*, and *C* in **Fig. 3.2**.

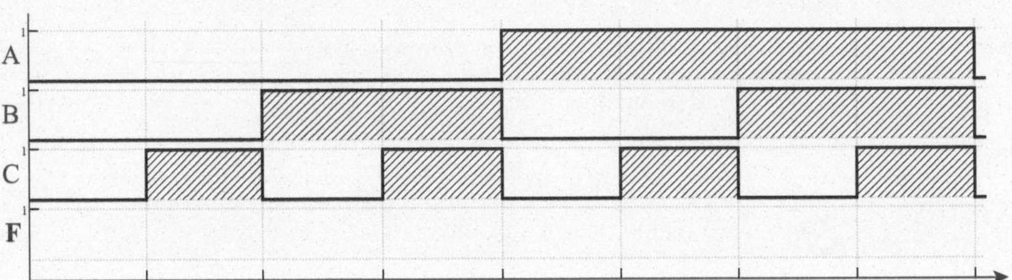

Figure 3.2: Waveform corresponding to the circuit in Fig. 3.1.

3.3.2 Wiring

Review **Appendix A** of the lab manual, covering basic wiring elements and techniques.

1. Complete **Table 3.1** with the appropriate resistor band colors, using the conversion chart in **Appendix A.1** and assuming a 5% tolerance.

Table 3.1: Resistor value to color conversion.

Value (Ω)	1st band	2nd	3rd	4th
330				

2. Draw wires on the breadboard in **Fig. 3.4**, based on the circuit in **Fig. 3.3**. LEDs and resistors have already been placed on the breadboard in their correct orientation.

   To determine locations of gates within the IC, use the 74LS08/74HC08 quad-AND gate IC data sheet in **Appendix J. Mark the IC pin numbers that will be used** (*e.g.*, 1, 2, 3, 4, etc.) for the gates in the dotted boxes in **Fig. 3.3.**

   Inputs *A*, *B*, and *C* should connect to the DIP switch. Intermediate signals (nets) should connect to the appropriately marked *LEDs 3..0* (these LEDs will verify the operation of the circuit).

5E ·· 15

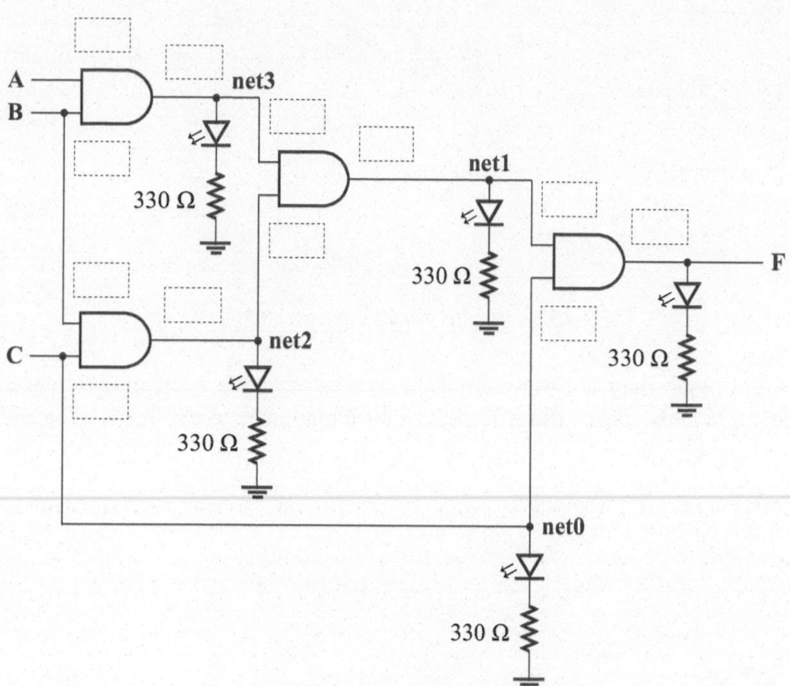

Figure 3.3: Laboratory circuit.

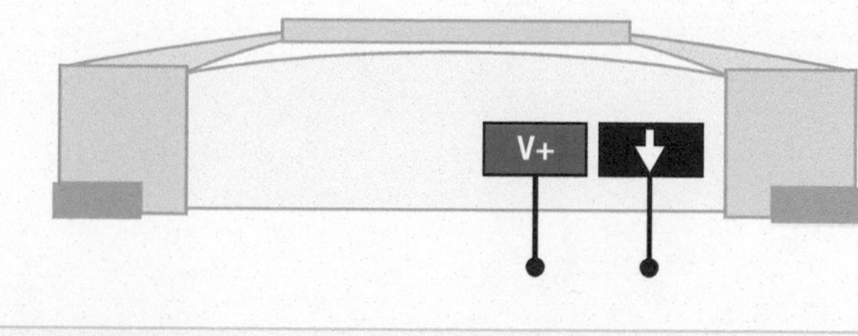

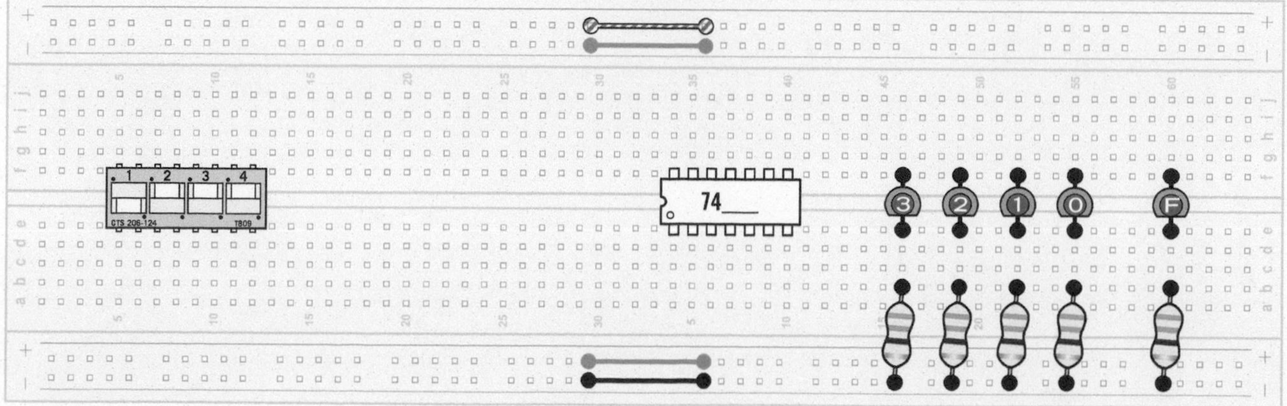

Figure 3.4: Laboratory breadboard wiring set up.

3.3.3 Quartus Block Diagrams

Read **Appendix D** of the lab manual, which illustrates the creation of block diagrams in Intel Quartus. Skip section **D.5**—this will be covered in later labs. If you need to refer to earlier steps (*i.e.*, creating a new project or running a simulation), refer to **Appendix C**.

1. Implement the circuit in **Fig. 3.5** as a block diagram. Create the inputs *A*, *B*, *C*, and output *F*. Also create outputs for intermediate connections *net3*, *net2*, *net1*, and *net0*.

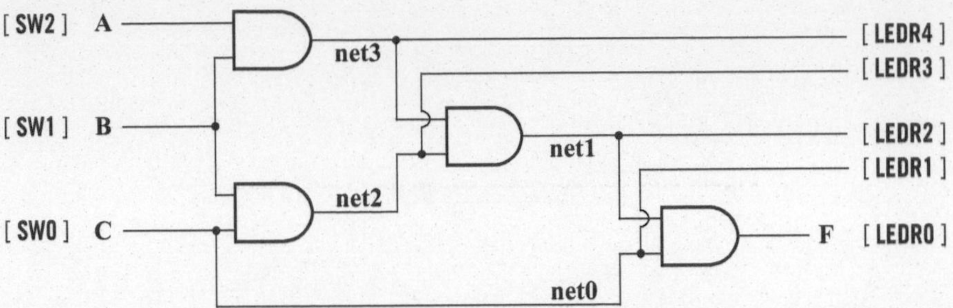

Figure 3.5: Quartus circuit implementation.

Save and synthesize the block diagram to ascertain that no errors have been made. Once synthesis completes successfully, **print and paste the block diagram below** (you may have to capture a screenshot for easier scaling).

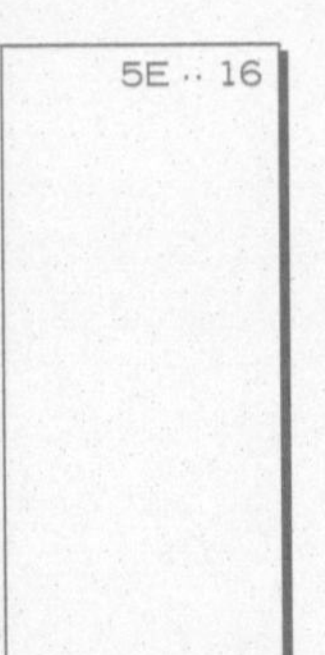

2. Simulate the block diagram. The simulated output will look similar to **Fig. 3.6**. Using the output, fill in the *Simulated* column of **Table 3.3** with your results.

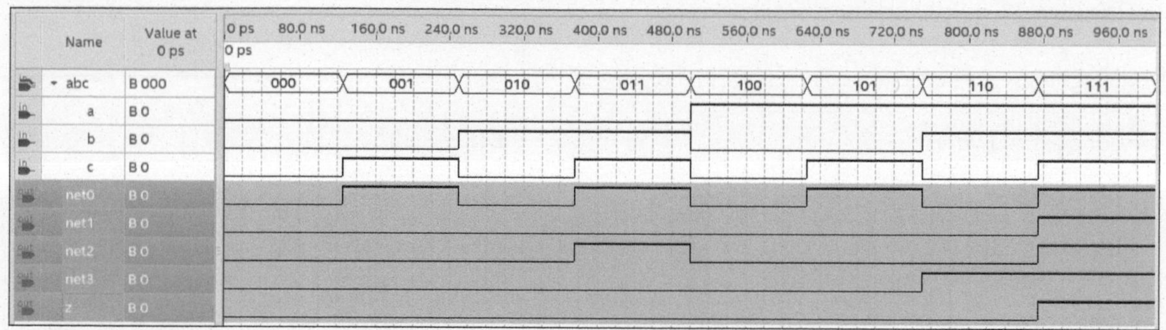

Figure 3.6: Sample simulation of the block diagram.

Print out a screenshot of the simulation and paste it below.

5E ·· 17

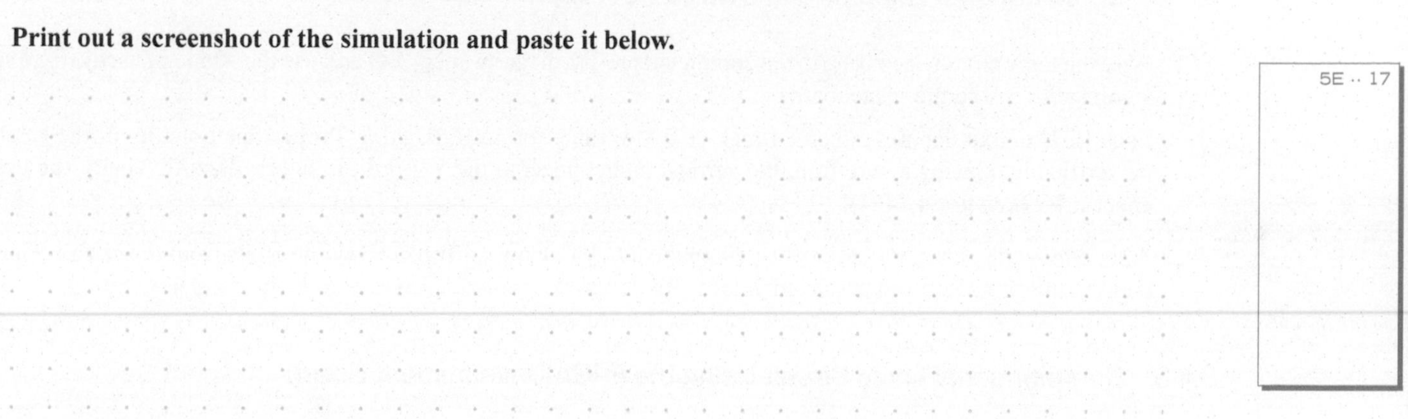

3. Complete the pin assignments in **Table 3.2** (refer to **Appendix H**).

5E ·· 18

Table 3.2: Pin assignments table.

Port Name	Port Function	Pin Location	Logic Level	Current Strength	Slew Rate
a	SW[2]	D12	3.3-V LVCMOS	2 mA	—
b	SW[1]				—
c	SW[0]				—
net3	LEDR4				2
net2	LEDR3				
net1	LEDR2				
net0	LEDR1				
f	LEDR0				

3.4 Laboratory

3.4.1 Required Equipment and Parts

The following items are needed to complete this laboratory:

- breadboard and wires
- 2x pin headers
- resistors (5x 330 Ω)
- 5x LEDs
- DIP switch
- 74XX IC (either HC or LS)
- FPGA development board, USB cable
- Analog Discovery scope

3.4.2 Combinational Logic Circuit Using 74XX ICs

1. Wire the logic circuit according to the completed pre-lab diagram (**Fig. 3.4**) and use the Analog Discovery to supply a voltage of 5 V to the breadboard.

   Each LED output denotes either a **1**/high or **0**/low value for *net 3..0* and *F*. Proper functionality of the LEDs can be verified by placing a wire from the vertical interconnect to the 5 V rail of the breadboard. **Verify the use of a correct IC (*i.e.*, not a 7404)!**

2. After confirming circuit functionality, fill in the *74XX* column of **Table 3.3** with results from the circuit. Compare them to the simulated and predicted values. **Demonstrate the functionality to a teaching assistant.**

3.4.3 Combinational Logic Circuit Using the FPGA Development Board

1. Open the Intel Quartus project from the pre-lab, containing your block diagram. Since synthesis and simulation have been completed, assign the pins based on **Table 3.2**.
2. Recompile the project and program the FPGA development board (refer to **Appendix C**).
3. Test the circuit by using switches **`SW2..0`**. The result should be displayed on LEDs **`LEDR4..0`**. Refer to **Fig. 3.5** to see how these correspond to specific inputs and outputs.

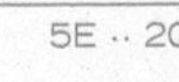

4. After confirming circuit functionality, fill in the *FPGA* column of **Table 3.3** with results from the circuit. Compare them to the simulated, predicted, and IC (74XX) values. **Demonstrate the functionality to a teaching assistant.**

Table 3.3: Laboratory data table

Inputs			Predicted					74XX					Simulated					FPGA				
			Intermediate					Intermediate					Intermediate					Intermediate				
A	**B**	**C**	net3	net2	net1	net0	**F**	net3	net2	net1	net0	**F**	net3	net2	net1	net0	**F**	net3	net2	net1	net0	**F**
0	0	0																				
0	0	1																				
0	1	0																				
0	1	1																				
1	0	0																				
1	0	1																				
1	1	0																				
1	1	1																				

3.5 Questions

1. Compare circuit output results between predictions, 74XX (IC) implementation, Quartus simulation, and FPGA hardware. Are the results identical? **Explain why or why not.**

2. Interpret the laboratory data in the context of the circuit. Does the behavior of the output make sense, given the components used? **Explain.**

LABORATORY 4

Seven-segment Display Logic

4.1 Overview

This laboratory will focus on creating a circuit that uses a binary-coded decimal (BCD) decoder to drive a seven-segment display. Data sheets for both devices will be used to determine the wiring between the inputs, decoder, and the display. After verifying the functionality of the driver circuitry, an additional circuit for blanking the seven-segment display will be created—allowing only values 0 through 9 to show up on the display.

GRADE SHEET DOWNLOAD
https://git.io/JeYMa

4.2 Objectives

At the conclusion of this lab, the student should be able to:

1. Interpret integrated circuit (IC) data sheets to determine gate input and output pins.
2. Describe the basic concepts behind driving a seven-segment display.
3. Interface standard ICs together to create a functional seven-segment display readout.
4. Use correct resistors to limit the current through LEDs.
5. Use a BCD to seven-segment decoder.
6. Create a logic circuit to output desired signals for blanking a seven-segment display.
7. Use Karnaugh maps and truth tables in the design of a logic circuit.

4.3 Pre-laboratory

Complete this pre-laboratory exercise prior to the laboratory period. All work must be completed **in pen**. To allow for revisions, circuit diagrams may be completed in pencil.

4.3.1 7-Segment Display

A seven-segment display consists of seven individual LEDs arranged in a figure-8 pattern, denoted by the letters ***a*** through ***g*** (**Fig. 4.1**). To display the desired number, some of the seven LEDs must be turned on. For instance, to display the numeral "1" will require LEDs labeled ***b*** and ***c*** to be illuminated.

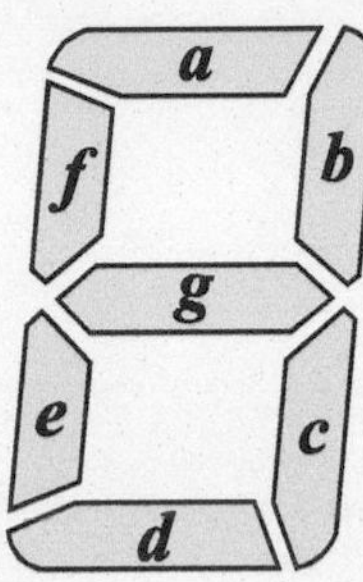

Figure 4.1: Diagram of a generic seven-segment display.

Review the 7447 IC (BCD decoder) and the 5166A (seven-segment display) data sheets in **Appendix J** and answer the following questions:

5E ·· 21

1. What is the 7447 IC and what does it do?

2. What is the purpose of the **BI/RBO** pin on the 7447 IC? What value must be asserted on the pin for the seven-segment display to not illuminate (blank)?

3. How many pins does the 5611A part (seven-segment display) have and what is the function of each individual pin?

4. What does it mean for a seven-segment display to be "common anode" and how does that affect the 7447 IC's outputs?

Complete **Table 4.1**, with the appropriate values of **H** or **L** for the individual elements of the seven-segment display (taking into account the common anode configuration of the seven-segment display).

Table 4.1: Individual LED states on the seven-segment display.

Digit	Display	*a*	*b*	*c*	*d*	*e*	*f*	*g*
0								
1								
2								
3								
4								

Digit	Display	*a*	*b*	*c*	*d*	*e*	*f*	*g*
5								
6								
7								
8								
9								

4.3.2 Wiring

Using information obtained from the data sheets, complete the breadboard wiring set up for the seven-segment display and decoder in **Fig. 4.2. Note that the datasheet uses *DCBA* (most significant bit [MSB] to least significant bit [LSB]). While in lab, we use *ABCD* (MSB to LSB).** Show connections from the switches to the decoder and from the decoder to the display. Make sure to power the IC from the Analog Discovery.

In order to limit the current on the LEDs inside the display, use a limiting resistor (similar to previous lab). Each LED needs a 330 Ω resistor connected between it and the 7447 decoder.

The common anode of the display is already connected to the power rail and segment ***g*** (pin 10 on the display) is connected to the decoder (pin 14 on the IC) through a limiting resistor.

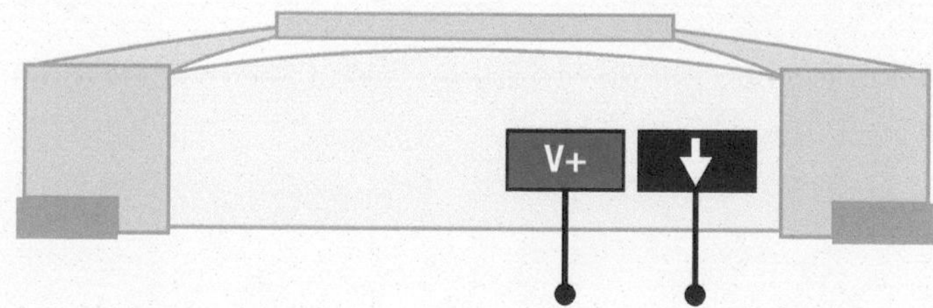

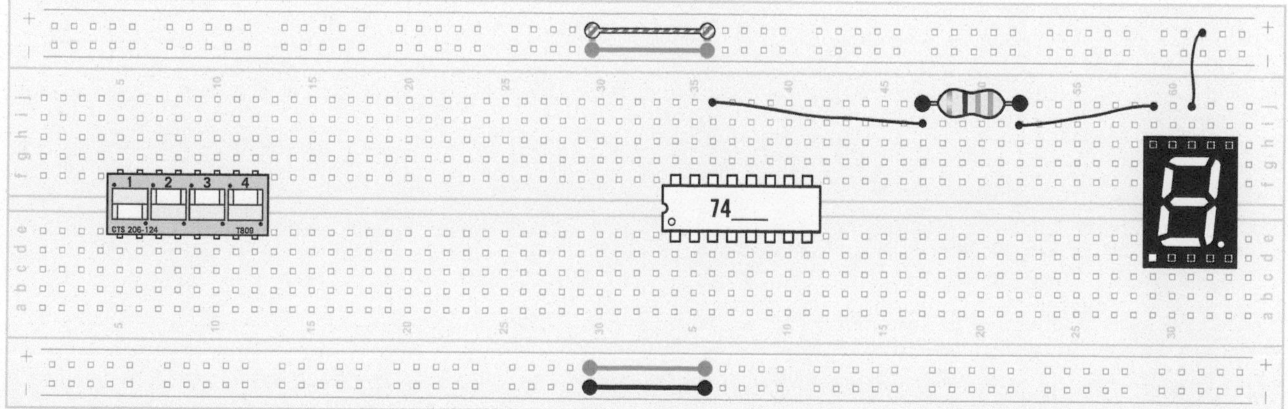

Figure 4.2: Laboratory breadboard wiring set up for driving the display. Do not place any components into the shaded area.

4.3.3 Combinational Blanking Logic

5E ·· 23

1. For the truth table **Table 4.2**, F is a logic-HIGH when a valid BCD code is being input, logic-LOW otherwise. Write out the unsimplified maxterm expansion (Boolean expression) for F.

Table 4.2: Blanking logic truth table.

A B C D	Decimal	F	A B C D	Decimal	F
0 0 0 0	0	1	1 0 0 0	8	1
0 0 0 1	1	1	1 0 0 1	9	1
0 0 1 0	2	1	1 0 1 0	10	0
0 0 1 1	3	1	1 0 1 1	11	0
0 1 0 0	4	1	1 1 0 0	12	0
0 1 0 1	5	1	1 1 0 1	13	0
0 1 1 0	6	1	1 1 1 0	14	0
0 1 1 1	7	1	1 1 1 1	15	0

2. Completely simplify the maxterm expression above using a Karnaugh map (if covered in class) or using Boolean postulates. Box your final answer.

3. Implement a minimal circuit from the Boolean expression you found using only a single gate type, either NAND (7400) or NOR (7402). Draw the circuit diagram of the combinational circuit in the space provided.

4.4 Laboratory

This laboratory consists of two parts: constructing the seven-segment display circuit using a decoder and adding a blanking logic circuit.

4.4.1 Required Equipment and Parts

The following items are needed to complete this laboratory:

- breadboard
- wires
- resistors (7x 330 Ω)
- 7447 IC
- NAND (7400) **or** NOR (7402) IC
- seven-segment display
- DIP switch
- Analog Discovery scope

4.4.2 Seven-segment Display and Decoder

1. Plug in the Analog Discovery and start Waveforms. Should any problems with the circuit occur, the voltmeter/logger functionality can be used as a powerful debugging tool (use the orange and orange/white scope leads for measurement).

2. Construct the circuit from the wiring diagram in **Fig. 4.2**. Leave ample room for an additional IC to the left of the BCD decoder IC when building the circuit on the breadboard.

   Use the Analog Discovery to provide a supply voltage of 5 V. Toggling the switches to a binary number should display this number on the display.

   After confirming the functionality of all parts of your circuit, **demonstrate the set-up to a teaching assistant**.

3. Test all binary values from 0 to 15 and record the results in **Table 4.3** (complete the truth table portion for switch combinations 10 through 15 and draw the segments as you see them on the display).

   The truth table should represent the logic level being asserted on the different pins (***a*** through ***g***) of the display, logic-LOW (**L**) or logic-HIGH (**H**).

   Leave the IC and display connected and proceed to the next part.

4.4.3 Combinational Logic Circuit for Blanking non-BCD values

1. Determine which IC (or ICs) will be needed to wire the combinational circuit derived in the pre-lab. From the pre-lab reading, the **BI** input of the 7447 IC will be used to blank the display whenever an integer decimal number is not entered.

   Draw the connections necessary to implement the logic you have created on **Fig. 4.3**. Be sure to specify the IC part number(s). **Verify your diagram with the instructor or teaching assistant.**

2. Add the additional IC and wiring to the existing breadboard set-up. When wired correctly, the seven-segment display should work for binary numbers 0 through 9 only.

   After confirming the functionality of all parts of the circuit, **demonstrate your set-up to a teaching assistant.**

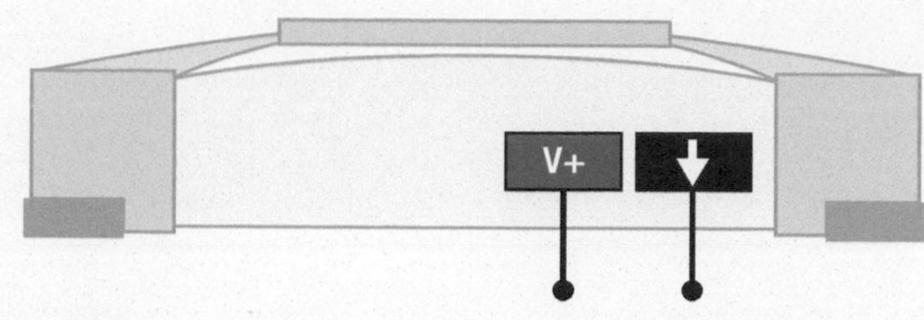

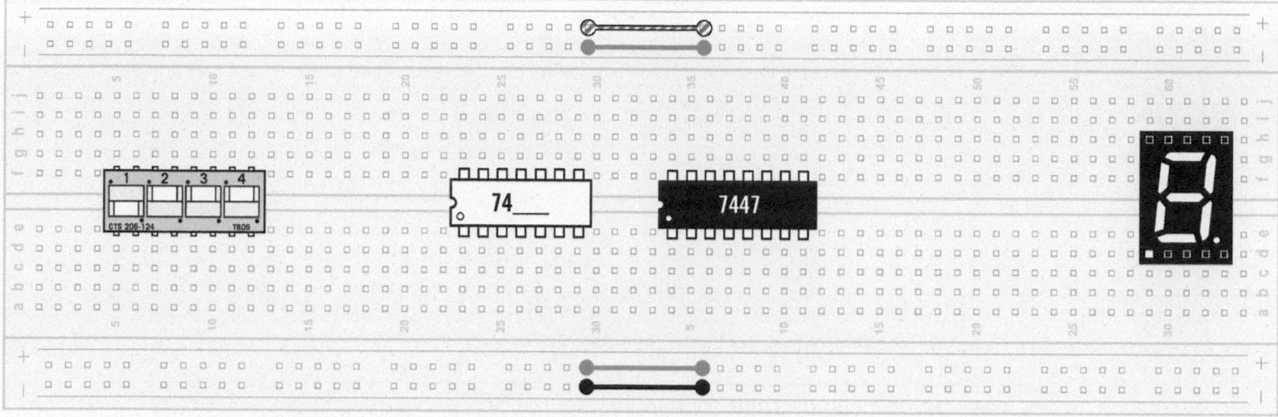

Figure 4.3: Blanking logic. Do not redraw existing connections from the previous part.

4.5 Questions

1. What is the purpose of creating a blanking circuit for the seven-segment display?

2. How would one create a combinational circuit to light the center bar (*g*) of the seven-segment display (resulting in a dash) instead of only blanking it? **Explain the process.** Hint: this can be accomplished with only one two-input gate.

Table 4.3: Seven-segment display truth table.

A B C D	Digit	Display	*a*	*b*	*c*	*d*	*e*	*f*	*g*
	10								
	11								
	12								
	13								
	14								
	15								

LABORATORY 5

Combinational Logic using VHDL

5.1 Overview

This lab focuses on developing two solutions to a four-person majority voting problem: one via an unsimplified minterm expansion and the other via a simplified expression. At the end of the laboratory, both solutions will be implemented in VHDL, simulated, and tested on the FPGA development board.

At the end of the laboratory, the output of both circuits will be compared to the simulation.

GRADE SHEET DOWNLOAD
https://git.io/JeYMr

5.2 Objectives

At the conclusion of this lab, the student should be able to:

1. Design, implement using VHDL, and test a logic circuit that satisfies certain conditions.
2. Simulate the circuit using a logic simulator and interpret the simulation results.
3. Interpret and explain experimental results, based on the behavior of a logic circuit.
4. Outline the steps necessary for translating combinational logic circuits to VHDL using a variety of approaches.

5.3 Pre-laboratory

Read the tutorial on implementing combinational circuits using VHDL in **Appendix C.2**. This tutorial will be a good reference during laboratory and pre-laboratory questions.

Complete this pre-laboratory exercise prior to the laboratory period. All work must be completed **in pen**. To allow for revisions, circuit diagrams may be completed in pencil.

5.3.1 Majority-four Voting Circuit

A majority-four voting circuit models an election process, in which four individuals cast their binary (yes/no) votes. Hence, to get a positive outcome, three or more individuals within the group must vote "yes".

1. Based on the information above, design a majority-four voting circuit. The voting circuit must only return a **1** at the output F when the majority of inputs (A, B, C, and D) are logic-HIGH.
2. Determine necessary logic-**1** outputs required, complete the truth table in **Table 5.1**, and sketch the output waveform in **Fig. 5.1**.

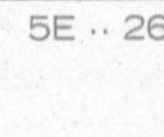

Table 5.1: Truth table for the majority voting circuit.

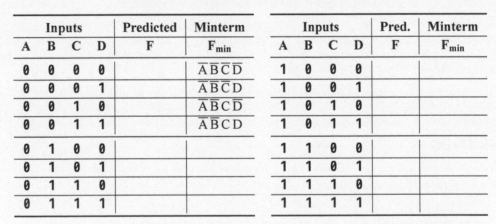

Inputs				**Predicted**	**Minterm**	**Inputs**				**Pred.**	**Minterm**
A	**B**	**C**	**D**	**F**	**F_{min}**	**A**	**B**	**C**	**D**	**F**	**F_{min}**
0	0	0	0		$\overline{A}\,\overline{B}\,\overline{C}\,\overline{D}$	1	0	0	0		
0	0	0	1		$\overline{A}\,\overline{B}\,\overline{C}D$	1	0	0	1		
0	0	1	0		$\overline{A}\,\overline{B}C\overline{D}$	1	0	1	0		
0	0	1	1		$\overline{A}\,\overline{B}CD$	1	0	1	1		
0	1	0	0			1	1	0	0		
0	1	0	1			1	1	0	1		
0	1	1	0			1	1	1	0		
0	1	1	1			1	1	1	1		

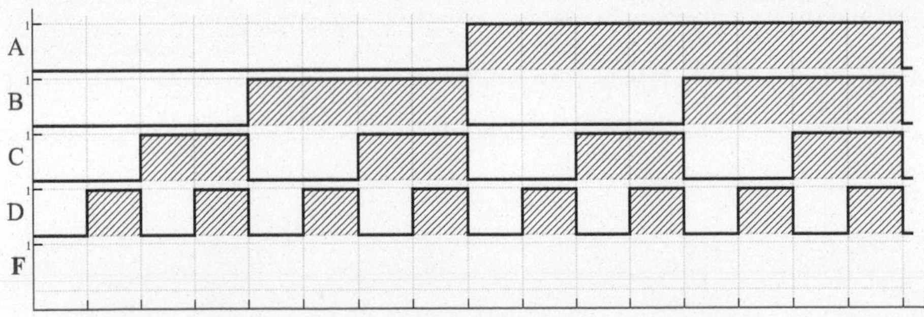

Figure 5.1: Waveform for the majority voting circuit.

3. Determine the minterm expansion for F, in terms of inputs A, B, C, and D (do not express in canonical form).

5E ·· 27

4. Sketch a logic circuit implementation of the minterm expansion using AND and OR gates. Separate inputs can be used for each gate (no connection to common inputs is necessary).

5. Use a Karnaugh map to simplify the minterm expansion derived in the previous steps, **box the final answer** (the output of this expression will be referred to as F_{Kmap}). If you have not yet covered Karnaugh maps in class, reference the appropriate chapter(s) in the textbook.

5E ·· 28

5.3.2 Breadboard Wiring

1. Draw a circuit diagram of the simplified expression (F_{Kmap}) obtained by using a Karnaugh map in previous steps. Group terms into a multi-level circuit to reduce gate usage.

2. Wire the circuit on the breadboard in **Fig. 5.2** according to the diagram above. You may not need to use all of the ICs on the breadboard.

5E ·· 29

   Indicate the ICs used by filling in the blanks in the diagram. You have the following devices available to you, with relevant data sheets reproduced in **Appendix J**.

   - **7400**: Quad 2-input NAND gates
   - **7402**: Quad 2-input NOR gates
   - **7404**: Hex inverter (NOT gates)
   - **7408**: Quad 2-input AND gates
   - **7432**: Quad 2-input OR gates
   - **7486**: Quad 2-input XOR gates

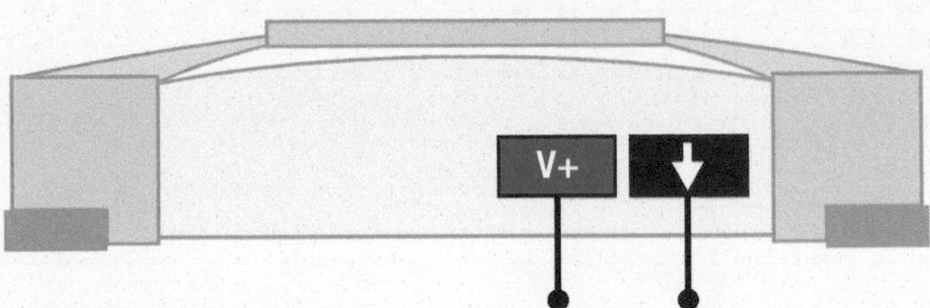

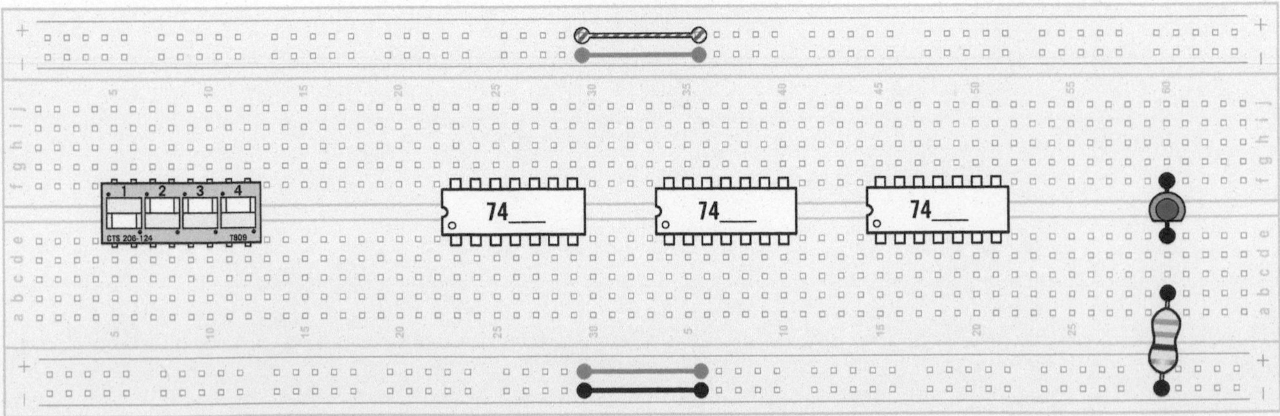

Figure 5.2: Laboratory breadboard wiring setup.

5.3.3 VHDL Primer

Answer the following questions based on **Appendix C.2**.

5E ·· 30

1. What is the purpose of an **`entity`** in VHDL?

2. What is the purpose of an **`architecture`**?

3. What are **`signal`**s and how can they be useful when implementing a design in VHDL?

4. How are "nets" used in the example circuit? What is the procedure for translating a logic circuit to VHDL?

5. What is the precedence of **`and`** / **`or`** operators in VHDL?

6. Which character(s) denote comments in VHDL code?

5.3.4 VHDL Combinational Logic

In this laboratory, two circuits will be implemented using VHDL. One circuit will represent a non-simplified minterm expansion (sum-of-products [SOP] terms) version of the majority-four voting circuit (five expansion terms total), while the other circuit will be based on the Karnaugh map-simplified version of the circuit.

Both circuits will be connected to the inputs A, B, C, and D, wired to switches **SW3**, **SW2**, **SW1**, and **SW0**, respectively. A simplified diagram for the circuit is given in **Fig. 5.3**.

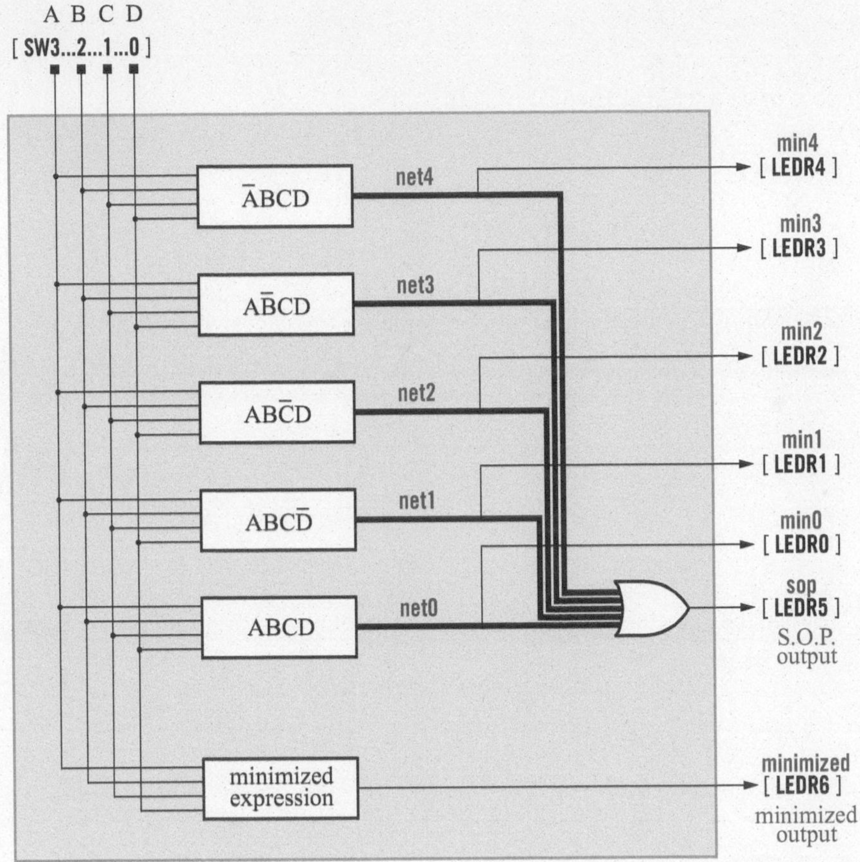

Figure 5.3: Block diagram of the circuit.

Since the unsimplified minterm expression is quite complex, intermediate signals will be used at the output of each smaller SOP term (remember that `signal`s go in the `architecture` portion of the VHDL code, prior to the `begin` statement).

Signals `net4..0` will be connected to the corresponding outputs **LEDR4..0**, respectively. This way, the output of each individual minterm expression will be visible for all possible inputs. The output of the OR operation of all the minterms should be connected to **LEDR5**.

Due to the low complexity of the simplified circuit, it may be directly connected to the output LED **LEDR6**.

1. Implement the circuit in **Fig. 5.3** in VHDL. Paste the code below.

   Make sure to synthesize the code first, in order to resolve any syntax and logical errors. With enough thought, most errors in VHDL are self-explanatory. Check for missing semicolons and general spelling errors.

   Make sure that your entity has outputs for minterms!

5E .. 31

5E ·· 32

2. Run a functional simulation of the code using *qsim*. Paste the simulation below.

3. Using the results of the simulation, fill in the *Simulated Outputs* portion of the results table (**Table 5.3**).

5.3.5 Pin Assignments

Complete the pin assignments in **Table 5.2** (refer to **Appendix H**).

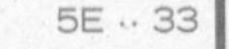

Table 5.2: Pin assignments table.

Port Name	Port Function	Pin Location	Logic Level	Current Strength	Slew Rate
a	SW3	C12	3.3-V LVCMOS	2 mA	—
b	SW2				—
c	SW1				—
d	SW0				—
minimized	LEDR6	E14	3.3-V LVCMOS	2 mA	2
sop	LEDR5				
min4	LEDR4				
min3	LEDR3				
min2	LEDR2				
min1	LEDR1				
min0	LEDR0				

(Optional) To minimize the time spent in lab, assign the pins based on the table above using the *Pin Planner* tool in Quartus. Save the project and have it readily available for the laboratory.

5.4 Laboratory

5.4.1 Required Equipment and Parts

The following items are needed to complete this laboratory:

- breadboard
- wires
- resistor (330 Ω)
- LED
- ICs (chosen in the pre-lab)
- DIP switch
- FPGA development board, USB cable
- Analog Discovery scope

5.4.2 FPGA Development Board Implementation

5E ·· 34

1. Assign the appropriate pins, compile the project, and program the FPGA development board. Based on the results obtained from interacting with the development board LEDs and switches, fill out the *FPGA Dev. Board Outputs* column of **Table 5.3**.

   Demonstrate the set up to the teaching assistant.

5.4.3 Wiring Implementation

1. Implement the simplified K-map circuit on the breadboard, based on **Fig. 5.2**. Run through the 16 possible switch combinations and note down the output status of the LED in the *Wired Output* column of **Table 5.3**. Don't forget to wire the LED in series with a 330 Ω resistor to prevent damage!

   Demonstrate the set up to the teaching assistant.

5E ·· 35

5.5 Questions

1. What do the **`LEDR4..0`** represent in the FPGA development board implementation?

2. Why is row/column ordering in a Karnaugh map not in ascending binary order?

3. Outline the steps necessary for implementing a circuit in VHDL.

4. Explain your experimental results.

Table 5.3: Results table for the majority-four voting circuit.

Inputs				**Simulated Outputs**							**FPGA Dev. Board Outputs**							**Wired**
A	B	C	D	F_{Kmap}	F_{min}	$\overline{A}BCD$	$A\overline{B}CD$	$AB\overline{C}D$	$ABC\overline{D}$	$ABCD$	F_{Kmap}	F_{min}	$\overline{A}BCD$	$A\overline{B}CD$	$AB\overline{C}D$	$ABC\overline{D}$	$ABCD$	**Output**
SW3	SW2	SW1	SW0	LEDR6	LEDR5	LEDR4	LEDR3	LEDR2	LEDR1	LEDR0	LEDR6	LEDR5	LEDR4	LEDR3	LEDR2	LEDR1	LEDR0	F_{Kmap}
0	0	0	0															
0	0	0	1															
0	0	1	0															
0	0	1	1															
0	1	0	0															
0	1	0	1															
0	1	1	0															
0	1	1	1															
1	0	0	0															
1	0	0	1															
1	0	1	0															
1	0	1	1															
1	1	0	0															
1	1	0	1															
1	1	1	0															
1	1	1	1															

LABORATORY 6

Multiplexed Displays

6.1 Overview

This lab will implement a multiplexed seven-segment LED display. A multiplexed display block will be driven by a counter module, in order to cycle through four display positions on the FPGA board. The binary-coded decimal (BCD) input to the LED displays will be provided as follows:

1. Constant 0 in the block diagram will provide input to displays **HEX3** and **HEX2**
2. **SW7..4** to display **HEX1**
3. **SW3..0** to display **HEX0**

Re-usable components in VHDL will be introduced to lay the groundwork for future laboratories. The multiplexed LED display driver module developed during this laboratory will be used in subsequent labs for the display of data.

GRADE SHEET DOWNLOAD
https://git.io/JeYMo

6.2 Objectives

At the conclusion of this lab, the student should be able to:

1. Design a decoder circuit for arbitrary functions.
2. Design, implement, and test a device for multiplexing seven-segment LED displays.
3. Use multiple VHDL files within a single project.
4. Recognize the hierarchy of VHDL entities.
5. Quickly create components, instances, and port maps.
6. Create frequency-scalable integer counters.
7. Package existing VHDL code into a block symbol file (**.bsf**).
8. Add custom block symbol files (**.bsf**) to a block diagram design.
9. Use custom global and local project libraries in a Quartus project.

6.3 Background

The seven-segment display on the Intel FPGA development board is arranged in a figure-8 pattern, with individual cathodes (negative terminals) representing the segments of each display. Positive terminals (anodes) are common to all segments. There are six display panels (**Fig. 6.1**), however only four rightmost displays will be used in this laboratory.

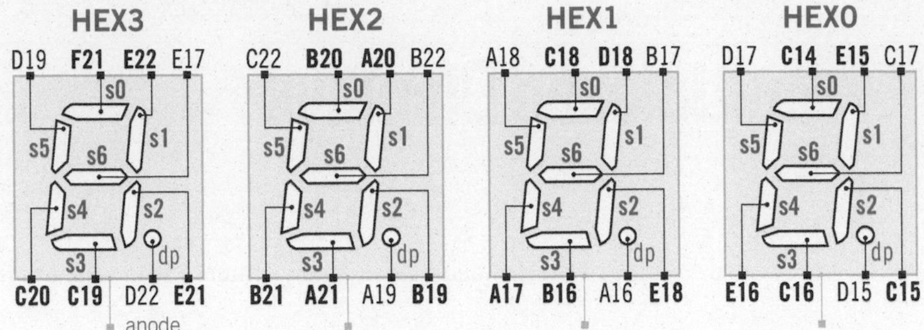

Figure 6.1: Diagram of the seven-segment displays on the Intel FPGA development board.

Due to the particulars of the driving transistor implementation, the cathodes are *active-LOW* (meaning that they turn on when driven by a logic-`0`, instead of a logic-1).

A detailed diagram and table of pin locations is given in **Appendix H**.

6.3.1 Display Multiplexing

To prevent flicker, the displays have to be multiplexed at a fairly high rate. If in **Appendix E**, the counter was reset every second (50 million cycles), the displays need to be refreshed about a thousand times faster (leading to a rate of refresh for the entire display of about 1 kHz).

Of course, multiplexing can be accomplished at a much slower rate (*e.g.*, 50-60 Hz), but the flicker would be perceivable to the human eye—leading to uncomfortable viewing experiences for those with light and strobe sensitivities.

One of the cardinal rules in VHDL is that **all bits of a bus have to be assigned at the same time**. In addition—to prevent crossfading between displays—**only one display can be on at one time**, when implementing multiplexing.

These important considerations leave only a limited number of implementation options, one of which is discussed below.

Concatenation and Slicing

Since only one display can be on at a time, the sequence of powering the displays should work similarly to the one in **Fig. 6.2**. For the example, assume that the number **`0123`** is being displayed.

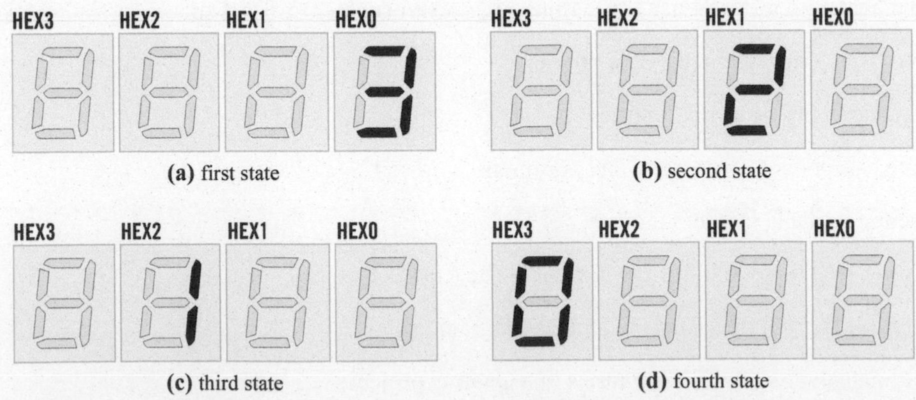

Figure 6.2: Firing sequence for four multiplexed displays.

Considering the limitations for multiplexing (one display at a time) and VHDL (all bits assigned at the same time), a bus with bits for all of the display segments has to be created. With seven segments per display, this would result in a 28-bit wide bus.

```
signal displays : STD_LOGIC_VECTOR(27 downto 0);
```

When multiplexing, only 7 of the 28 bits will have segment information. The rest of the bit positions will have **1**s—the corresponding segments will be off (**Fig. 6.3**).

The **segments** output of the decoder can either be concatenated with manually entered **1**s or with a single seven-bit vector containing **1**s (**off <= "1111111"**).

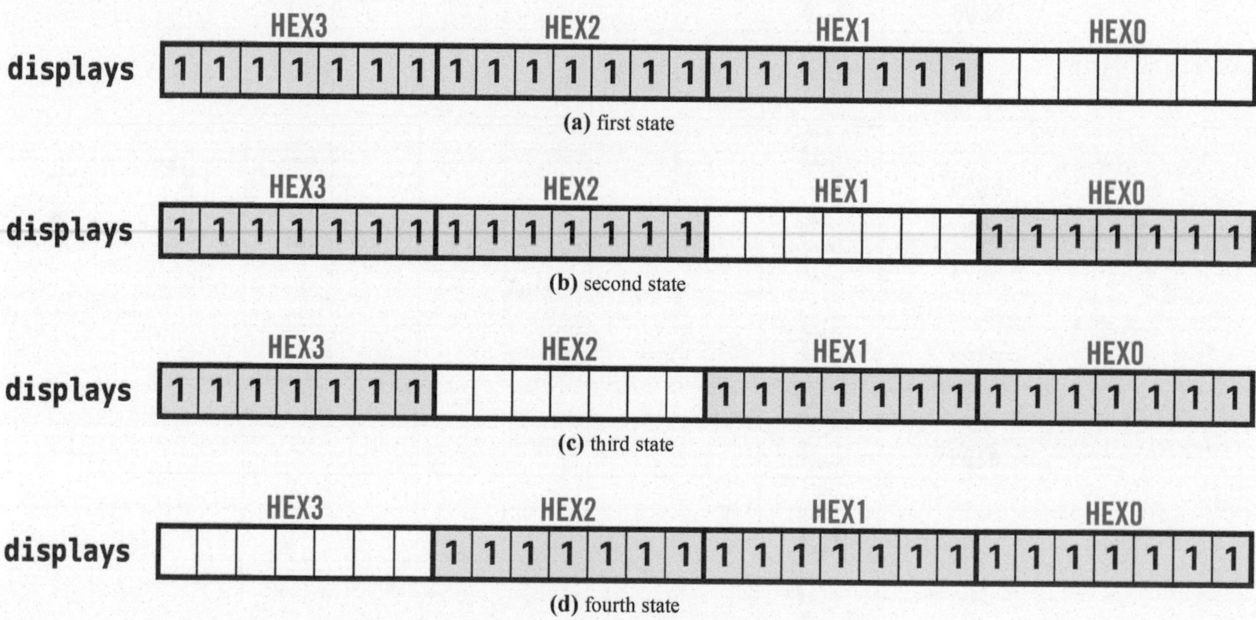

Figure 6.3: Bus population sequence for three displays.

```
displays <= off & off & off & segments;        -- First state
```

In the final step, the **displays** signal will need to be sliced between the four different displays (where **hex3(6 downto 0)**, **hex2(6 downto 0)**, **hex1(6 downto 0)**, and **hex0(6 downto 0)** are the outputs to the individual displays.

```
hex3 <= displays(27 downto 21);
hex2 <= displays(20 downto 14);
hex1 <= displays(13 downto 7);
hex0 <= displays(6 downto 0);
```

6.4 Pre-laboratory

Read the tutorial on multiplexers and decoders in **Appendix E**. This will serve as a good reference during laboratory and pre-laboratory questions. Reading and understanding the tutorial will greatly minimize the time spent in the lab. If VHDL was not yet covered in class, review **Appendix C.2**.

6.4.1 Seven-segment Decoder Circuit

1. Fill in the truth table for each of the segments, given in **Table 6.1**. Remember that to "turn on" a segment, it has to be driven **LOW**. Refer to **Fig. 6.1** for **`s(N)`** segment locations.

Table 6.1: Truth table for individual display segments.

number(3..0)	Symbol	s(6)	s(5)	s(4)	s(3)	s(2)	s(1)	s(0)
0000	0							
0001	1							
0010	2							
0011	3							
0100	4							
0101	5							
0110	6							
0111	7							
1000	8							
1001	9							
others	-							

2. The next steps will involve creating a 4:7 display decoder named **`decoder.vhd`**, shown in **Fig. 6.5**.

   Open a new project, create the **`decoder.vhd`** VHDL file, and name the top-level entity **`decoder`**. The multiplexer will be added to this project at a later stage.

3. Using VHDL, implement the 4:7 decoder for seven-segment displays based on **Table 6.1**. Use the code at the end of **Appendix E** for reference. Make sure to adjust and verify the port widths—the decoder in the appendix is only intended as an example.

   Synthesize the decoder and resolve any syntax errors.

   Paste the VHDL code on the following page.

Decoder VHDL code.

5E .. 37

4. Simulate the decoder. Verify that the simulation output (signal levels) matches the decoder simulation in **Fig. 6.4**. If the output does not match, troubleshoot the issue by looking at which segments are on or off.

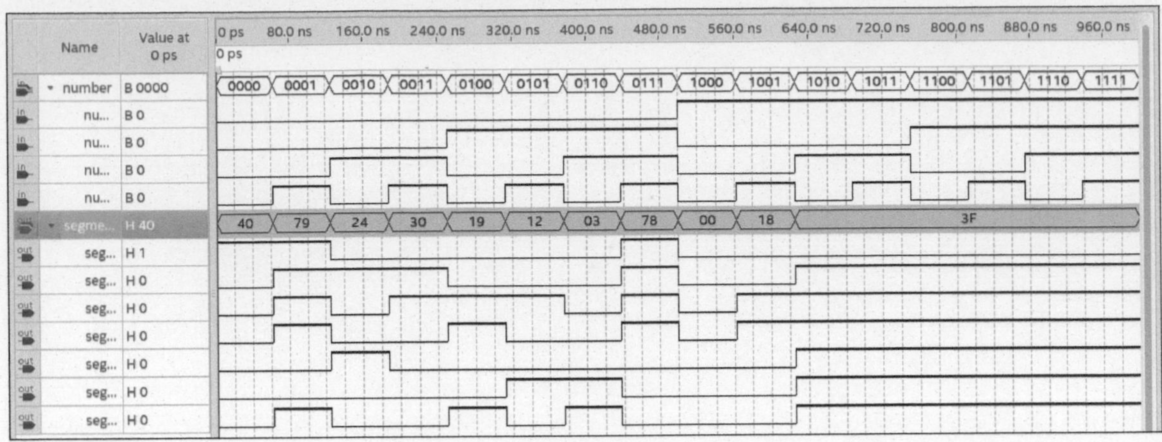

Figure 6.4: Seven-segment display decoder simulation (provided for verification purposes).

Since 16 possible values are being simulated and the default simulation runtime is 1000 ns, it would be advisable to use the "counter" function in the simulator. Increment every 1000/16 ns (or 62.5 ns).

Paste a screenshot of the simulation below.

5E ·· 38

6.4.2 Multiplexing

1. Brainstorm the structure of the VHDL code for the multiplexer (do not enter it into your Quartus project yet). The implementation diagram is given in **Fig. 6.5**. The "/" over a signal indicates the number of elements within the bus.

   Complete the VHDL code by hand in your lab notebook using **Fig. 6.7**.

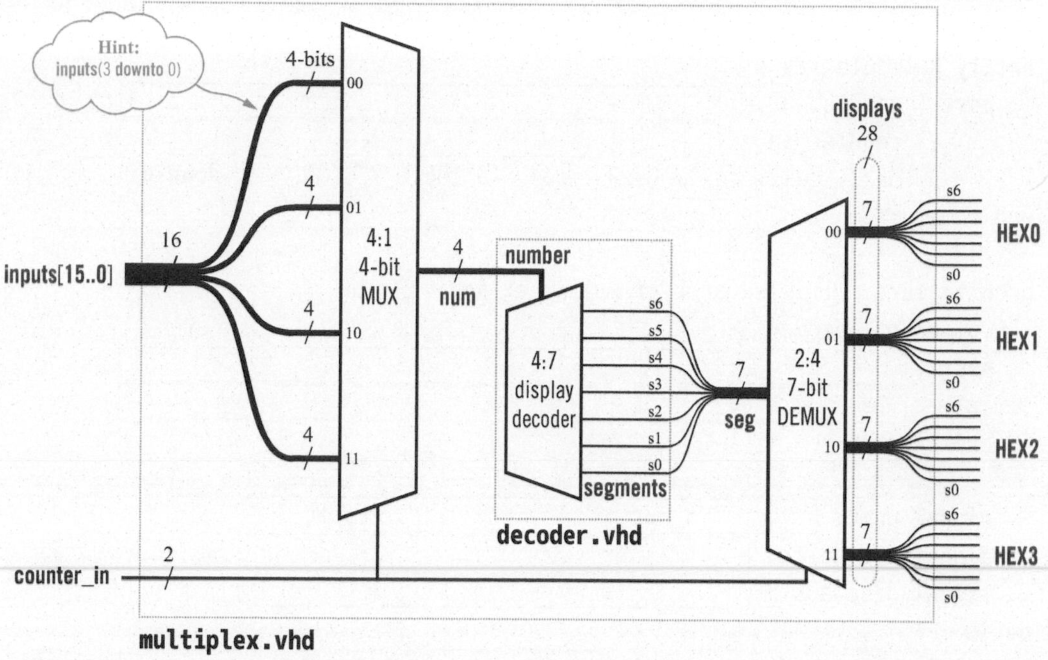

Figure 6.5: Multiplexer/decoder circuit for reading inputs and driving seven segment displays.

2. Add a new VHDL file to your Quartus project that already has **decoder.vhd**. Enter the code from the brainstorming portion of the lab into the new file. If everything is done correctly, Quartus should automatically update the hierarchy and place **decoder.vhd** underneath **multiplex.vhd** after you save the file and attempt to run synthesis.

   If the hierarchy does not get updated automatically, look at the component definition and the corresponding port map. You may have to right-click on the **multiplex.vhd** and select **Set as top-level entity**.

   Attempt to resolve any of the errors that appear during synthesis before coming to the laboratory. With enough thought, most errors in VHDL are self-explanatory. Check for missing semicolons, bus width consistency, and general spelling errors.

3. **Paste your completed code on the following page.**

   If there are errors that cannot be resolved prior to the laboratory, highlight the line causing the error (from the error description) on the printout and annotate the highlighted line with an abbreviated error that was received (example in **Fig. 6.6**).

```
architecture decoder_arch of decoder is
begin
    segments <= "1000000" when number = "0000" else
                "1111001" when number = "0001" else
                "0100100" when number = "0010" else
```

Width mismatch expecting 10 bits

Figure 6.6: Example code error annotation.

```
library IEEE;
use IEEE.STD_LOGIC_1164.ALL;
use IEEE.STD_LOGIC_UNSIGNED.ALL;

entity multiplex is
   port ( inputs       : ____ ____________________ ;
          counter_in   : ____ ____________________ ;
          hex3, hex2, hex1, hex0 : out STD_LOGIC_VECTOR(____ downto ____) );
end entity;

architecture multiplex_arch of multiplex is
   component decoder
   port ( ________ : ____ ____________________ ;
          ________ : ____ ____________________ );
   end component;

   signal num : ____________________ ;
   signal seg, off : ____________________ ;
   signal displays : ____________________ ;
begin
   dec_inst : decoder port map ( ________ => num, ________ => seg);
   off <= "1111111";

   with counter_in select
   num <= ________________ when "00",
          ________________ when "01",
          ________________ when "10",
          ________________ when "11",
          "0000" when others;

   with counter_in select
   displays <= ______ & ______ & ______ & ______ when "00",
               ______ & ______ & ______ & ______ when "01",
               ______ & ______ & ______ & ______ when "10",
               ______ & ______ & ______ & ______ when "11",
               off & off & off & off when others;

   hex3 <= displays( ____________ );
   hex2 <= displays( ____________ );
   hex1 <= displays( ____________ );
   hex0 <= displays( ____________ );
end architecture;
```

Figure 6.7: Multiplexer code brainstorming.

Multiplexer VHDL code.

5E .. 40

6.4.3 Pin Assignments

Complete the pin assignments in **Table 6.2** (refer to **Appendix H**). **Hint**: the location of the clock is given on the first page of the appendix. Pick either one of the pins specified.

Table 6.2: Pin assignments table.

Port Name	Port Function	Pin Location	Logic Level	Current Strength	Slew Rate
sw[7]	SW7				—
sw[6]	SW6				—
sw[5]	SW5				—
sw[4]	SW4				—
sw[3]	SW3				—
sw[2]	SW2				—
sw[1]	SW1				—
sw[0]	SW0				—
clk	CLOCK				—

Segment	Display hex0	hex1	hex2	hex3	Logic Level	Current Strength	Slew Rate
s6 [6]	C17	B17	B22	E17	3.3-V LVCMOS	2 mA	2
s5 [5]							
s4 [4]							
s3 [3]							
s2 [2]							
s1 [1]							
s0 [0]							

6.5 Laboratory

6.5.1 Required Equipment and Parts

The following items are needed to complete this laboratory:

- FPGA development board, USB cable

6.5.2 Symbol Block Creation

Read **Appendix D.5**, skipping section **D.5.2**.

If the directory structure requirements have not been followed thus far, organize the directory structure on the drive according to the guidelines in the appendix.

1. Once the code from pre-laboratory synthesizes correctly, generate a symbol file for the multiplexer/decoder (**Fig. 6.8**) by following the instructions given in **Appendix D.5.1**.

   Copy the **.bsf** and **.vhd** files into the `/cec222/blocks` directory. Remember that there are two VHDL files: **`multiplex.vhd`** and **`decoder.vhd`**.

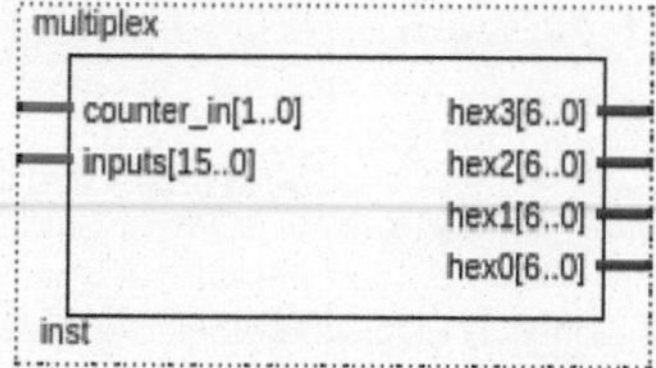

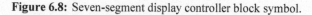

Figure 6.8: Seven-segment display controller block symbol.

   At this point, the directory structure should resemble **Fig. 6.9**.

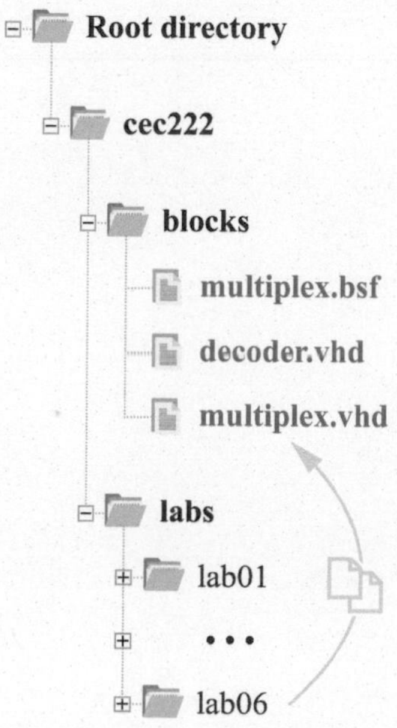

Figure 6.9: Directory structure.

2. **Demonstrate the directory structure to a teaching assistant.**

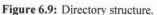

5E ·· 42

6.5.3 Supporting Files

1. Download **blocks.zip**—a file containing two blocks: a 2-bit 1 kHz counter, necessary to drive the multiplexer block, and a port breakout block that pads the upper eight bits on the multiplexer block inputs with zeros and passes through the lower eight bits (as switch inputs). The link is given in the GitHub box in the margin.

Code available @ GitHub
https://git.io/JvupZ

2. Unarchive the files into the `/cec222/blocks` directory. Make sure to place the **.bsf** and **.vhd** files directly into the **blocks** folder.

   Your directory structure should look similar to **Fig. 6.10**.

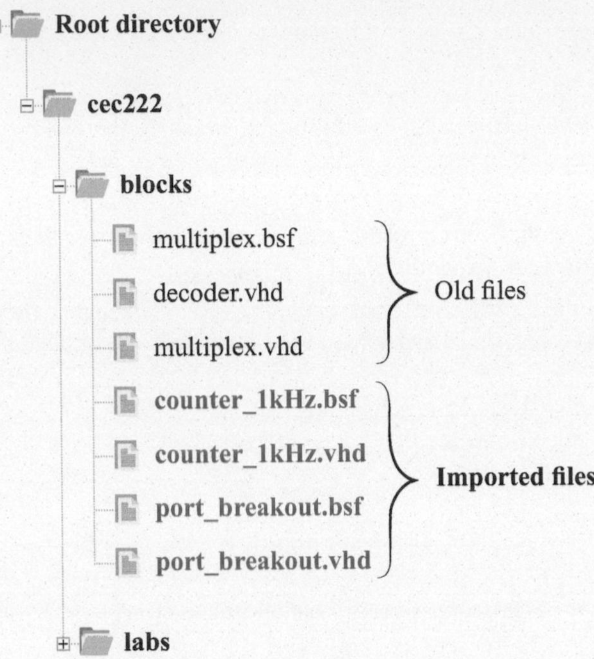

Figure 6.10: Directory structure.

6.5.4 Using Custom Symbol Libraries

All of the symbol blocks created to date will be integrated within a single block diagram.

1. Open a new Quartus project and create a blank block diagram.
2. Read **Appendix D.5.2** and follow the steps to create the block diagram in (**Fig. 6.11**).

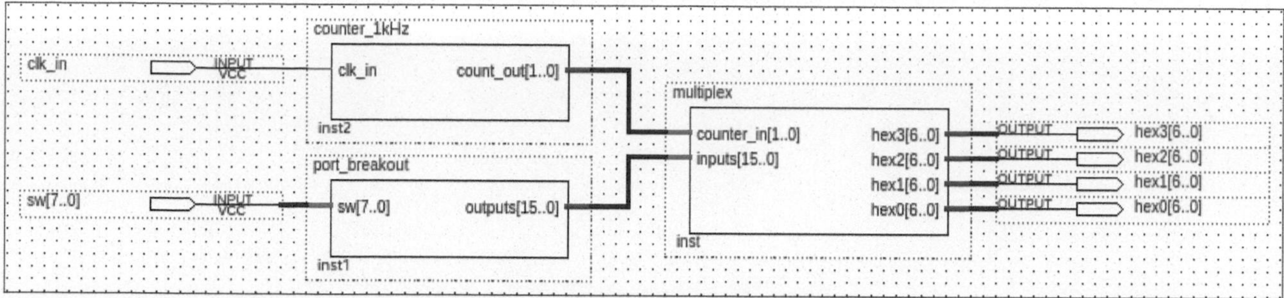

Figure 6.11: Multiplexed displays block diagram.

3. Synthesize the block diagram, assign pins using *Pin Planner*, and program the FPGA development board. Resolve any issues with the code, should synthesis fail. **Note that it is possible to edit the code for the block directly by double-clicking it. The original laboratory files do not have to be modified** (and your changes will be saved in your `/cec222/blocks` directory).
4. Paste the working block diagram and VHDL code for the multiplexer (if modified during laboratory) on the following pages.
5. **Demonstrate the set-up to a teaching assistant.**
6. Take pictures of the FPGA development board in operation with the following switch settings and paste them on the page following the VHDL code.

   - **31** (*i.e.*, switches set to **`0011 0001`**, should display **`0031`**)
   - **FE** (should display **`00--`**)
   - Last two digits of your **sort number** (if assigned), shown with two leading zeros

   Scale the printouts so they fit in the space provided. Make sure that both the display and switches are visible.
7. **If the multiplexer or decoder code was revised during laboratory, please paste the new version into the appropriate pre-laboratory section.**

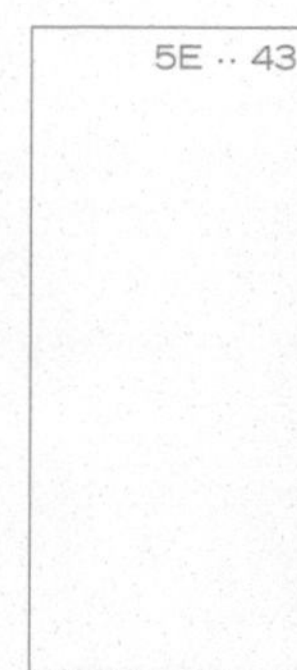

Paste the block diagram below. Don't forget to include a footer.

FPGA development board images.

31 (switches set to **`0011 0001`**, should display **`0031`**)

FE (should display **`00--`**)

Last two digits of sort no., padded with leading zeros

6.6 Questions

1. When implementing blanking for the seven-segment display that was created using hardware (previous laboratory), a combinational circuit had to be developed. What would need to be changed in order to implement blanking on the FPGA?

2. What would need to be changed in order to display hexadecimal (**A-F**) digits?

3. What is the function of a multiplexer (summarize, as if explaining to a child)? Give two real-world applications of multiplexers.

Servo Motor Control

7.1 Overview

The goal of this laboratory is to create a servo motor controller that uses pulse width modulation (PWM) to communicate with the motor. A PWM generator will be designed, implemented, and its performance will be evaluated by observing the behavior of the servo and capturing the PWM waveform using the oscilloscope.

GRADE SHEET DOWNLOAD
https://git.io/JeYMK

7.2 Objectives

At the conclusion of this lab, the student should be able to:

1. Use the general purpose input/output (GPIO) port for interfacing with peripherals.
2. Design VHDL code containing concurrent arithmetic operations and number conversions.
3. Use pulse width modulation (PWM) for controlling a servo motor.
4. Analyze the PWM waveform and determine its compliance with design requirements.
5. Use an oscilloscope to capture time-varying signals.
6. Implement conversions and counters in VHDL.
7. Implement sequential processes and concurrent statements in VHDL.

7.3 Background

Prior to reading this section, read the tutorial on dimming LEDs with PWM in **Appendix F**.

7.3.1 Servo Motors

This lab will use a 9-gram micro servo motor with plastic gears, TowerPro SG90. This model is used extensively in hobby RC aircraft building, since it is durable, inexpensive, and lightweight.

In servo motors, PWM is used for communicating the required motor shaft position. Based on the duty cycle of the PWM signal received, the motor control system automatically adjusts the position of the shaft with constant feedback from an internal potentiometer (**Fig. 7.1**).

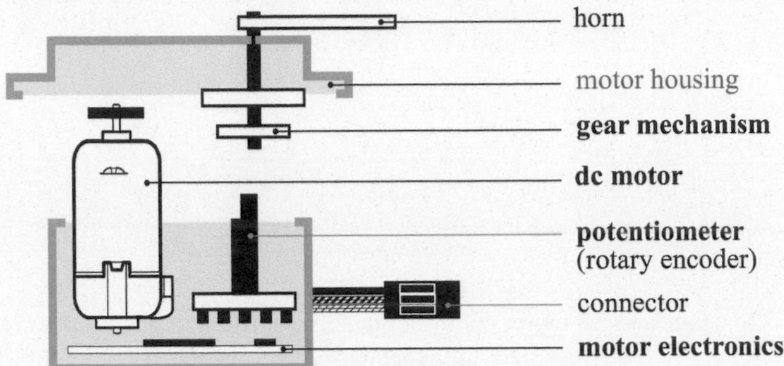

Figure 7.1: An exploded view of a servo motor.

A servo motor has four main components:

1. **direct current (dc) motor**
2. **gearbox** (to "gear down" the dc motor, so that it provides more torque)
3. **potentiometer** (rotary encoder) for measuring the angle of the servo motor shaft
4. **electronics**, implementing a feedback control system

The period T of the PWM waveform for most servo motors is 20 ms, with a changing duty cycle (just like with LED dimming). In the case of the TowerPro SG90, a t_{on} of 0.75 ms results in 0° positioning, while 2.5 ms results in the motor shaft rotating into the 180° position (despite the fact that the official datasheet states ≈1-2 ms.. **the information given in the datasheet is incorrect**, but such sloppy tolerances are expected from a $2 servo motor).

Most servos have three connections, as shown in **Fig. 7.2**.

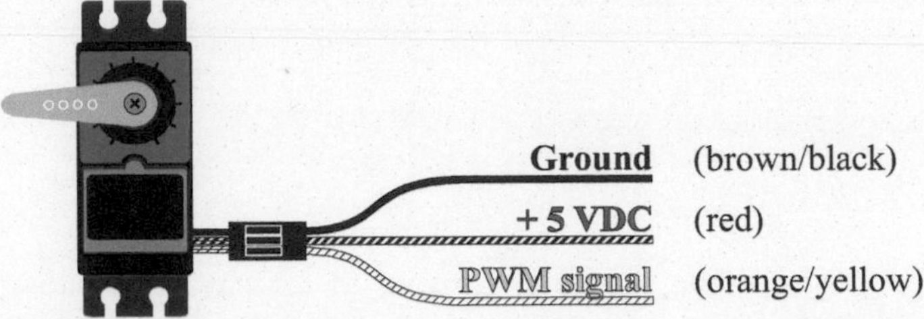

Figure 7.2: View of the connections for a typical servo motor.

7.4 Pre-laboratory

Read all of **Appendix F**. It is an essential reference when completing the pre-lab assignments and the laboratory itself.

7.4.1 Duty Cycle and Transition Calculations

1. Based on the fact that the FPGA development board has a 50 MHz clock (and knowing that for the SG90 servo a t_{on} of 0.75 ms results in 0° positioning, while 2.5 ms results in the motor shaft rotating into the 180° position), fill out **Table 7.1** below and determine the number of clock cycles for each period T (20 ms).

5E ·· 44

Table 7.1: Position vs. duty cycle calculations.

Position	`SW9..0`	Duty cycle	Timing	Clock cycles
0°	`00 0000 0000`	3.75%	0.75 ms / 20 ms	37,500
45°				
90°				
135°				
180°	`00 1011 0100`		2.5 ms / 20 ms	

Cycles per period = ______________________ cycles

2. Derive a general formula for calculating the cycle, during which the PWM waveform should drop down to a logic-LOW (similar to the approach discussed in the appendix). This formula should relate the converted decimal input from 10 slide switches **`SW9..0`** to the number of cycles required for proper motor shaft positioning from **Table 7.1**.

5E ·· 45

```
transition = CONV_INTEGER(inputs) * ______________________
```

7.4.2 VHDL Code and Simulations

5E ·· 46

1. Implement your PWM servo motor controller in VHDL. Name the top-level entity **`servo`**, instead of **`dimmer`**. Synthesize the code to make sure that it does not contain any errors (resolve the errors if they appear during synthesis). Paste the code below.

2. Read **Appendix G**, which covers the ModelSim simulation tool. Simulate your design using ModelSim for two periods of the PWM signal (switch positions for 0° and 180° on a single waveform). Paste a screen capture of the simulation below. Make sure the entire simulation is visible, along with port names.

5E .. 47

3. Complete the pin assignments in **Table 7.2** (refer to **Appendix H**).

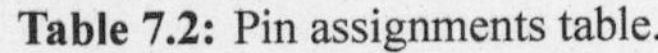
Table 7.2: Pin assignments table.

Port Name	Port Function	Pin Location	Logic Level	Current Strength	Slew Rate
inputs[9]	**SW9**		3.3-V LVCMOS	2 mA	—
inputs[8]	**SW8**				—
inputs[7]	**SW7**				—
inputs[6]	**SW6**				—
inputs[5]	**SW5**				—
inputs[4]	**SW4**				—
inputs[3]	**SW3**				—
inputs[2]	**SW2**				—
inputs[1]	**SW1**				—
inputs[0]	**SW0**				—
clk	clock				—
pwm	**GPIO1**				2

(Optional) To minimize the time spent in lab, assign the pins based on the table above using the *Pin Planner* tool in Quartus. Save the project and have it readily available for the laboratory.

7.5 Laboratory

7.5.1 Required Equipment and Parts

The following items are needed to complete this laboratory:

- male-to-female jumper wires
- TowerPro SG90 servo motor
- Analog Discovery scope
- FPGA development board, USB cable

7.5.2 Implementation and Testing

1. Synthesize, assign pins (if not already done), and compile the code for the PWM servo controller. Program the FPGA development board with your code.
2. Connect channel 1 of the Analog Discovery scope to pin 1 and ground of the GPIO port (refer to **Appendix H** for the location of the grounding pins of the GPIO port). Use only the oscilloscope inputs on the Analog Discovery. **Do not connect the power supply wires of the Analog Discovery to the power and ground pins of the FPGA board!** This could permanently damage either the Analog Discovery of the FPGA board.

   Display more than one, but less than two periods of the PWM waveform (see **Appendix F** for some examples of perfect triggering and waveform display). Test each of the five degree combinations completed in **Table. 7.1**, take automatic measurements using the Waveforms software and fill in **Table. 7.3**. The time results between the two tables should closely match.

Table 7.3: Position vs. t_{on} pulse width (experimental results).

Position	`SW9..0`	**Timing** (calculated)	**Timing** (experimental)
0°	`00 0000 0000`	0.75 ms / 20 ms	
45°			
90°			
135°			
180°	`00 1011 0100`	2.5 ms / 20 ms	

Troubleshooting.. If the results do not match, troubleshoot the transition calculation. Incorrectly implementing the order of operations (multiply first, then divide) is the number one error that students make when implementing this code. This will cause the transition period to be completely incorrect.

Since VHDL is performing integer division, dividing a smaller number by a larger number (*i.e.*, 1000/1001) will result in a zero. Dividing 3 by 2 would result in a 1 (the decimal would be truncated).

3. Capture the PWM waveform for positions 0° and 180° using the Analog Discovery scope and paste the screen captures in the space below.

4. Connect the servo motor to the FPGA development board, as indicated in **Fig. 7.3**. Male-to-female jumper cables should be used between the GPIO port and the servo motor.

    - **ground** (brown/black) wire of the servo should be connected to the **GND** pin.
    - **power** (red) wire should be connected to the **5V** pin.
    - **signal** (orange/yellow) wire should be connected to pin 1 of the GPIO port.

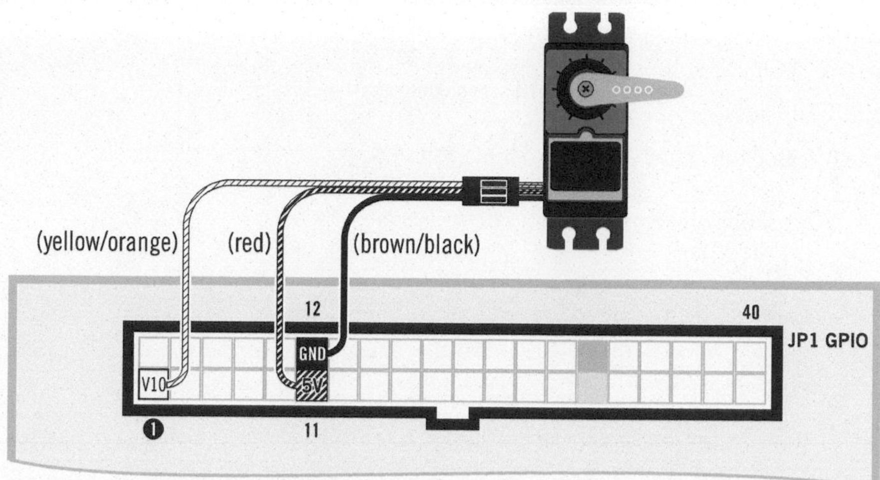

Figure 7.3: Connections between the FPGA development board and the servo motor.

5. Verify the functionality of the design: when the switches are set to `00 0000 0000` (0°), the motor horn should turn to the right. When the switches are set to `00 1011 0100` (180°), the horn should turn to the left.

6. Once the functionality of your design has been verified, **demonstrate the set up to a teaching assistant.** 5E ·· 49

    Do not close the Quartus project and proceed to the next section (after code).

7. **If the servo controller code was revised during laboratory, please paste the new version into the appropriate pre-laboratory section.**

7.5.3 Symbol Block Creation

1. Generate a symbol file for the PWM controller (**Fig. 7.4**) by following the instructions given in **Appendix D.5.1**. Copy the **.bsf** and **.vhd** files into the `/cec222/blocks` directory.

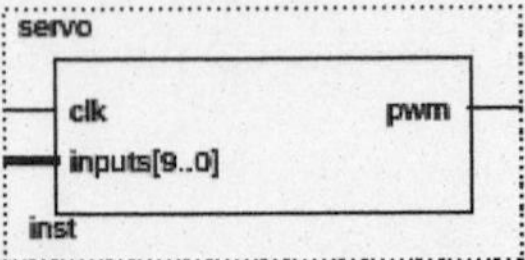

Figure 7.4: PWM servo controller block symbol.

At this point, the directory structure should resemble **Fig. 7.5**.

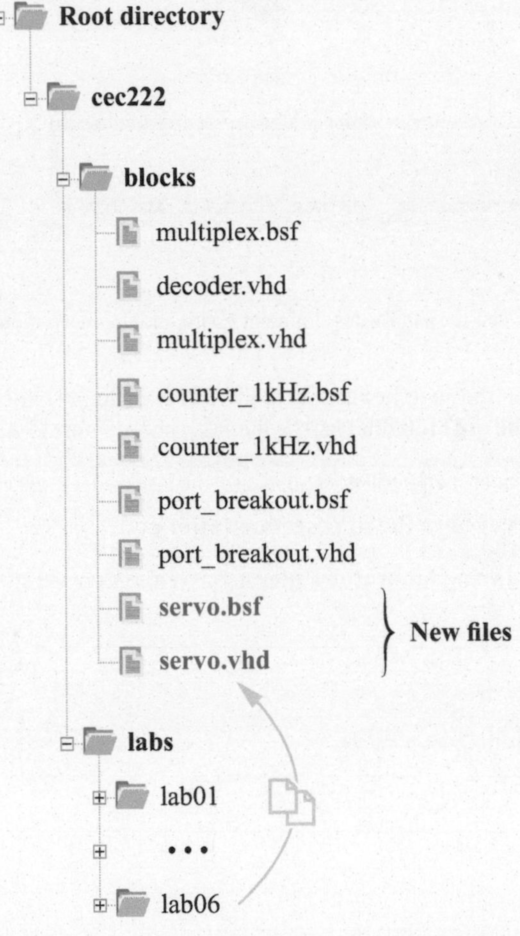

Figure 7.5: Directory structure.

5E ·· 50

2. **Demonstrate the directory structure to a teaching assistant.**
   This may also be the time to synchronize the lab files (**cec222** directory) with a partner.

LABORATORY 8

Accelerometer Interfacing

8.1 Overview

This laboratory will introduce the use of serial peripheral interface (SPI) for communicating with a 3-axis MEMS accelerometer. The format for accelerometer readings will be explored and a concurrent arithmetic block will be created, allowing the conversion of uncalibrated two's complement accelerometer data into unsigned degree measures 0° to 180°.

As a final step of the implementation, a block diagram will be used to implement a real-time open-loop feedback system, which will capture accelerometer readings and drive a servo motor.

GRADE SHEET DOWNLOAD
https://git.io/JeYN6

8.2 Objectives

At the conclusion of this lab, the student should be able to:

1. Use the SPI interface for communicating with an accelerometer.
2. Analyze accelerometer data, determine the relationship between accelerometer positioning and axis data.
3. Implement a conversion block, which translates from uncalibrated 2's complement accelerometer output to an unsigned degree measure.
4. Design VHDL code containing concurrent arithmetic operations and number conversions.
5. Integrate previously created block symbols with the current design.

8.3 Background

8.3.1 Concurrent arithmetic

In VHDL, all calculations can be executed concurrently, instead of sequentially. As soon as there is data on the input port, an immediate result can be obtained. If multiple calculations are required, all of them can be executed at once (although this requires careful thought).

Sequential operations increase the area utilization on an FPGA and are many times larger (area-wise) than their concurrent counterparts.

An additional library **STD_LOGIC_UNSIGNED** was used in the previous labs. This library contains mathematical operations pertaining to unsigned integers.

8.3.2 2's Complement Measurements

The on-board ADXL345 accelerometer is configured to take measurements every 200 ms (five times per second). The data that is returned represents a 10-bit 2's complement (signed) binary number. Sample measurements can be seen in **Fig. 8.2**.

In the figure, the FPGA development board is tilted from $-90°$ to $+90°$. The accelerometer measures in ranges **0255..0**, **1023..0768**. Recall from in-class discussions that "signed number representations" are just that: representations. Computers still operate with purely positive binary numbers. If the ranges were translated into signed decimal representations using the 2's complement scheme (invert all bits, add 1), the range would be **255..0,-1..-256**.

The accelerometer data can represent $256 + 256$ levels, or 512 levels in total (**Fig. 8.1**).

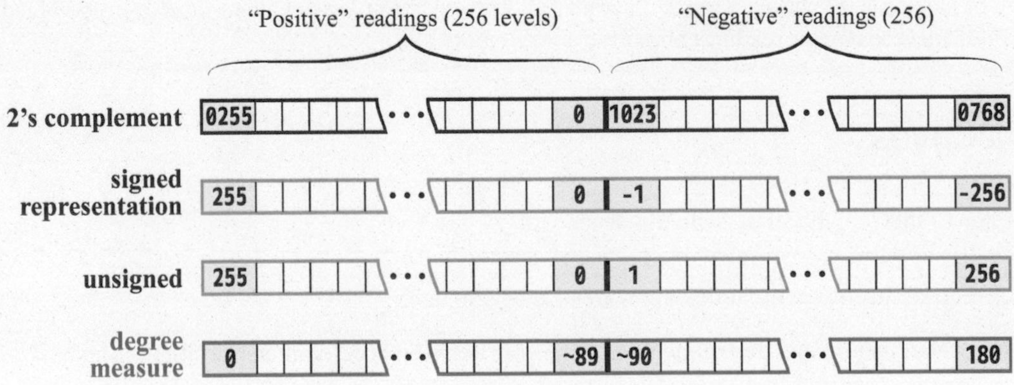

Figure 8.1: Different representations (conversion goal is at the very bottom).

For the code sample below, assume that there is a **signal temp(8..0)** and an input port for 2's complement accelerometer data **axl_in(9..0)**. To convert the input to an unsigned integer, the following steps should be followed:

1. Determine whether or not the number is negative by examining the sign bit [the most significant bit—in this case, **axl_in(9)**].
2. If **positive** (sign bit is zero), do nothing and propagate lower magnitude bits into **temp**.
3. If **negative** (sign bit is 1), invert all magnitude bits and add 1. Propagate into **temp**.

```
with axl_in(9) select
temp <= axl_in(8 downto 0) when '0',
       (not axl_in(8 downto 0) + 1) when '1',
       (others => 'X') when others;
```

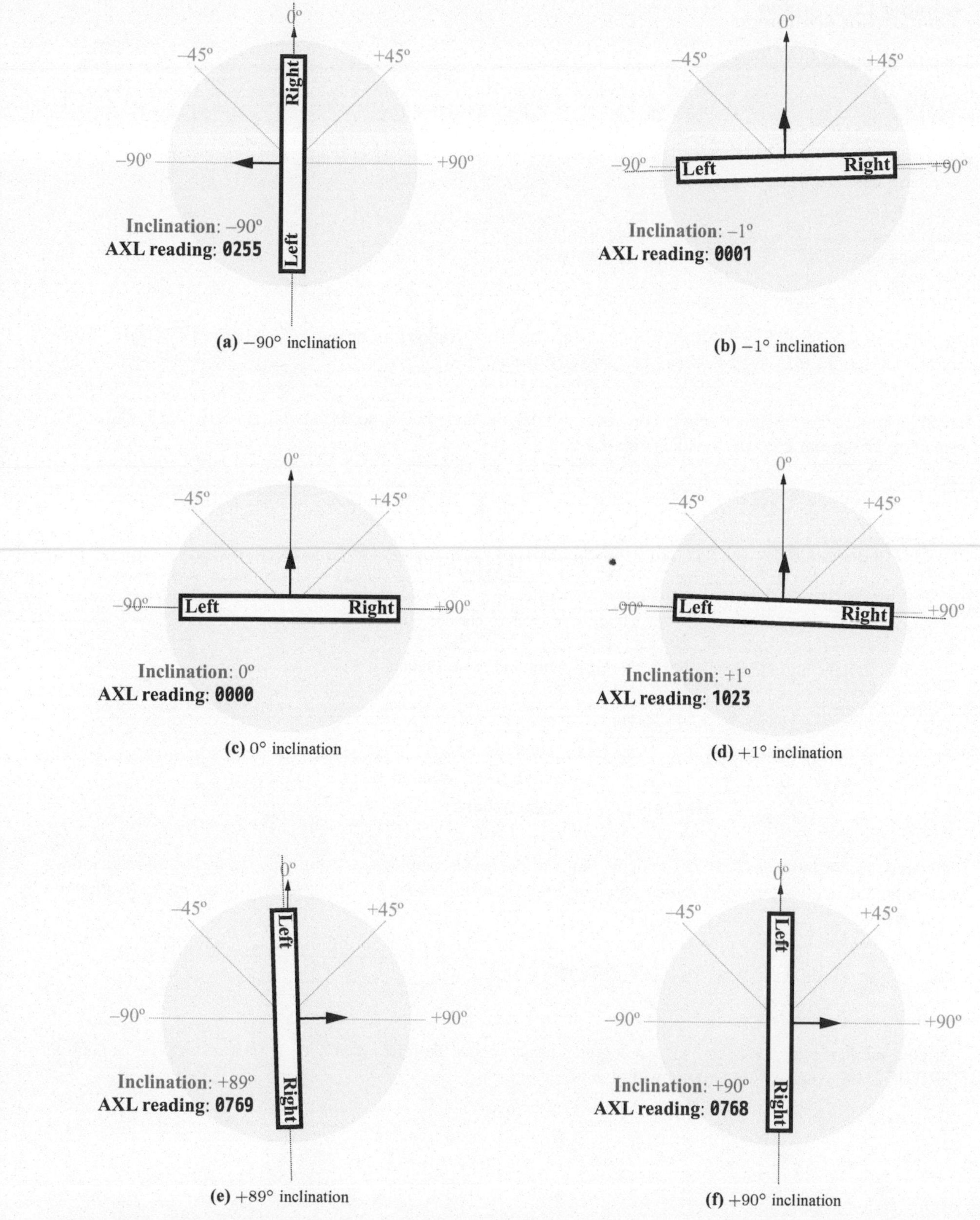

The **black** rectangle represents the FPGA development board. Left and right sides are marked. The readout occurs on the X axis of the accelerometer. Readings are approximate, designed to illustrate the "big picture". $1° \neq$ **001**.

Figure 8.2: Accelerometer inclination vs. data readout

8.4 Pre-laboratory

8.4.1 Number Conversion

Assume the following entity declaration:

```
library IEEE;
use IEEE.STD_LOGIC_1164.ALL;
use IEEE.STD_LOGIC_UNSIGNED.ALL;
use IEEE.STD_LOGIC_ARITH.ALL;

entity axl_interface is
    Port ( axl_in : in STD_LOGIC_VECTOR (9 downto 0);
           degrees : out STD_LOGIC_VECTOR (9 downto 0) );
end entity;
```

Side note: the **STD_LOGIC_UNSIGNED** library supports arithmetic operations on unsigned numbers; **STD_LOGIC_ARITH** library contains functions to convert between vectors and integers.

1. Recalling the 2's complement conversion code, modify the code below so the output spans **0..255,256..511**, instead of the current **255..0,1..256** (Fig. 8.3).

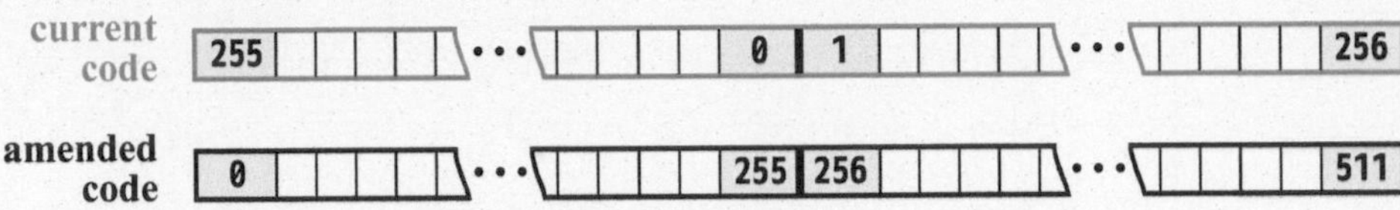

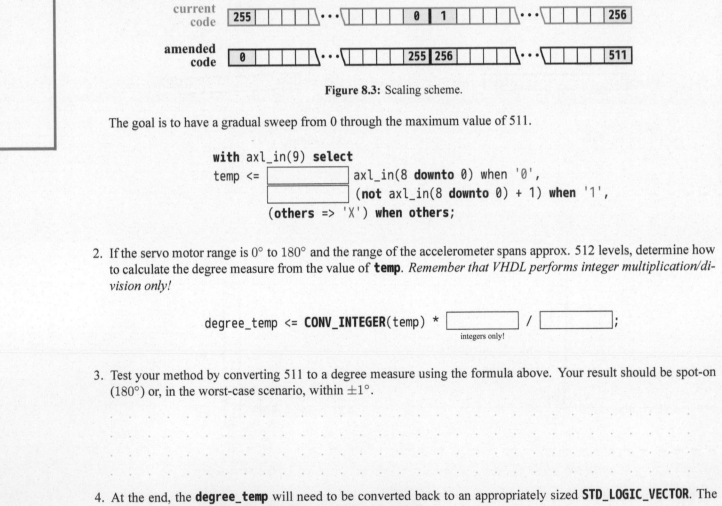

Figure 8.3: Scaling scheme.

The goal is to have a gradual sweep from 0 through the maximum value of 511.

```
with axl_in(9) select
temp <= [          ] axl_in(8 downto 0) when '0',
        [          ] (not axl_in(8 downto 0) + 1) when '1',
        (others => 'X') when others;
```

2. If the servo motor range is 0° to 180° and the range of the accelerometer spans approx. 512 levels, determine how to calculate the degree measure from the value of **temp**. *Remember that VHDL performs integer multiplication/division only!*

```
degree_temp <= CONV_INTEGER(temp) * [          ] / [          ];
```

integers only!

3. Test your method by converting 511 to a degree measure using the formula above. Your result should be spot-on (180°) or, in the worst-case scenario, within $\pm 1°$.

4. At the end, the **degree_temp** will need to be converted back to an appropriately sized **STD_LOGIC_VECTOR**. The width should be 10 bits (specified by the second argument):

```
degrees <= CONV_STD_LOGIC_VECTOR(degree_temp, 10);
```

5. Develop your code in Quartus (synthesize and resolve any errors). **Paste it below.**

5E · · 52

6. Simulate the **axl_interface** code with *qsim*.

   Add the two ports (**axl_in** and **degrees**) to the simulation. Right click on each port and select **Radix** > **Unsigned Decimal**—this way, it is possible to enter and view signal values directly in decimal.

   Two simulations should be generated:

   a) Test the "positive" range of input values **0255..0000** (should return approx. 0° to 90°).
   b) Test "negative" range **1023..0768** (returns approx. 90° to 180°).

This can be accomplished by forcing a counter (increment every 350 ns), see **Fig. 8.4**.

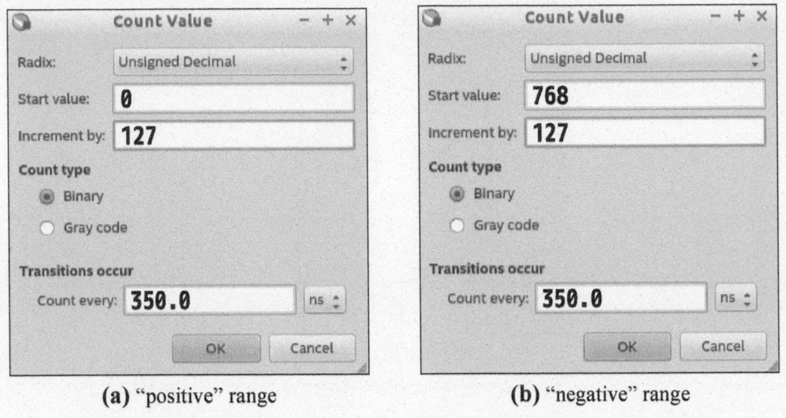

(a) "positive" range **(b)** "negative" range

Figure 8.4: Simulation settings (forcing an unsigned decimal counter).

Sample simulations are given in **Fig. 8.5**.

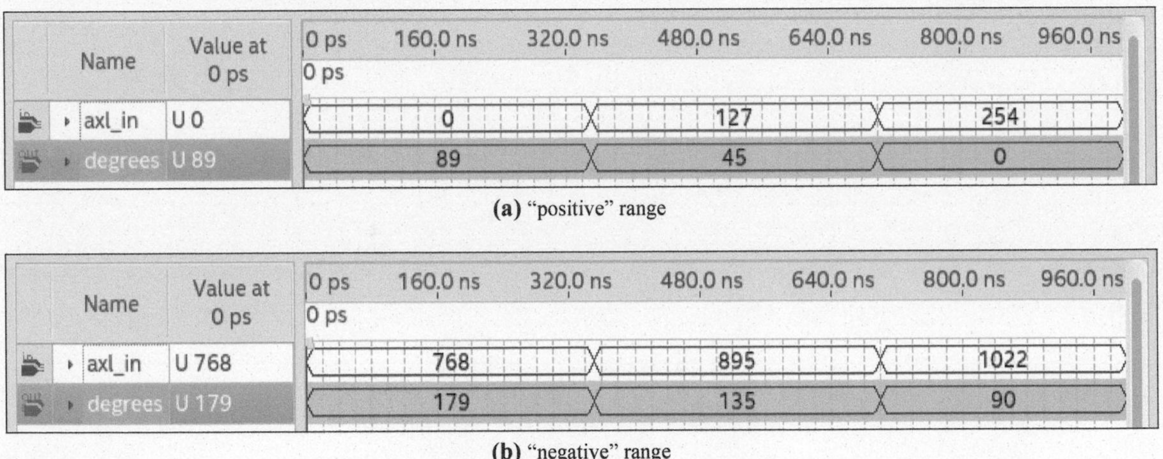

(a) "positive" range

(b) "negative" range

Figure 8.5: Sample simulations.

Paste the simulations on the following page. After simulating your code, do not quit Quartus or close the project. Move on to the next step.

Simulations for `axl_interface`.

5E .. 53

8.4.2 Symbol Block Creation

1. Generate a symbol file for the AXL interface (**Fig. 8.6**) by following the instructions given in **Appendix D.5.1**. Copy the **.bsf** and **.vhd** files into the `/cec222/blocks` directory.

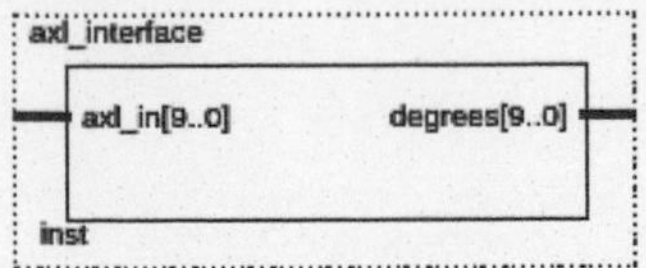

Figure 8.6: AXL interface block symbol.

8.4.3 Supporting Files

1. Download **`blocks.zip`**—a file containing two blocks: one for communicating with the accelerometer over the SPI interface, along with all supporting VHDL files, and another for converting from a 10-bit binary number to a 16-bit binary-coded decimal (BCD) number. The link is given in the GitHub box in the margin.

2. Unarchive the files into the `/cec222/blocks` directory. Make sure to place the **.bsf** and **.vhd** files directly into the **blocks** folder.

   Your directory structure should look similar to **Fig. 8.7**.

Code available @ GitHub
https://git.io/JeYDs

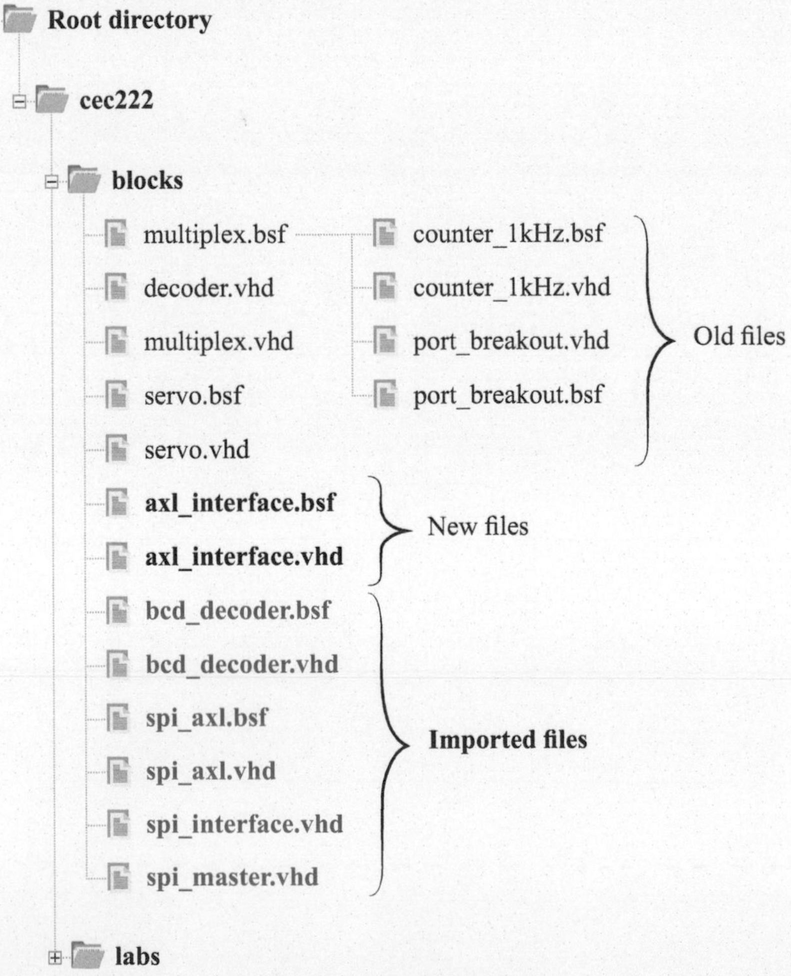

Figure 8.7: Directory structure.

8.4.4 Using Custom Symbol Libraries

All of the symbol blocks created to date will be integrated within a single block diagram.

1. Open a new Quartus project and create a blank block diagram.
2. Read **Appendix D.5.2** and follow the steps to create the block diagram in **(Fig. 8.8)**.

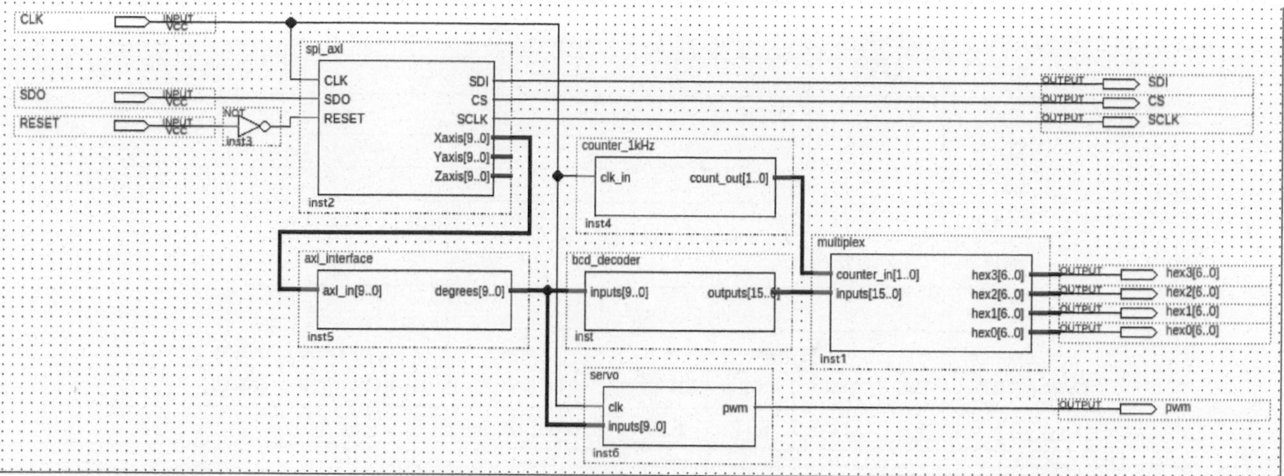

Figure 8.8: Accelerometer-based servo control block diagram.

Note that the **RESET** input has an inverter connected to it. This is to account for the fact that the **KEY0** pushbutton is normally closed (NC), which makes it logic-LOW whenever it is depressed.

3. Save the project and have it readily-accessible for lab. **Print and paste the block diagram below.** Don't forget to include a footer.

8.4.5 Pin Assignments

Complete pin assignments in **Table 8.1** (refer to **Appendix H**, look closely at the section covering the accelerometer).

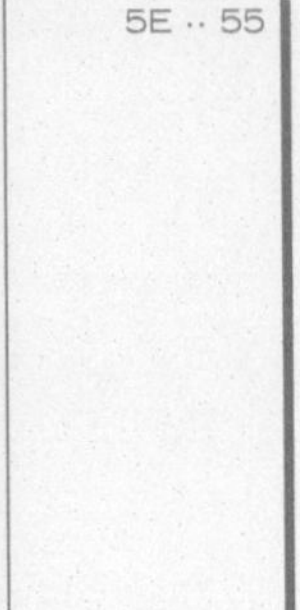

Table 8.1: Pin assignments table.

Port Name	Port Function	Pin Location	Logic Level	Current Strength	Slew Rate
CLK	CLOCK		3.3-V LVCMOS	2 mA	—
RESET	KEY0				—
SDO	—				—
SDI	—				2
CS	—				2
SCLK	—				2
pwm	GPIO1				—

Segment	Display				Logic Level	Current Strength	Slew Rate
	hex0	hex1	hex2	hex3			
s6 [6]	C17	B17	B22	E17	3.3-V LVCMOS	2 mA	2
s5 [5]							
s4 [4]							
s3 [3]							
s2 [2]							
s1 [1]							
s0 [0]							

(Optional) To minimize the time spent in lab, assign the pins based on the table above using the *Pin Planner* tool in Quartus. Save the project and have it readily available for the laboratory.

8.5 Laboratory

8.5.1 Required Equipment and Parts

The following items are needed to complete this laboratory:

- FPGA development board, USB cable
- TowerPro SG90 servo motor
- Male-to-female jumper wires

8.5.2 Testing

1. Synthesize the project, assign pins (if they haven't been assigned during the pre-laboratory portion), compile, and program the FPGA development board.

   You should observe numbers from `000` to `180` displayed as the board is tilted side-to-side. The count should be smooth (chunks of numbers should not be skipped). If the board is stuck on a number, press the pushbuttons on the right side of the board to reset it. If this does not correct the issue, verify the block diagram connections (no connections should be shorted together or missing).

   Troubleshooting. If the numbers are "jumping over" a certain range (especially around the 90° mark, when the board is pointing upward), your `axl_interface` was not designed correctly. Go back to the `axl_interface` project and troubleshoot your code (remember to re-create your symbol files after the code is fixed).

2. After ascertaining that the code is working properly, connect the servo motor to the FPGA development board, as shown in **Fig. 8.9**. Male-to-female jumper wires should be used between GPIO pins and the servo motor.

   - **ground** (brown/black) wire of the servo should be connected to the **GND** pin.
   - **power** (red) wire should be connected to the **5V** pin.
   - **signal** (orange/yellow) wire should be connected to pin 1 of the GPIO port.

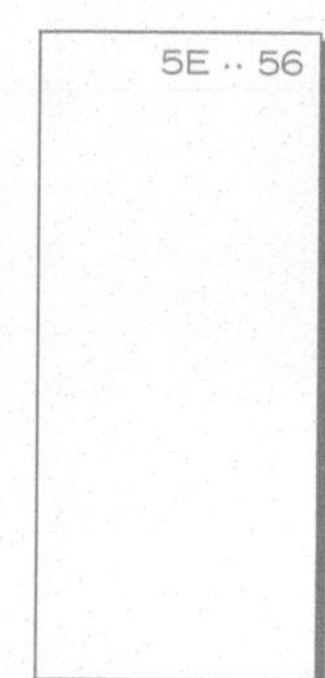

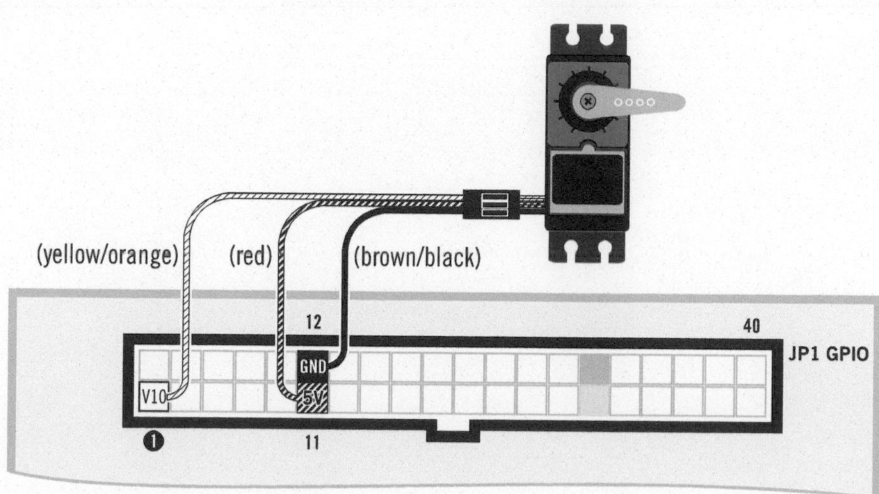

Figure 8.9: Connections between the FPGA development board and the servo motor.

3. As you tilt the FPGA development board from side to side, the servo motor should instantly respond and drive the horn to the appropriate degree position.

   Demonstrate the operation of your circuit to the TA.

4. **If block diagrams or code were updated during the lab, paste them into the appropriate pre-laboratory sections.**

LABORATORY 9

SPDT Switch De-bouncing, Multiplexers

9.1 Overview

This laboratory focuses on the development of a *de-bounce* circuit for a single-pole double-throw (SPDT) switch. Both the debounced and the non-debounced signal waveforms will be captured using an Analog Discovery scope (using the digital signal analyzer functionality) and the de-bouncing circuit will be integrated with a counter and multiplexer.

At the end of the laboratory, the performance of both circuits will be evaluated to determine whether or not they have similar functionality.

GRADE SHEET DOWNLOAD
https://git.io/JeYNi

9.2 Objectives

At the conclusion of this lab, the student should be able to:

1. Interpret and explain experimental results, based on the behavior of a logic circuit.
2. Implement a single-pole double-throw (SPDT) switch de-bounce circuit using a combinational logic circuit of an S-R latch in VHDL.
3. Integrate the de-bounce circuit with other components, such as counters.
4. Implement de-bouncing circuit using standard components, integrate it with counter ICs.
5. Trigger the Analog Discovery oscilloscope either on the rising or falling edge (in digital mode), in order to capture circuit behavior.

9.3 Background

9.3.1 SPDT Switches and Mechanical Bounce

Switches are mechanical devices—when the contacts of the switch touch one another under the force of actuation, contact is not established instantaneously. There is no "crisp" transition from the *on* state to the *off* state. What typically happens (due to the elasticity of contact materials) is that the contacts encounter a "bounce", where the switch alternates between the on and off states for some period of time, before finally coming to rest in the final state.

In most applications, the switch bounce happens so quickly that the millisecond-long pulses of alternating states do not affect the final outcome. With digital circuits, however, since a single cycle of the clock measures 20 ns (or much less with state-of-the-art machines), switch bounce can be erroneously interpreted as multiple inputs. Consider a keyboard that transmits a dozen or so characters every time a single key is pressed—this would be problematic.

This laboratory will use a single-pole double-throw (SPDT) switch, which means that there are 3 switch contacts (a typical SPDT switch is shown in **Fig. 9.1**): (1) common connection (**COM**), (2) normally-open (**NO**)—logic-HIGH when depressed, and (3) normally-closed (**NC**)—logic-LOW when depressed.

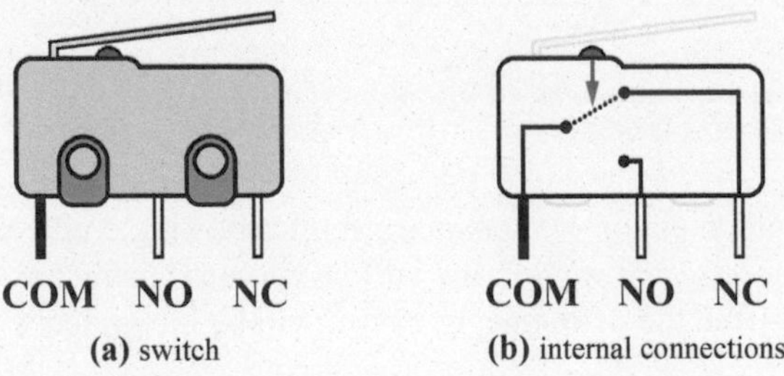

Figure 9.1: SPDT switch and internal connections.

These switches can be directly integrated with an S-R latch to provide "clean" output. This is called *de-bouncing* the switch (**Fig. 9.2**).

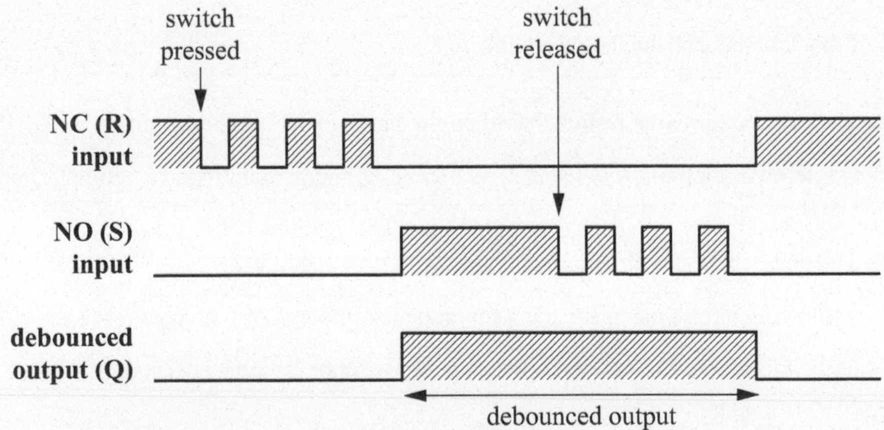

Figure 9.2: Debounced pushbutton output using an S-R latch.

Fig. 9.3 illustrates the wiring schematic for a typical SPDT application.

This configuration connects the common terminal (**COM**) to power. Whenever the **COM** is connected with **NC**, power is provided to the **NC** terminal (resulting in a logic-HIGH signal). Once the connection is broken, the **NC** terminal is grounded (logic-LOW). Same is true for **NO**.

Switch bounce (and *de-bounced* output) is shown in **Fig. 9.4**.

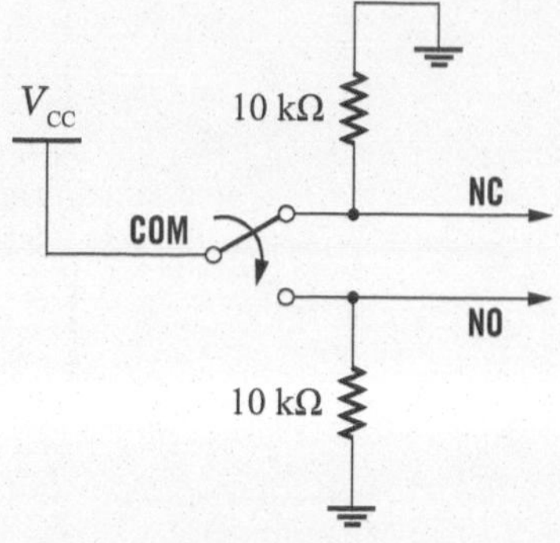

Figure 9.3: A circuit diagram for connecting an SPDT switch.

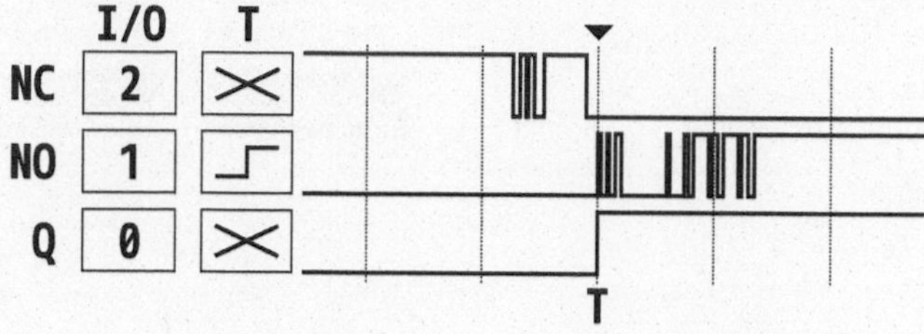

Figure 9.4: Waveform from **NC** and **NO** terminals, along with de-bounced signal.

9.4 Pre-laboratory

Complete this pre-laboratory exercise prior to the laboratory period. All work must be completed **in pen**. To allow for revisions, circuit diagrams may be completed in pencil.

9.4.1 Circuit Implementation

Wire the circuit in **Fig. 9.6** on the breadboard diagram in **Fig. 9.5**. Reference the appropriate data sheets in **Appendix J** to determine IC pinouts. All of the necessary components have already been placed onto the breadboard. Run the appropriate connections to the analog discovery scope.

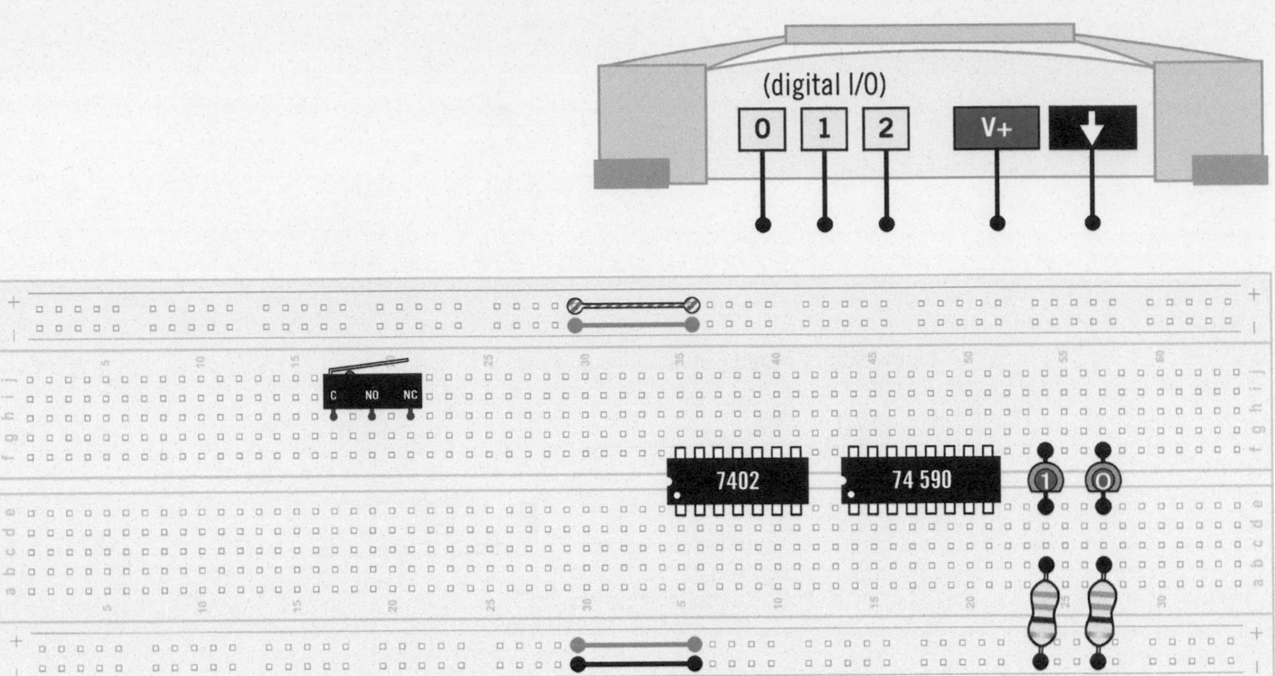

Figure 9.5: Laboratory breadboard wiring set up.

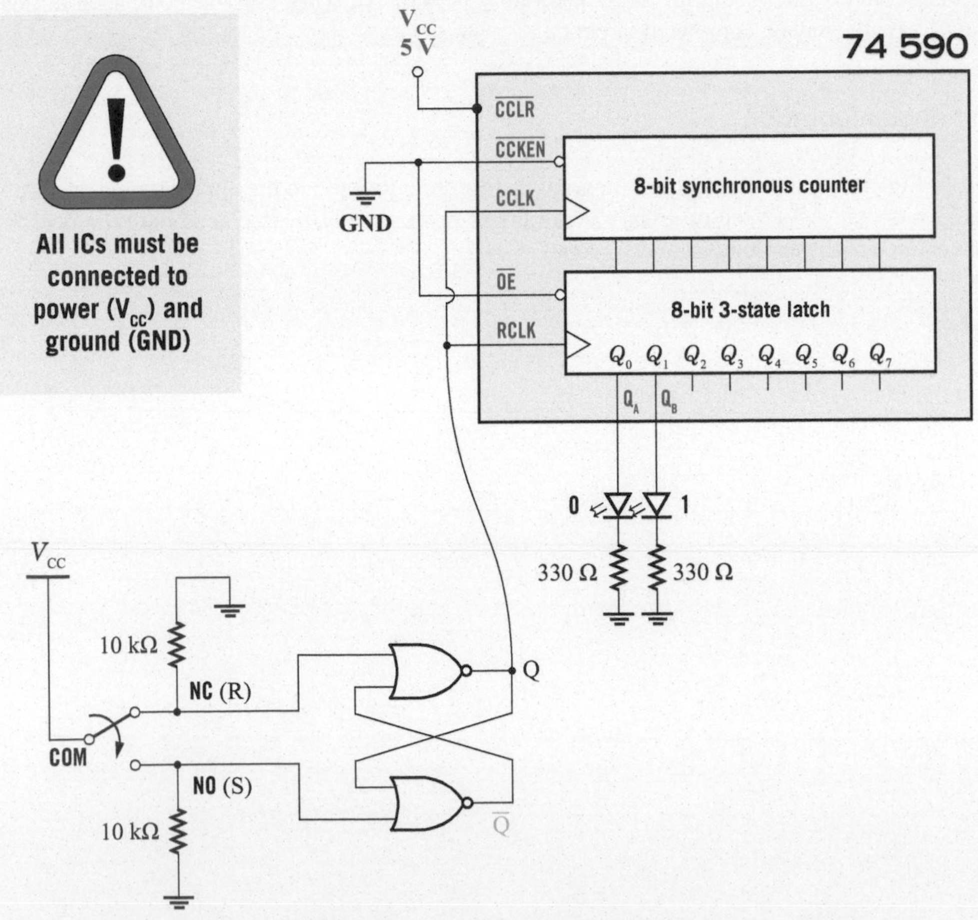

Figure 9.6: Laboratory circuit diagram.

9.5 Laboratory

9.5.1 Required Equipment and Parts

The following items are needed to complete this laboratory:

- resistors (2x 10 kΩ, 2x 330 Ω)
- ICs (1x 7402, 1x 74590)
- SPDT switch
- 2x LEDs
- breadboard
- wires
- Male-to-female jumper wires
- Analog Discovery scope

9.5.2 NOR Debounce Implementation

1. Wire just the NOR debounce circuit (the 7402 part of your diagram). Do not wire the rest of the circuit at this point in time. Connect the power and ground rails of the breadboard to the Analog Discovery voltage supply and power the 7402 IC.

   Practice a crucial engineering approach called *"Build a little, test a little"*. This will eliminate the possibility of errors propagating into the next steps of the laboratory.

2. Open the digital signal analyzer (**Logic**) portion of the Waveforms software. Connect the Analog Discovery to the computer.

   Examine the **NC** (normally closed switch output), **NO** (normally open switch output), and **Q** (latch output) signals using the Analog Discovery digital channels 2, 1, and 0, respectively. The scope should be grounded to the common ground rail on the breadboard, using the black (down arrow) lead on the pigtail. Trigger the **NO** output on the rising edge of the waveform.

   Run the digital signal analyzer and depress the switch. A de-bounced waveform should be visible on channel 0. If it does not resemble a waveform that was expected, troubleshoot the circuit (is the 5 V Analog Discovery power supply connected and operating?).

3. Take screen shots of pressing the SPDT switch and letting it go (two captures total). **Paste the captures on the following page.**

9.5.3 Full Wiring Implementation

1. Now that the latch is constructed, implement the remainder of the circuit. Remember to use the build-a-little, test-a-little principle.

   Use the LEDs and the Analog Discovery scope for debugging the circuit.

2. Once the circuit is wired and functionality has been verified, **demonstrate the set-up to a teaching assistant.**

5E ·· 58

Paste the two SPDT debounce captures below.

LABORATORY 10

Brushless DC Motor Control

10.1 Overview

This laboratory introduces Moore finite state machine-based control of brushless dc motors (BLDC). The design will first be implemented on paper and converted to VHDL code.

Three channels will be used—each corresponding to an individual coil in the BLDC motor.

GRADE SHEET DOWNLOAD
https://git.io/JeYMX

10.2 Objectives

At the conclusion of this lab, the student should be able to:

1. Test the resistance of individual coils of the brushless dc (BLDC) motor and determine their function based on relative resistances.
2. Create a Moore-type finite state machine to control a BLDC motor by sending pulses on 3 channels.
3. Determine the optimal period of the waveform required for driving the BLDC motor at maximum (rated) speed.
4. Measure the period of the optimal driving waveform using a digital signal analyzer.

10.3 Background

10.3.1 BLDC motors

A typical brushless dc motor (electronically commutated motor, ECM) consists of three electromagnetic coils. The rotor of this motor contains a permanent magnet, which is either attracted to or repelled from the coils depending on whether or not they are energized. In this motor configuration, the rotor spins, while the coils remain stationary. A highly simplified diagram of the motor coils is given in **Fig. 10.1**.

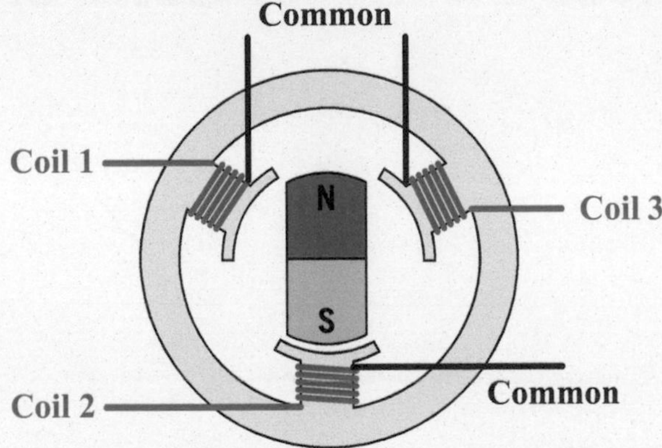

Figure 10.1: Simplified BLDC motor configuration diagram.

By pulsing each of the coils in sequence (*i.e.*, **1**, **2**, **3**, **1**, etc), it is possible to make the permanent magnet of the rotor spin. The higher the frequency of the transitions, the higher the number of revolutions per minute (RPM).

Electrically, the coils are connected in a fashion similar to **Fig. 10.2**. The common terminal provides a connection to one side of the coil, while the other three terminals are connected to the individual coils.

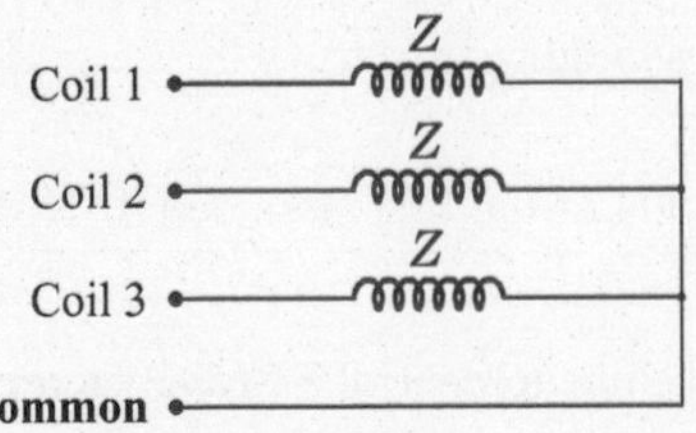

Figure 10.2: Circuit diagram of coil connections.

Each coil has an impedance Z (which can be thought of as the resistance). Suppose that the impedance of the connection between **Coil 1** and **Common** is Z. If the impedance between the terminals for **Coil 1** and **Coil 2** were to be measured, the total measured impedance would be $2Z$. This is one way of determining the function of each pin of the BLDC motor: exhaustively measure the resistance between each pin and the connections with the least resistance would indicate a common-to-coil connection).

The signals output by the control board of a hard drive are shown in **Fig. 10.3**. These signals are used to drive the hard drive BLDC motor.

Figure 10.3: BLDC controller board signals.

Overlapping pulses make the BLDC motor vibrate less, as the permanent rotor magnet does not have to make huge jumps from one coil to the next—the transition is gradual. In addition, this gives the motor the ability to self-start, without outside intervention.

The high-frequency transitions from 0 to 1 and back are implemented as a power-saving measure—the inertia of the motor rotor will keep the motor spinning, allowing the control board to deliver the least power possible.

BLDC motors are also used to propel electrically-powered RC aircraft (along with a PWM controller, which translates the PWM signal into the pulses required to spin the motor).

10.3.2 Power Transistors

In this laboratory, a power transistor will be used. The FPGA development board cannot deliver sufficient power to drive the motor, therefore a transistor will act as a high-frequency switch for the coils, drawing power from the external clock/power module on the breadboard.

A common transistor package is called *TO-220* (**Fig. 10.4**). With the transistor facing upward, the pins are: base, collector, emitter, arranged from left to right. Be mindful of this when using the transistor in the wiring set up.

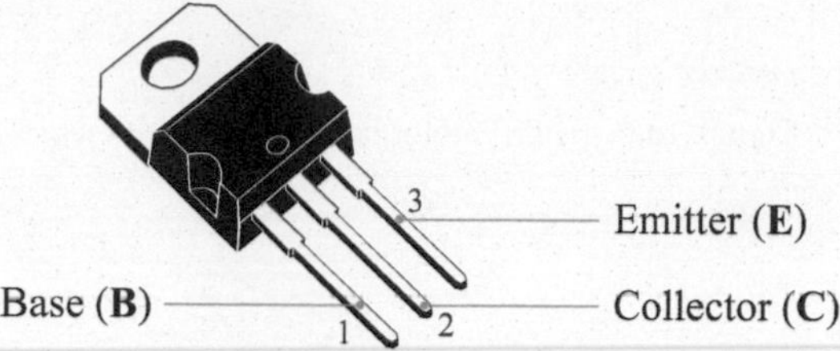

Figure 10.4: Transistor pin diagram (TO-220 plastic package).

Most power transistors have *protection diodes* already built in, so they are not necessary when wiring the circuit (**Fig. 10.5**). For details on the Darlington pair power transistors used in this laboratory (TIP122), see **Appendix J**.

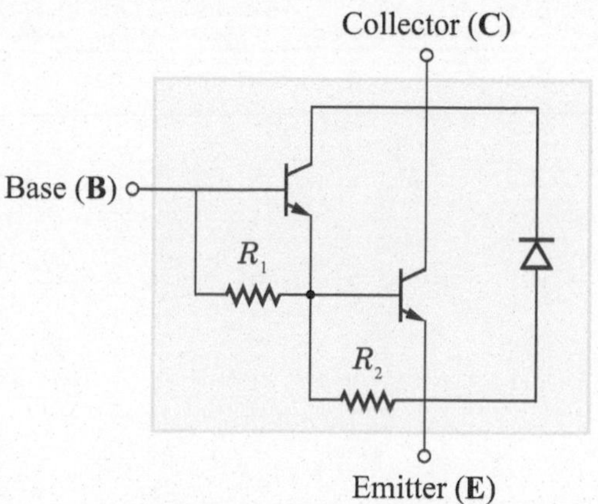

Figure 10.5: Transistor internals.

10.4 Pre-laboratory

1. Design a state transition diagram for a seven-state Moore finite state machine that implements the BLDC motor controller in **Fig. 10.6**.

   Note that **S0** should be an initial state (all **`coils`** set to **`0`**), when **`rst`** is logic-HIGH. The next state for **S0** should be **S1**. State **S0** should be entered when **`rst`** is logic-HIGH. States should advance when **`rst`** is logic-LOW (you may implement **`not rst`** as **`input`** to the FSM).

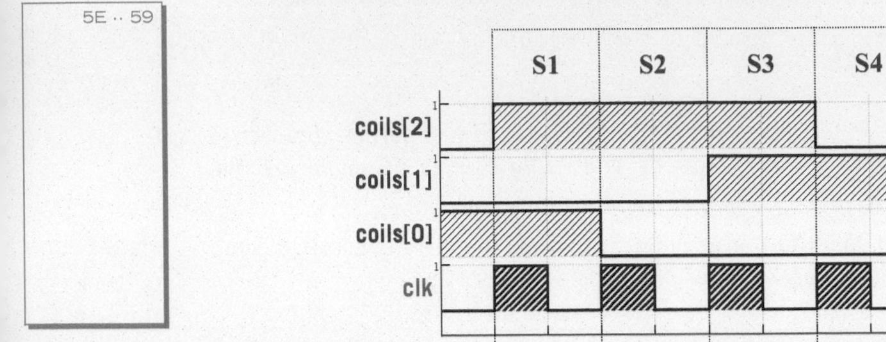

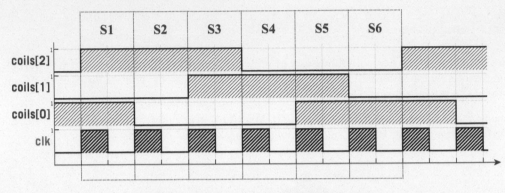

Figure 10.6: BLDC motor controller transitions.

2. Implement your design in VHDL. Take the following entity declaration as a starting point:

```
entity bldc_controller is
    Port ( clk, rst : in STD_LOGIC;
           coils : out STD_LOGIC_VECTOR(2 downto 0) );
end entity;
```

`rst`—pulling this pin logic-HIGH should reset the motor controller to a **`000`** output on **`coils`** (state **S0**). Once the pin is set to logic-LOW, the controller should resume the pulse pattern in **Fig. 10.6**.

Paste your VHDL code below. Make sure to run synthesis and resolve any errors.

5E .. 60

3. Generate a simulation of the code for approximately two full cycles of the FSM. **Paste it below**. The simulation should look similar to (**Fig. 10.7**). A good way to generate the clock signal would be to force counter on `clk` every 50 ns.

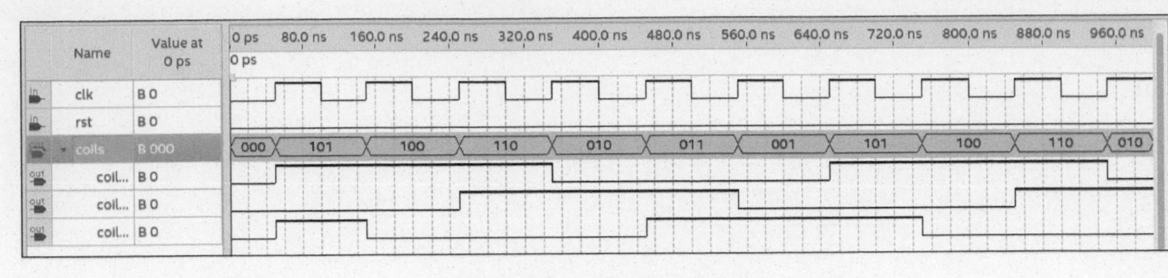

Figure 10.7: Sample simulation.

4. Generate a symbol file for the BLDC motor controller (**Fig. 10.8**) by following the instructions given in **Appendix D.5.1**. Copy the **.bsf** and **.vhd** files into the `/cec222/blocks` directory.

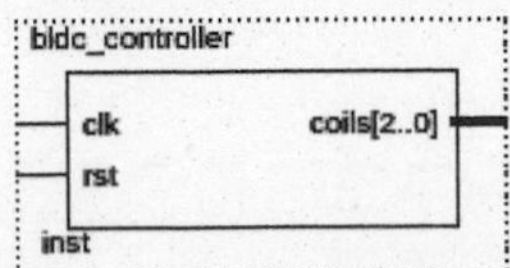

Figure 10.8: BLDC motor controller block symbol.

10.4.1 Supporting Files

1. Download **`blocks_2.zip`**—a file containing a frequency scaler block (converting a 50 MHz signal into a clock with a 2 ms period), along with the supporting VHDL file. The link is given in the GitHub box in the margin.

2. Unarchive the files into the `/cec222/blocks` directory. Place the **.bsf** and **.vhd** files directly into the **blocks** folder. Your directory structure should look similar to **Fig. 10.9**.

Code available @ GitHub
`https://git.io/fN5Hg`

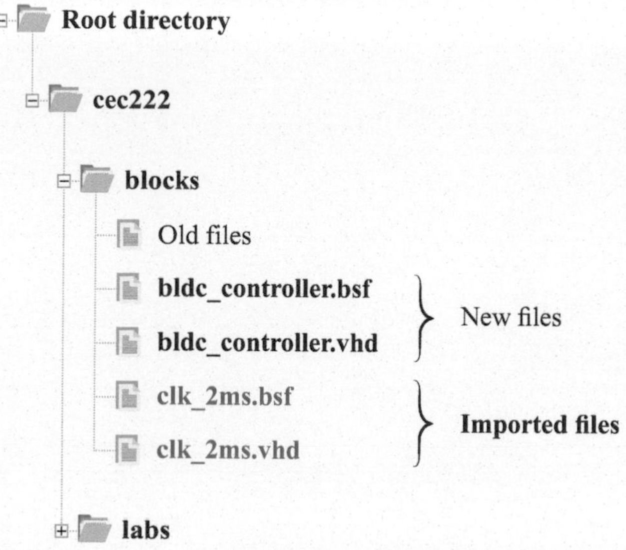

Figure 10.9: Directory structure.

10.4.2 Block Diagram Design

1. Open a new Quartus project and create a blank block diagram.

2. Read **Appendix D.5.2** and follow the steps to build the block diagram in (**Fig. 10.10**).

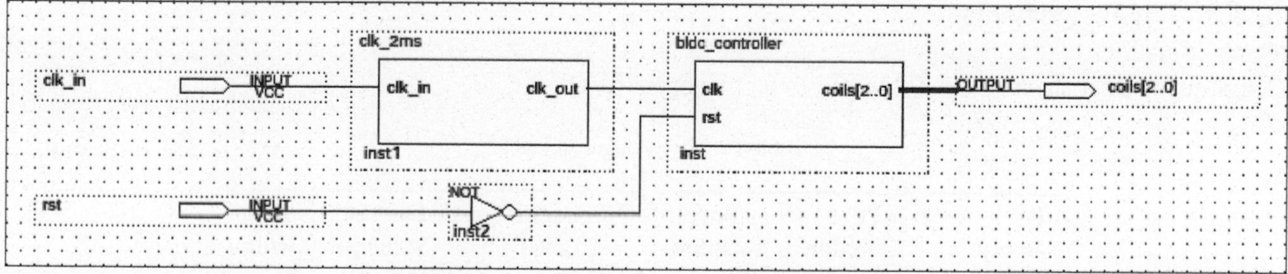

Figure 10.10: Brushless dc motor control block diagram.

The **`rst`** input has an inverter connected to it due to the **`KEY0`** pushbutton being normally closed (NC), which makes it logic-LOW whenever it is pressed.

3. Save the project and have it readily-accessible for lab. **Print and paste the block diagram below..** Don't forget to include a footer.

5E ·· 62

10.4.3 Pin Assignments

Complete the pin assignments in **Table 10.1** (refer to **Appendix H**).

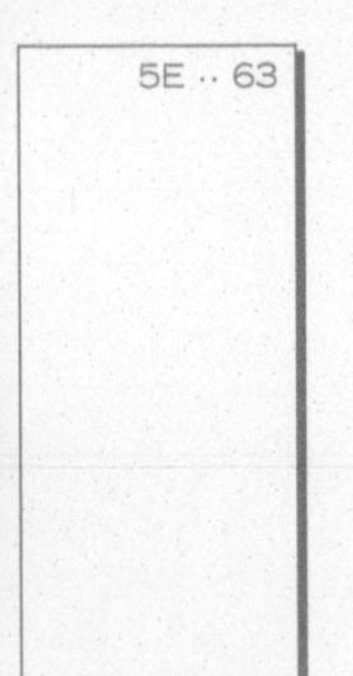

Table 10.1: Pin assignment table.

Port Name	Port Function	Pin Location	Logic Level	Current Strength	Slew Rate
`clk_in`	CLOCK		3.3-V LVCMOS	2 mA	—
`rst`	`KEY0`				—
`coils[2]`	`GPIO3`				2
`coils[1]`	`GPIO2`				2
`coils[0]`	`GPIO1`				2

(Optional) To minimize the time spent in lab, assign the pins based on the table above using the *Pin Planner* tool in Quartus. Save the project and have it readily available for the laboratory.

10.4.4 Circuit Wiring

Wire the circuit in **Fig. 10.11** on the breadboard diagram in **Fig. 10.12**. Refer to the lab background information and the TIP122 data sheet in **Appendix J**. This lab will require the use of the power/clock module, information for which is found in **Appendix A**.

5 V (from clock/power module)
common terminal
motor coils
FPGA development board outputs
1 kΩ
C
B
E
1 kΩ
1 kΩ
coils[0]
coils[1]
coils[2]
GPIO12
(ground)

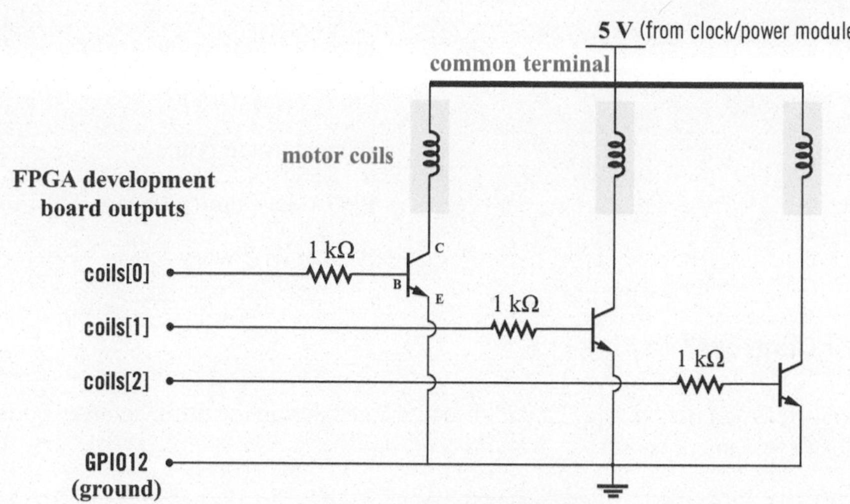

Figure 10.11: Circuit diagram.

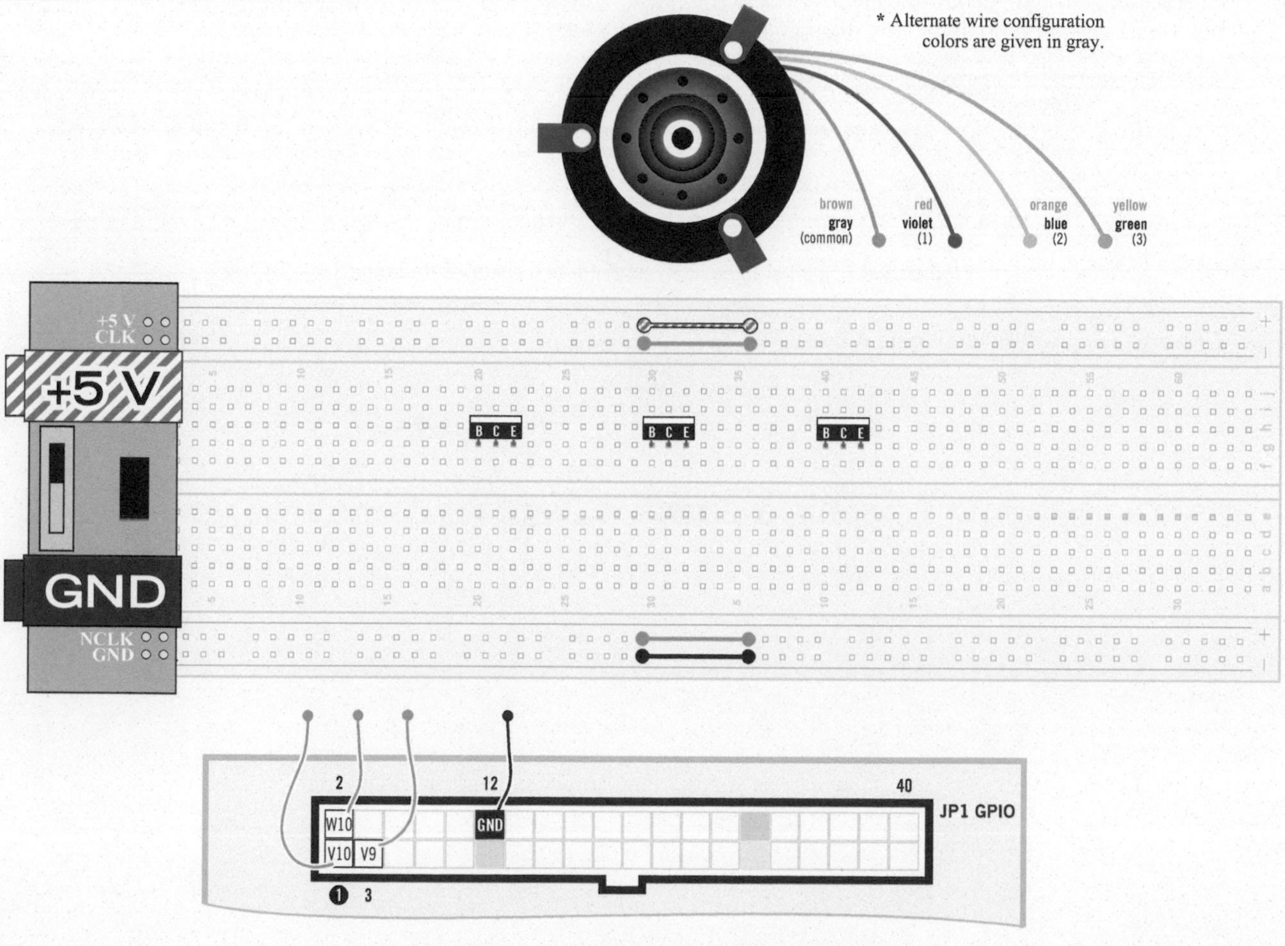

* Alternate wire configuration colors are given in gray.
brown
gray
(common)
red
violet
(1)
orange
blue
(2)
yellow
green
(3)
+5 V
CLK
+5 V
GND
NCLK
GND
B C E
B C E
B C E
2
12
40
JP1 GPIO
W10
GND
V10
V9
1
3

Figure 10.12: Laboratory breadboard wiring set up.

10.5 Laboratory

10.5.1 Required Equipment and Parts

The following items are needed to complete this laboratory:

- resistors (3x 1 kΩ)
- 3x TIP122 power transistors
- pin headers
- breadboard
- wires
- male-to-female jumper wires
- brushless dc motor
- power/clock module
- FPGA development board, USB cable
- Analog Discovery scope

10.5.2 BLDC Motor Controller Testing

1. Synthesize the project, assign pins (if they haven't been assigned during the pre-laboratory portion), compile, and program the FPGA development board.

2. Examine the signals on GPIO pins 1, 2, and 3 using the Analog Discovery digital channels 0, 1, and 2, respectively. The scope should be grounded to GPIO pin 12, using the black (down arrow) lead on the pigtail. Trigger channel 0 on the rising edge of the waveform.

   Make sure that the waveform matches the design requirements (**Fig. 10.13**). If it does not (*i.e.*, the timing is incorrect), troubleshoot the block diagram or your VHDL code.

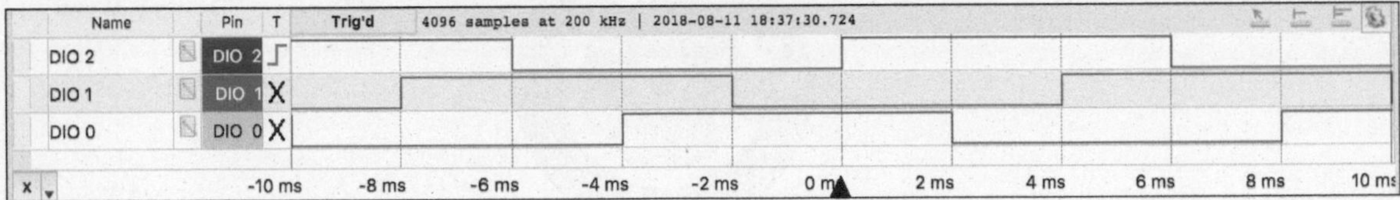

Figure 10.13: Digital logic analyzer output on channels 1, 2, and 3.

Capture the waveform and paste it below:

10.5.3 Full Circuit Testing

Since the FPGA development board cannot supply the necessary current to drive the BLDC motor, we will have to use a TIP122 Darlington transistor pair device to act as a high-speed switch. The signals from the development board will turn the transistor either on or off, which would in turn pass the current through the individual coils of the BLDC motor.

1. Identify the common terminal on the motor by measuring the resistance between all of the leads. Write down the measured resistance in **Table 10.2** below and (based on the pre-laboratory reading) determine which lead colors represent which terminals.

Table 10.2: Measured resistance between terminals.

Color 1	Color 2	Resistance (Ω)

2. Construct the circuit in **Fig. 10.12**. **Check with the TA to ensure that the circuit has been wired correctly prior to connecting the power supply**. The transistors drop a lot of current and severe damage can occur to the components or the FPGA development board, should the circuit be wired incorrectly.
3. An electronic speed controller (ESC) for brushless dc motors typically ramps up the frequency, in order to get the motor to self-start. Since the implemented design operates at a single frequency, initially, **only one GPIO port wire (pin 1) should be connected.**

   If power is applied to the circuit, the motor should hum. Attempt to start the motor by quickly spinning the rotor (in a motion similar to launching a small spinning top).

   Once the motor is spinning, gradually connect GPIO pin 2, followed by GPIO pin 3. Take note of the pitch change as you connect more signals to the motor.
4. Once the circuit is fully functional, **demonstrate the set up to a teaching assistant.**
5. **If any changes were made to the code during the lab, paste a new version of the code in the appropriate pre-laboratory section.**

10.6 Questions

1. Assuming that the motor spins at 7,200 RPM when the period of one full rotation is 231.17 μs, calculate the approximate speed of the motor if the period is 12 ms (six states of 2 ms each). Show your calculations or dimensional analysis.

2. How does the pitch of the motor change as you connect more signal leads? Explain why.

3. Can the motor be started from a stopped state with all three signal leads connected? Why or why not? Provide a detailed explanation.

Basic Electrical Components

This appendix describes some basic electrical components that will be used during this laboratory. The list given here is by no means exhaustive and specialized components will be described within each laboratory where they are used.

A.1 Resistors

The resistor is one of the most common electrical components. Resistors are two-terminal components, which resist the flow of current. This component has numerous applications: from simple voltage division to transistor biasing. A resistor is represented on a circuit diagram with a symbol in **Fig. A.1**.

R_1

47 kΩ

Figure A.1: Circuit schematic symbol for a resistor.

A.1.1 Color Code

In the United States, color code is the most popular method for marking resistors with their values during the manufacturing process. A series of four bands are painted on the outside of the component, indicating the resistivity, as well as the tolerance. In rare circumstances, a fifth band (indicating failure rate) is included. Marking resistors with bands is more reliable than printing the digits, as the bands are less likely to be completely rubbed off.

Examine the four-band resistor color code chart in **Fig. A.2a**. The tolerance band for typical resistors is gold-colored, indicating a $\pm5\%$ tolerance (meaning that the measured value of the resistor can deviate $\pm5\%$ from the marked value). Resistor color bands are read from left to right, with the tolerance band on the right. The sample resistor given in the figure is valued at 47,000 Ω, or 47 kΩ.

Despite resistors being organized into labeled drawers, some of them may be placed into the wrong drawer by others. **Always verify the actual resistor value from the color bands!**

One easy way of remembering the resistor color code sequence is given in **Fig. A.2b**.

XKCD's Randall Munroe has a relevant cartoon to remember the resistor color code, in addition to some bad advice of applying electrical engineering knowledge to the great outdoors.

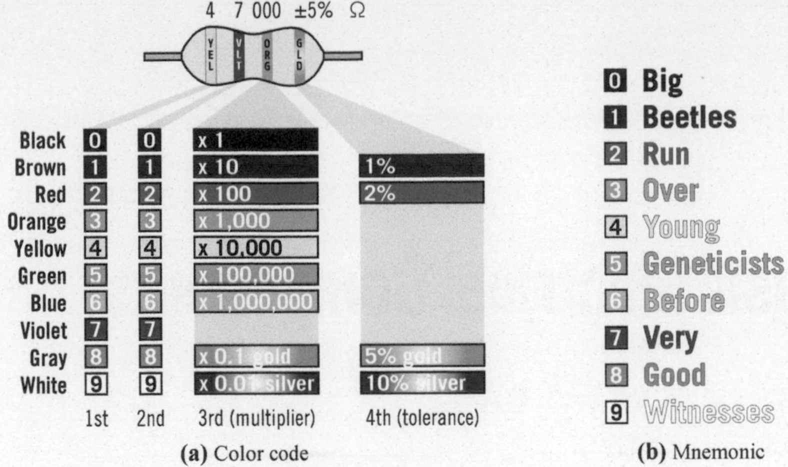

(a) Color code **(b)** Mnemonic

Figure A.2: Four-band resistor color code and appropriate mnemonic. Color version: **`https://git.io/JfLvM`**

A.1.2 Standard Resistor Values

In order to limit the number of resistors that are kept in stock (and are manufactured), in 1952 the International Electrotechnical Commission (IEC) introduced a set of standard resistor values, which are evenly spaced in a logarithmic progression. These vary by tolerance value; **Fig. A.3** demonstrates the standard 5% tolerance resistor values.

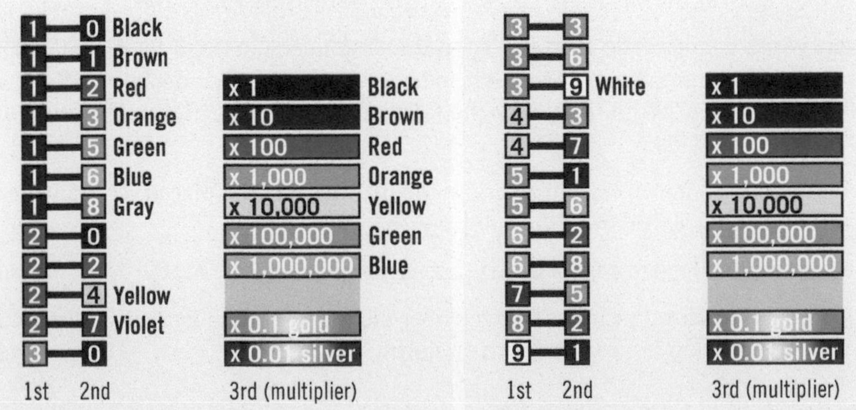

Figure A.3: Standard values for resistors with a 5% tolerance.

A.2 Diodes and Light-Emitting Diodes (LEDs)

A diode is a two-terminal device capable of restricting the flow of current in one direction only. Light-emitting diodes (LEDs) are essentially diodes that have an additional capability of emitting light when current is passed through them. LEDs can serve as logic indicators.

When connecting diodes, it is important to remember that—unlike resistors—diodes have polarity. Power must be connected to the **anode** (positive terminal) and ground to the **cathode** (negative terminal). An easy way to remember this is by recalling that **black cat**s have a **negative** connotation.

Fig. A.4 demonstrates how to identify the positive and negative leads on a diode; **Fig. A.5** does the same for the LED.

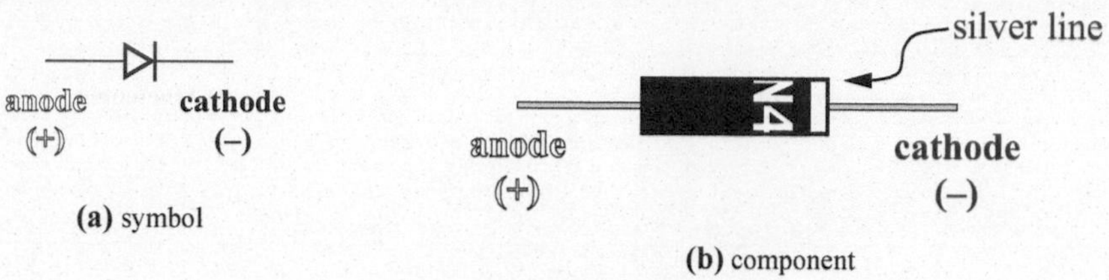

Figure A.4: Diode pin identification and symbol.

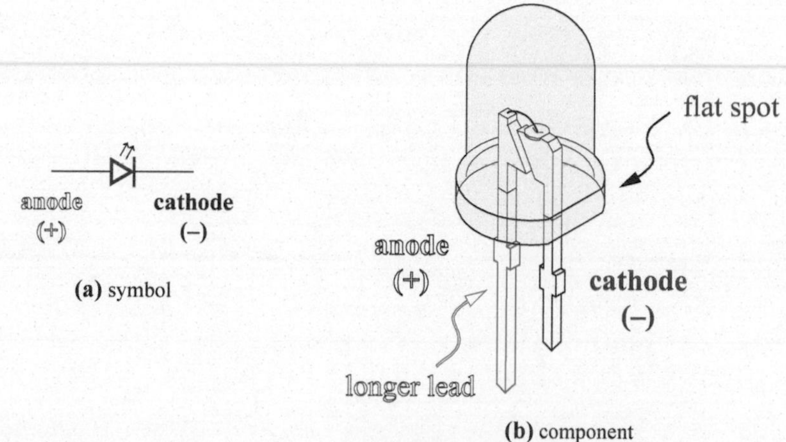

Figure A.5: LED pin identification and symbol.

Important note: The LEDs are typically connected in series with a resistor to ensure the correct amount of current flow (passing more than the designed amount of current through an LED will destroy it).

Be sure to check both the polarity and the series resistor value when connecting these devices to the breadboard and troubleshooting. A typical value of the resistor connected in series with a standard LED is 330 Ω. **Fig. A.6** demonstrates the resistor-LED connection.

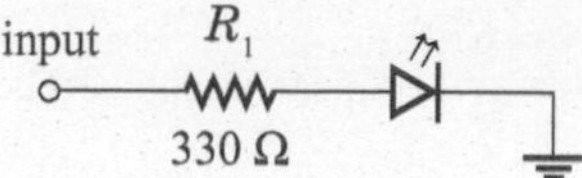

Figure A.6: Resistor connected in series with the LED.

A.3 Solder-less Breadboards

All circuits built in the laboratory will be prototyped on "solder-less breadboards". These devices have hundreds of holes, which are interconnected in certain ways. By inserting components into the holes, it is possible to *prototype* circuits without ever having to touch the soldering iron or manufacture a printed circuit board (PCB). A typical breadboard and the corresponding connection diagram are shown in **Fig. A.7**.

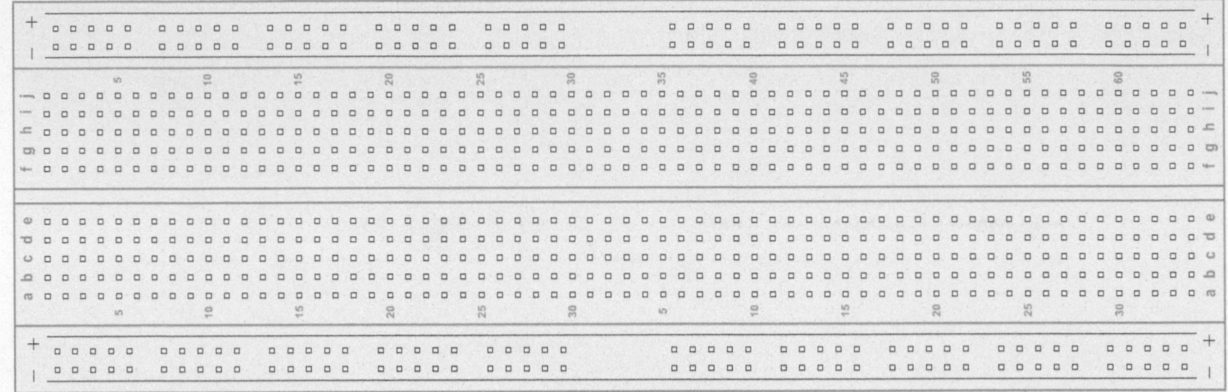

(a) Breadboard

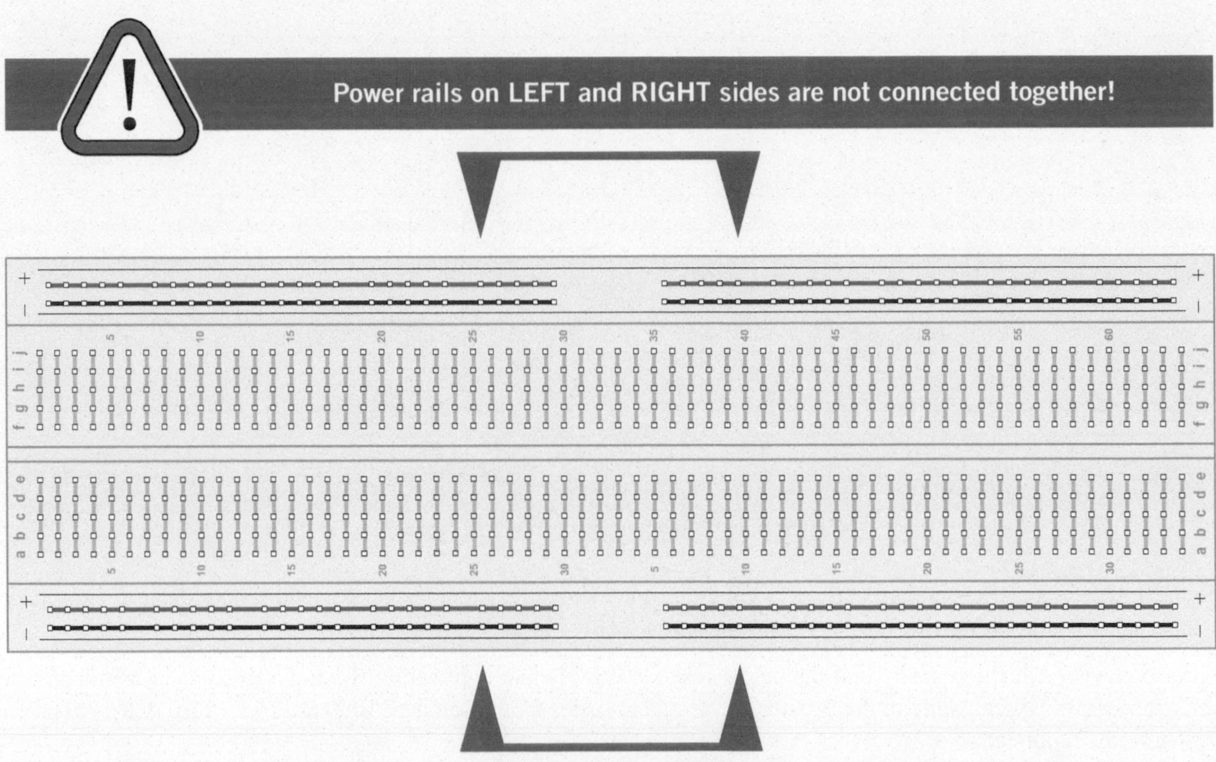
Power rails on LEFT and RIGHT sides are not connected together!

(b) Internal interconnections

Figure A.7: Typical breadboard layout.

The way the internal interconnections are configured is that all groups of five vertical holes are connected together. The division across the middle between the top and bottom provides isolation from the top and bottom groups of holes (allowing the construction of more compact circuits, in addition to plugging in standard integrated circuits in a DIP package).

Note that the top and bottom power rails on the right and left sides of the breadboard are <u>not connected</u>! If the rails need to span the entire breadboard, then a jumper wire must connect the right and left sides.. This is the one common mistake that students make when building circuits on a breadboard.

A.3.1 Wiring Components

If multiple components need to be wired together (*i.e.*, there is a node in the circuit diagram), simply plug the components into holes within a single connected group of five (marked in blue in **Fig. A.7b**).

A sample breadboard setup is shown in **Fig. A.8**, along with a corresponding circuit diagram. Placing components at 90 degrees when drawing on a breadboard (see **Fig. A.8b**) is good practice and will help when wiring the circuit with real components.

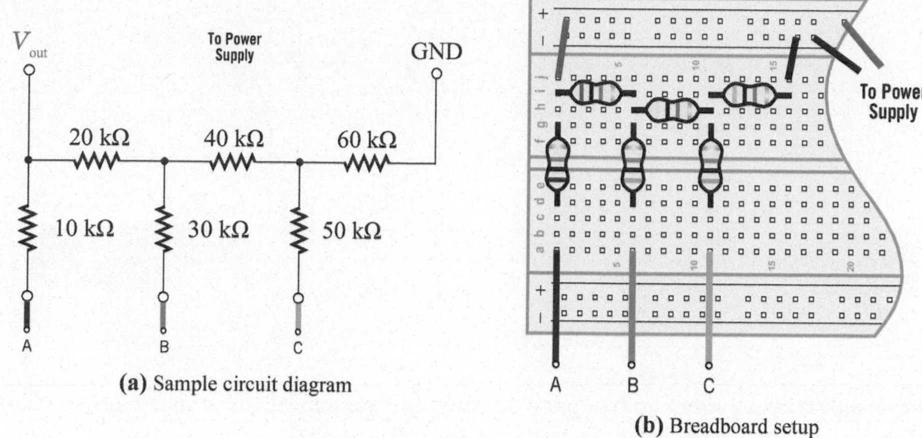

(a) Sample circuit diagram

(b) Breadboard setup

Figure A.8: Sample breadboard setup.

If the breadboard diagram is carefully drawn ahead of time, wiring using the breadboard should be quite easy in the laboratory—the diagram can serve as a 1:1 model of how real components should be placed.

Don't "cram" components together on the breadboard diagram or the breadboard itself. **The more spread out the components are, the easier it is to test and troubleshoot the circuit.**

Fig. A.9 demonstrates what the circuit would look like when drawn on a breadboard template. This level of detail and neatness is **expected** when completing pre-laboratory exercises.

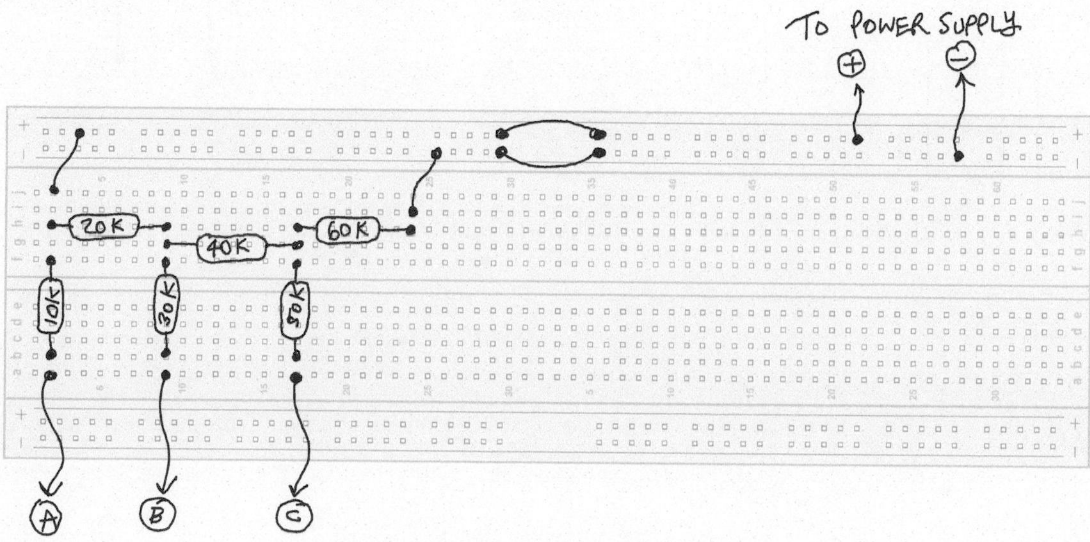

Figure A.9: Sample breadboard drawing.

A.4 DIP Switch Module

The switch module provides four toggle switches. These types of switch will be used in a number of the laboratories.

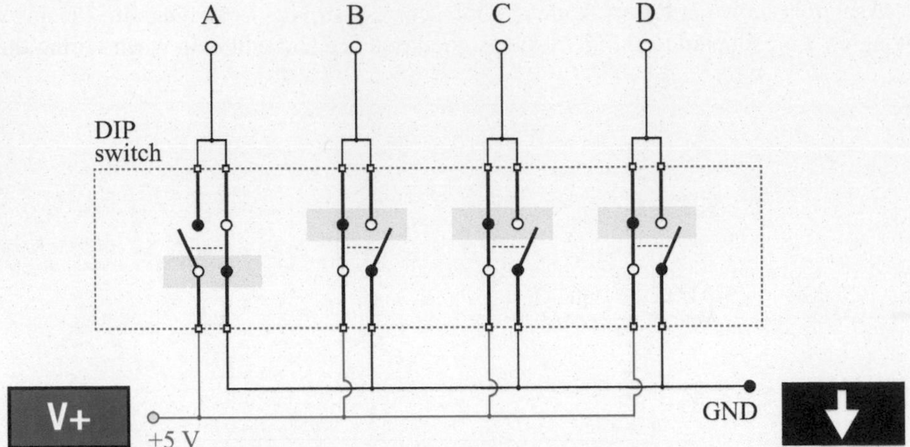

Figure A.10: DIP switch module internals.

By toggling the individual switches either up (on) or down (off), either a logical 1 or 0 can be provided to the circuit. The switch module in **Fig. A.10** is set to binary `0111` (down, up, up, up).

Internally, the switch is wired with 4 pairs of toggle switches. Each pair has a normally-open (NO) switch on the left and a normally-closed (NC) switch on the right. Every pair of contacts on the top must be shorted together to provide the output, while the contacts on the bottom must alternate between power and ground.

A sample wiring diagram is given in **Fig. A.11**, where power is sourced from the Analog Discovery scope.

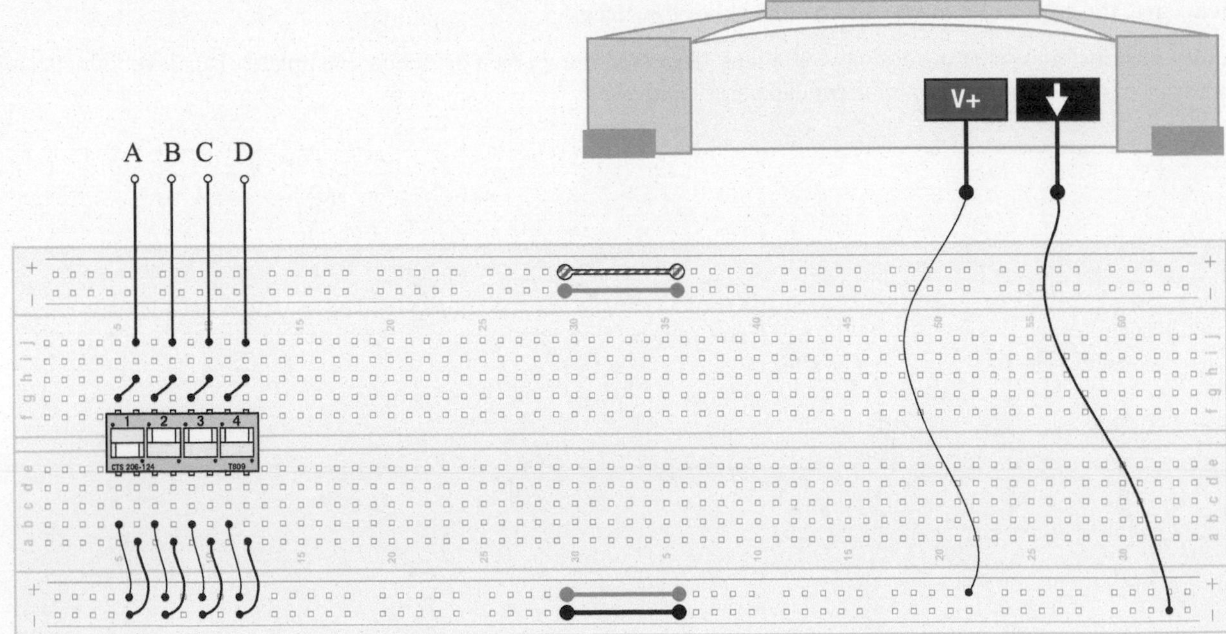

Figure A.11: DIP switch module wiring.

A.5 Power/Clock Module

The power/clock module provides power to the breadboard and should be inserted as shown in **Fig. A.12**.

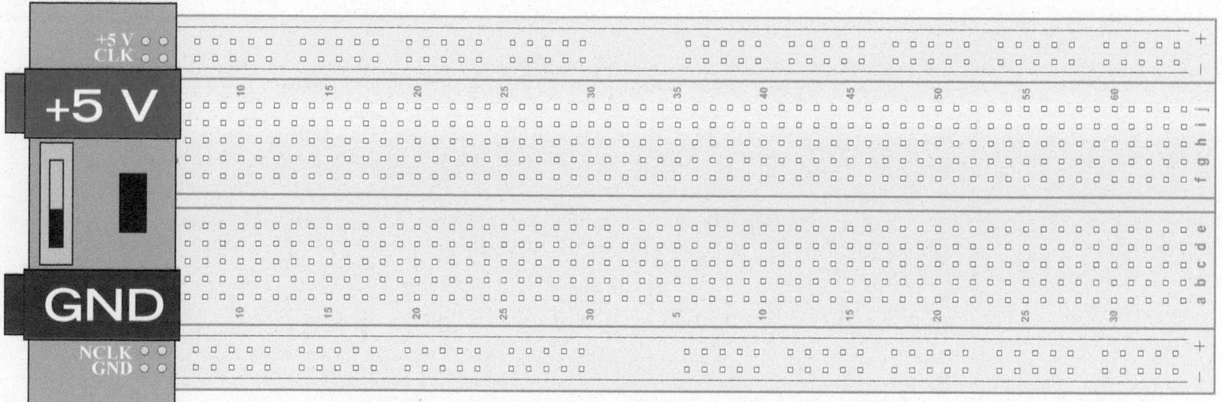

Figure A.12: Clock and switch module connections.

The power/clock module requires an external supply of 5 VDC. Once the module is powered, an indicator on the module should be lit/blinking. Four connections are provided by the clock module to the breadboard power rails, listed from top to bottom:

1. **5 VDC**, labeled as **+5V** on the clock module.
2. **Clock signal**, labeled as **CLK** and changeable using the switch on the clock module. There are three positions for the switch: the topmost position will provide the highest frequency clock, while the bottom position will provide the lowest (approximately 1 Hz).
3. **Negative clock signal**, **NCLK**. Provides the inverted version of the clock signal.
4. **Common ground**, **GND**.

A.6 Pin Headers

A *pin header* is a connector, which consists of a single row of pins, spaced similarly to the holes on a breadboard. When connecting to/from the Analog Discovery scope, pin headers will make it easier to connect the scope to various signals on the breadboard. A typical pin header is shown in **Fig. A.13**.

Figure A.13: Pin header.

Analog Discovery Scope

The Analog Discovery (AD) is a versatile measurement instrument that allows for the measurement, visualization, and generation of analog and digital signals. Housed in a tiny package, this device contains all of the tools required in a typical lab setting for digital circuits.

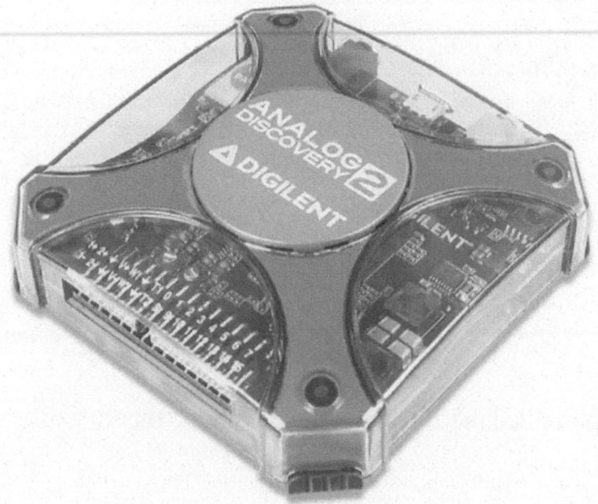

Figure B.1: Analog Discovery device

The housing contains all of the ports for interfacing with a computer (only the micro-USB port will be used in this laboratory, as additional power capacity is not required) on one side, as seen in **Fig. B.2a**, and a place to plug in the pigtail connector on the opposite side, **Fig. B.2b**.

(a) Rear connections for the AD (left to right: external power, USB, audio signal generator).

(b) Pigtail connector on the front of the AD.

Images courtesy of Digilent, Inc.

Figure B.2: Analog Discovery connections.

The pigtail connector has individual wire breakouts, which make it easy to interface the device with circuits for measurement and signal generation. The pigtail connector layout is given in **Fig. B.3**.

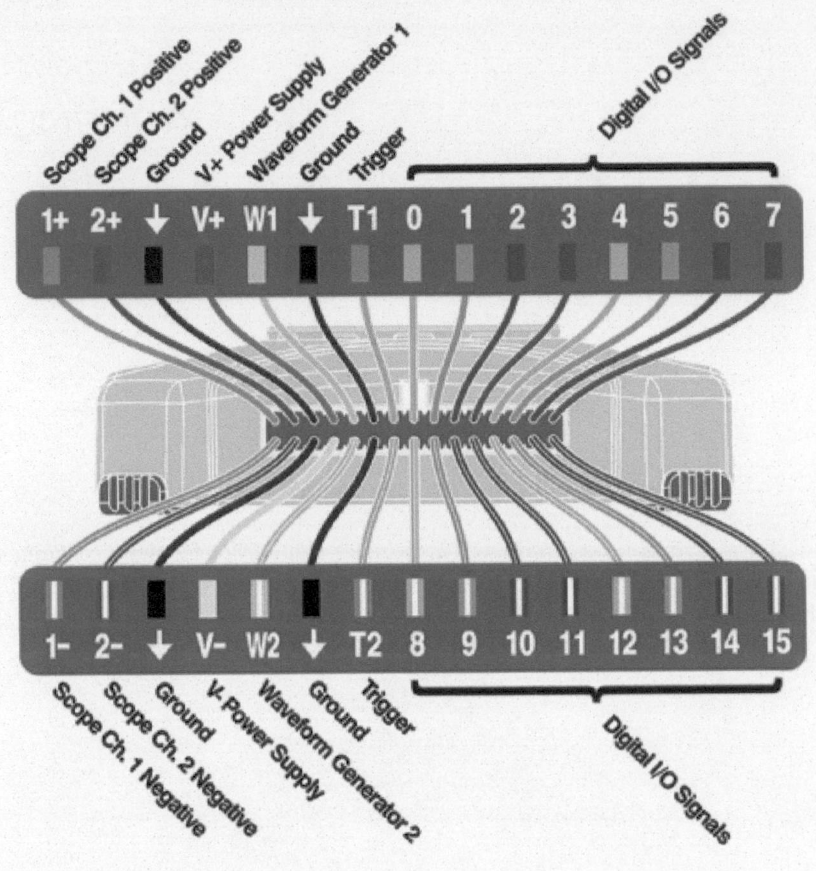

Image courtesy of Digilent, Inc.

Figure B.3: Pigtail connector wire description. Color version: **`https://git.io/JfLvM`**

Digilent Waveforms software and pigtail connectors have the following functionality:

- **Scope and Voltmeter (Logger)**: used for measuring voltages or displaying time-varying signals using the oscilloscope.
- **DC Power Supply**: the device is capable of producing an arbitrary dc voltage, from 0 to ±5 V DC. The current output is rated for 800 mA, which is enough to power reasonably-sized discrete gate circuits and components. The wires that should be used in this case are **V+** (positive 0-5 VDC), **V-** (0 to –5 VDC), and ground (↓).
- **Waveform Generator**: this functionality allows the device to produce arbitrary waveforms, ranging from 0 to 5 V in magnitude. There are two channels present: **W1** (channel 1) and **W2** (channel 2).
- **Digital Signal Analyzer**: allows for logging and viewing of digital logic signals. There are 16 individual inputs, numbered 0 through 15.
- **Digital Signal Output**: the device is capable of generating arbitrary digital waveforms on 16 channels, marked 0 through 15. The Waveforms software automatically determines whether the 0–15 connections are used in input or output mode.

B.1 Voltmeter (Logger) Functionality

When the Waveforms software is first started, a popup window will appear, where the appropriate Analog Discovery scope can be selected (**Fig. B.4**). Make sure to select a device with a serial number, instead of the *DEMO* designation. If *DEMO* is selected, random simulated values will be shown, instead of actual measurements.

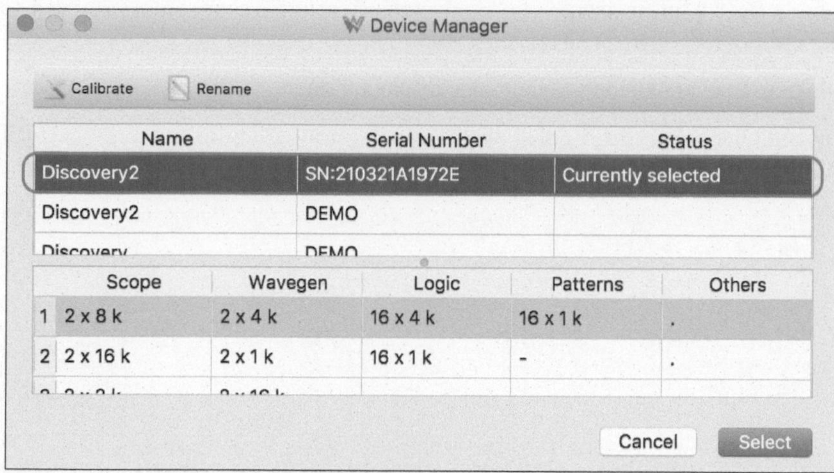

Figure B.4: Device listing.

To measure DC voltage, start the **Logger** by clicking the Logger button on the main screen. An interface, similar to **Fig. B.5** will appear. Click the Run button to start capturing data. Click Stop to stop sampling.

1+, 1-, **2+**, and **2-** pigtail connectors are used to provide two fully-differential inputs to the logger (two channels).

Since this is a "data logger", it will plot data over a selected interval (1 min by default)—this is sometimes useful for troubleshooting. Numerical values can be observed in the *Value* column under the appropriate channel (either *C1 DC* or *C2 DC*). By unchecking the *Plot* checkboxes, unused values, such as *RMS*, can be hidden from the logger plot.

If only a *single* reading needs to be collected, click Single.

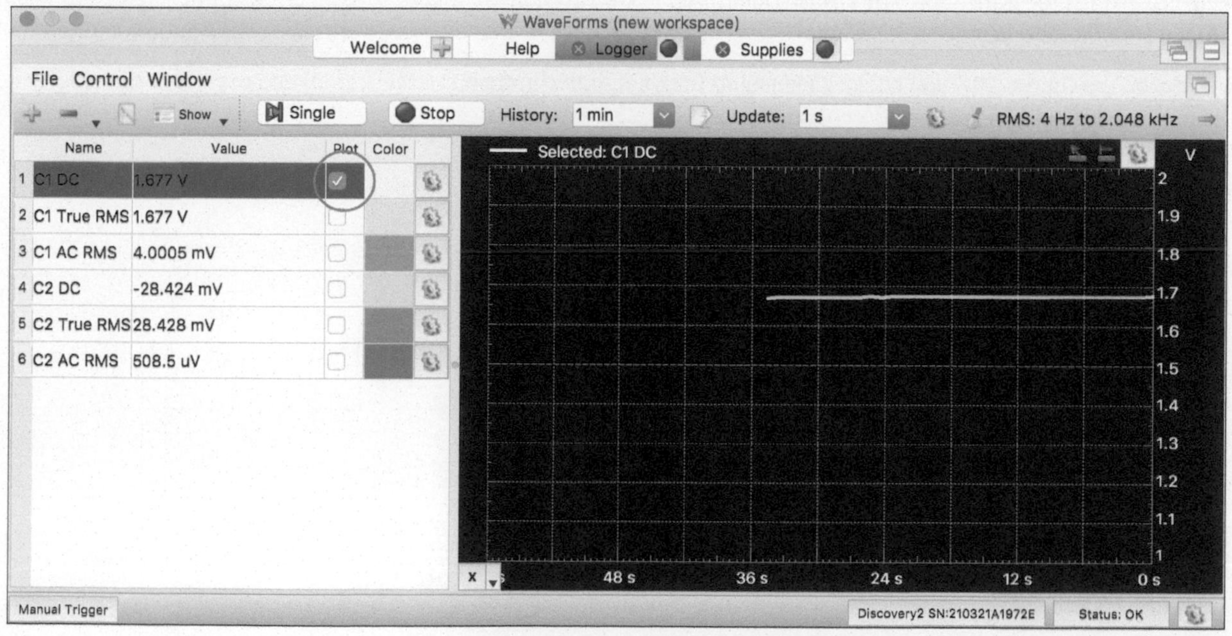

Figure B.5: Waveforms Logger user interface.

B.2 Oscilloscope (Scope) Functionality

Click on the Scope button on the main screen of the Waveforms software. To start capturing data, click the Run button. An interface, similar to **Fig. B.6** should appear.

AD provides two channels for capturing data. 1+, 1-, **2+**, and **2-** pigtail connectors are used to provide two fully-differential inputs to the oscilloscope (two channels).

Deselect the box for any unused channels on the right side of the interface.

To reduce ink usage, change the background color of the waveform by going to **Settings** > **Options** > **Analog color** dropdown, and choose **Light**. **Points will be deducted for using a dark background color!**

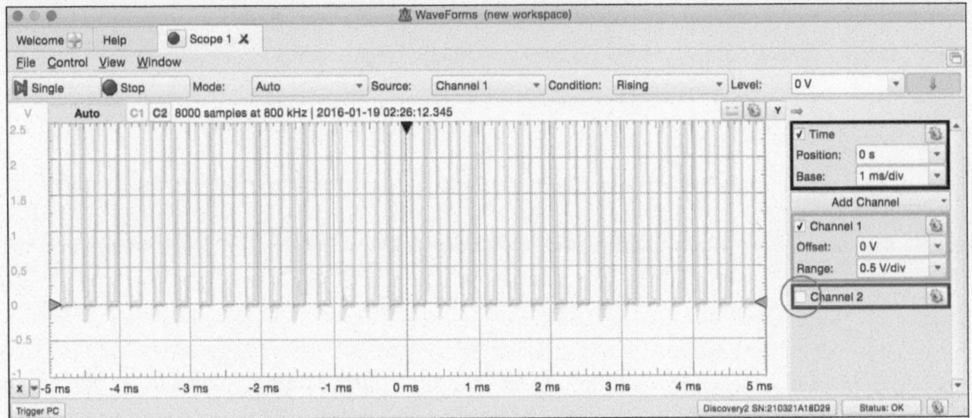

Figure B.6: Capturing the signal on Channel 1.

B.2.1 Triggering the Oscilloscope

If the signal is jittery and not stable (in the case of a periodic waveform), the signal may not be properly *triggered* (or locked-in). Adjust the horizontal **Time Base** (measured in sec/division) so that only 1-2 periods of the signal are visible and make sure that the **Range** (V/division) is chosen appropriately, so that the waveform isn't clipped on top or bottom.

The slider on the right will adjust **Triggering** (move it to the midpoint of the signal) and the slider on the left will adjust the **Offset** (vertical position of signal), **Fig. B.7**.

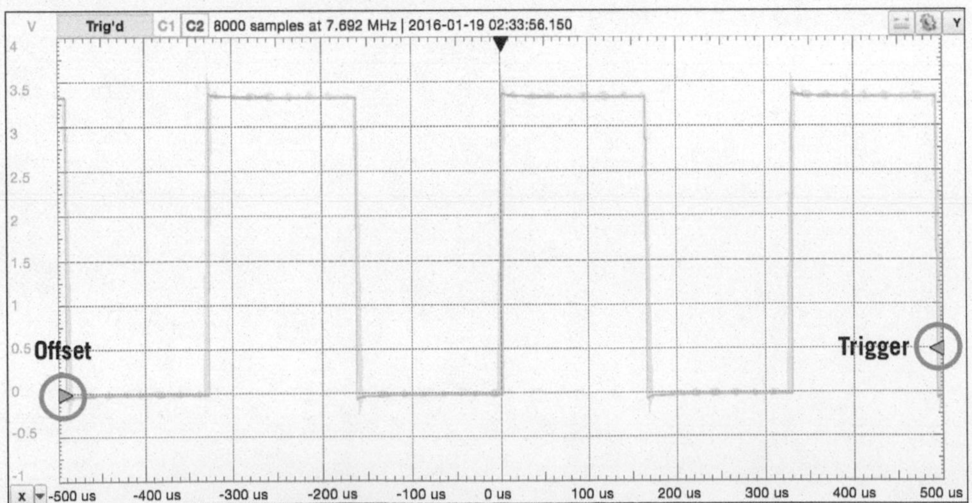

Figure B.7: Offset and Trigger sliders.

B.2.2 Signal Measurements

Waveforms provides a quick way to measure signals (even when the scope is capturing data). Simply double-click on the first peak of the waveform and drag it to the next one. The frequency and period of the signal will be displayed in real-time (**Fig. B.8**).

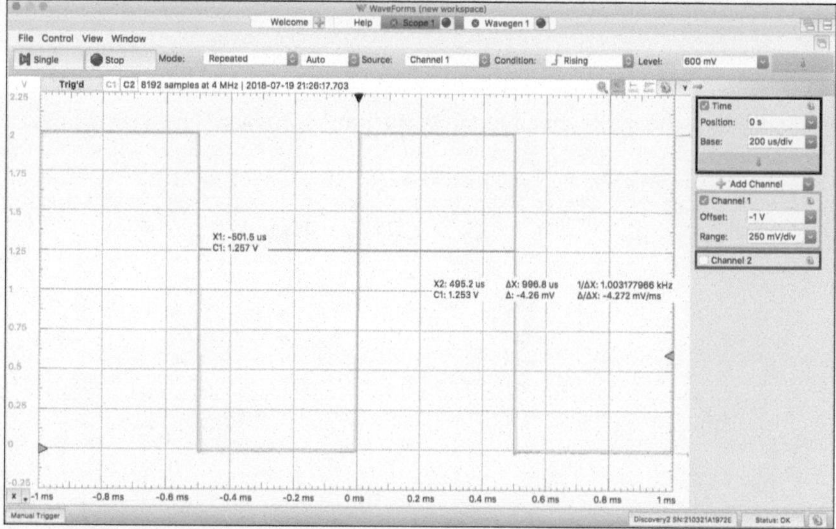

Figure B.8: Signal measurements displayed over the signal in real-time.

The period of the sample signal is approximately 1 msec (frequency of 1 kHz). From the vertical scale, it is apparent that the amplitude of the signal is approximately 2 V.

B.3 Voltage Supply Functionality

The Analog Discovery scope is capable of producing an arbitrary dc voltage, from −5 V to +5 V DC. The current output is rated for 800 mA, which is enough to power reasonably-sized discrete gate circuits and components. The wires that should be used in this case are **V+** (positive 0-5 VDC), **V-** (0 to −5 VDC), and ground (↓).

Click on the Supplies button on the main screen of the Waveforms software. The voltage supply interface will appear (**Fig. B.9**).

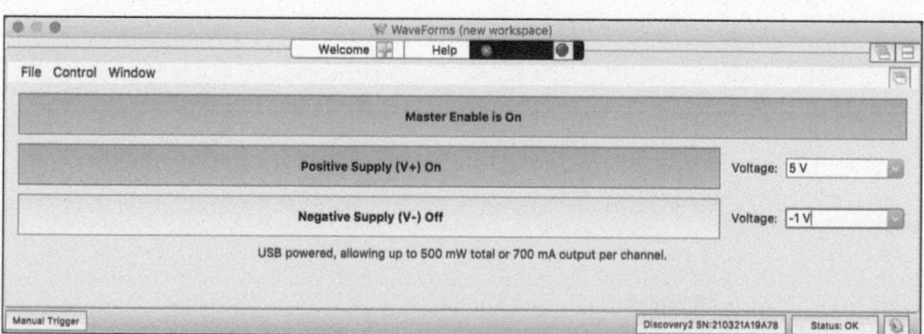

Figure B.9: Voltage Supplies user interface.

To enable the positive voltage supply, click on **Master Enable**. It is possible to enable/disable the positive and negative supplies individually. Voltage is adjusted by entering a new voltage into the **Voltage** box.

The voltage supply on the Analog Discovery can run concurrently with data capture and other functions.

B.4 Digital Signal (Logic) Analyzer Functionality

In addition to measuring analog voltages, the Analog Discovery also doubles as a digital signal analyzer, supporting up to 16 individual digital channels. This is useful for troubleshooting circuits, as intermediate outputs can be examined while the circuit is powered.

This feature will be used for troubleshooting circuits with discrete components, as well as circuits implemented on the FPGA development board.

Click on the Logic button on the main screen of the Waveforms software. The logic analyzer interface will appear (**Fig. B.10**).

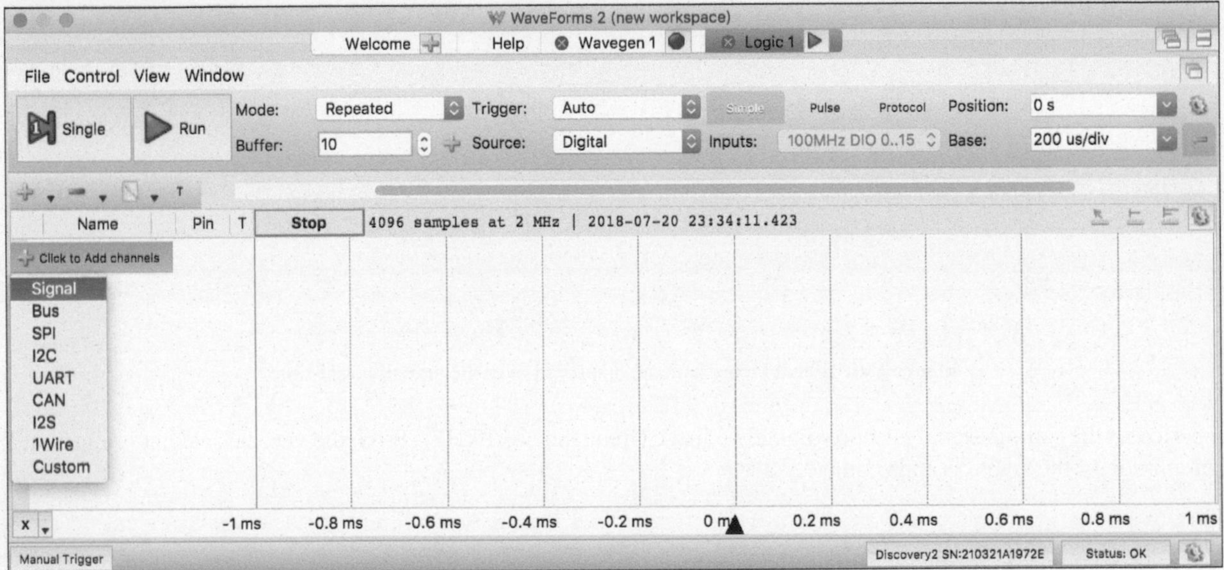

Figure B.10: Digital signal (Logic) analyzer user interface.

To add signals, click and choose **Signal**. Depending on the inputs you are using, select **DIO0** through **DIO15**. The pinout of the AD pigtail connector is given in **Fig. B.3**. To remove signals, click . Once the signals are added, click Run to start capturing data.

If the signals are not triggered, the following triggering options are available. In order to set the trigger, select the signal and press the appropriate key on the keyboard or set it using the triggering drop-down. **Only one channel should be triggered at any given time.**

- X Ignore X **No triggering**
- 0 Low L **Logic-low** (0)
- 1 High H **Logic-high** (1)
- Rise R **Rising edge**
- Fall F **Falling edge**
- Edge E **Any edge**

Fig. B.11 shows triggering on channel **DIO0**. Note that the signal on **DIO1** remains un-triggered.

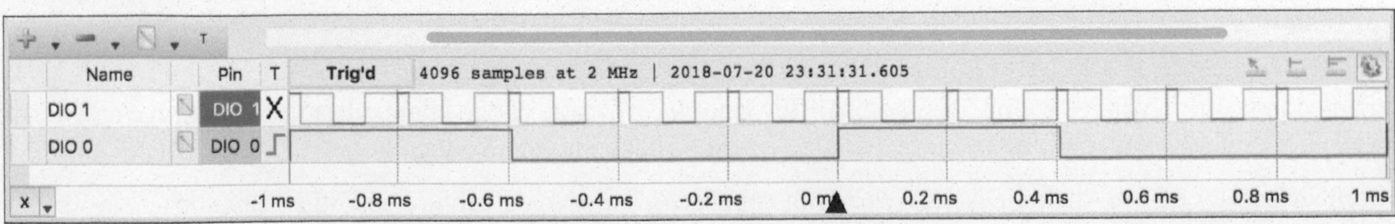

Figure B.11: Triggering on **DIO0**.

HDL Design Using Intel Quartus

This tutorial covers the Intel Quartus Prime workflow for FPGA design: implementing a combinational logic circuit using a hardware description language (HDL), simulating the circuit, running synthesis, assigning pins, and programming the FPGA. For students, who have had previous experience with Xilinx Vivado, this design flow should be fairly straightforward.

A brief introduction of VHDL (the HDL used in this class) is given. If more information is desired, Free Range VHDL is a good starter text, available at **http://bit.ly/2nKnJqH**.

Note: Quartus software is freely downloadable from Intel for installation on personal machines and is available for use on most University machines. It is strongly recommended that you install Quartus on your personal machine to complete lab and class assignments. Quartus is available for Windows and Linux platforms; you would have to use a virtualization environment—such as Oracle VirtualBox—to run the software within a Linux (or Windows, although it is not recommended) VM on a Mac.

C.1 Objectives

After completing this tutorial, the student will be able to:

- Translate a circuit into VHDL.
- Create a new Quartus project from scratch, which targets an Intel Max 10 FPGA device located on the DE10-Lite development board (part no. **10M50DAF484C7G**).
- Simulate the circuit using the academic version of the simulator.
- Synthesize and implement the circuit.
- Assign pins to the inputs and outputs within the design.
- Generate the bitstream and program the FPGA using the generated bitstream to verify circuit functionality.

C.2 VHDL Primer

This section will cover the implementation of a simple combinational logic circuit, given in **Fig. C.1**. The circuit has three inputs (connected to slide switches **SW2..0**) and one output (connected to LED **LEDR0**). Circuit functionality will be verified by both simulation and hardware testing on the Intel FPGA board against the circuit truth table.

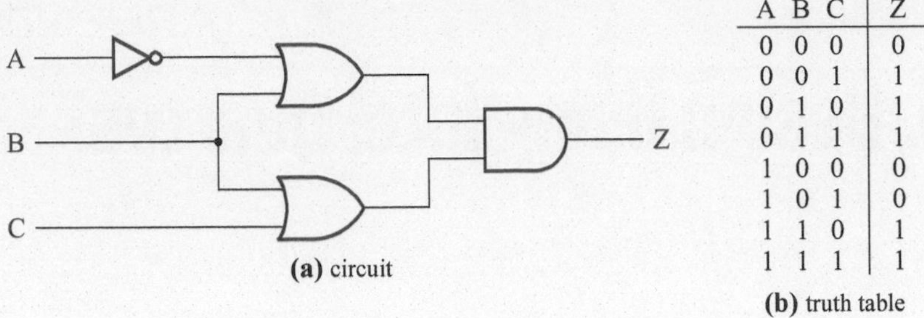

(a) circuit

A	B	C	Z
0	0	0	0
0	0	1	1
0	1	0	1
0	1	1	1
1	0	0	0
1	0	1	0
1	1	0	1
1	1	1	1

(b) truth table

Figure C.1: Basic combinational logic circuit and the corresponding truth table.

Unlike student opinions that VHDL is a **V**ery **H**ard and **D**ifficult **L**anguage (note: not the actual acronym), it is surprisingly simple to understand and use. The biggest difference from other languages that you've seen before is that **it is not sequential**. What this means is that instead of being executed line-by-line, all of the lines in VHDL run at the same time.

VHDL is a hardware description language—it is a language that describes hardware and is **not** a "programming language". Think of it as taking the circuit in **Fig. C.1** and implementing it in code. If an LED was connected at the output of every gate, the state of all LEDs would change as soon as the input switches were flipped. It would not happen gradually.

C.2.1 VHDL Design Units

Code available @ GitHub
https://git.io/fNXsJ

```
1  library IEEE;                  -- Library definitions
2  use IEEE.STD_LOGIC_1164.ALL;   -- Note: Comments are denoted using '--'
3
4  entity tutorial is
5     Port ( a, b, c  : in STD_LOGIC;
6            z        : out STD_LOGIC);
7  end entity;
8
9  architecture tutorial_arch of tutorial is
10    signal net2, net1, net0 : STD_LOGIC;   -- Constants, signals, entity references
11 begin
12    net2 <= not a;                         -- Circuit behavior
13    net1 <= net2 or b;
14    net0 <= b or c;
15    z <= net1 and net0;
16 end architecture;
```

This might seem like a lot, but the code is (very logically) broken down into something called *design units*: independent parts of the code, which can be compiled separately. Two of the most important design units will be discussed: **entity** and **architecture**. For now, take the first two lines at face value—these are library definitions that will be discussed at a later time (for more complex VHDL designs).

Entity

Just like functions in a programming language, the main design needs to be broken up into smaller blocks (otherwise, it will be very difficult to create, maintain, and troubleshoot). An **entity**, lines 4 through 7, in VHDL serves precisely this purpose: it creates a black box with a declaration of interfaces (**in**puts and **out**puts).

Aside from input and output declarations, an entity does not contain anything else. There is a corresponding **architecture**, which specifies the functionality of the black box.

Ports may be listed individually, or together like in the example above (separated by a comma). Each port must have a direction (either **in** or **out**). There is no internal semicolon after the last **STD_LOGIC**. **This is important!**

Architecture

Much like a function definition, the **architecture**, lines 9 through 16, defines the design and is tied to an existing entity. The space before the **begin** statement can be used to define other components, signals, or constants, while the code after the **begin** statement defines the design and behavior of the architecture.

In the code above, *intermediate wires* (or *nets*) are being defined, referred to as **signals**, as well as the behavior of each of the LEDs, based on the individual inputs **a**, **b**, **c**, and **d**.

C.2.2 Translating Circuit Schematics to VHDL

In order to convert combinational logic circuit schematics to VHDL, intermediate connections (connections that do not act as an input or output) have to be labeled as a *net*. These will be declared as **signals** before the **begin** statement in the **architecture** section of your code.

Start from the nets closest to the output and work toward the input (**Fig. C.2**).

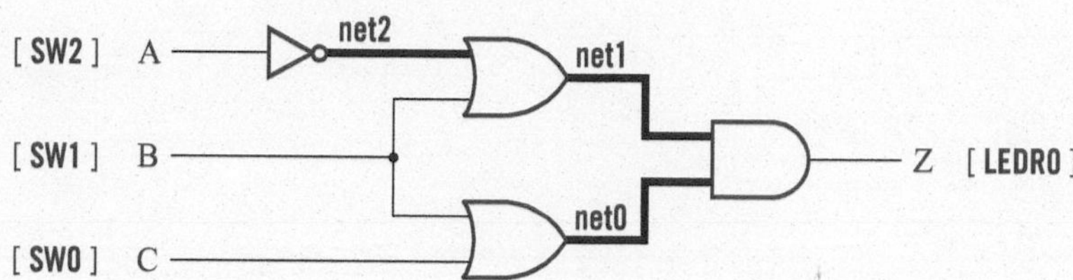

Figure C.2: Basic combinational logic circuit with labeled nets.

Add the required libraries to your code:

```
library IEEE;
use IEEE.STD_LOGIC_1164.ALL;
```

Define the entity with all of the inputs and outputs:

```
entity tutorial is
   Port ( a, b, c  : in STD_LOGIC;
          z        : out STD_LOGIC);
end entity;
```

Insert all of the nets before the **begin** statement in the architecture. Define the behavior of the circuit after the **begin**.

Note that the **end** statements can either be followed by **entity/architecture** or the name of the entity or architecture (*i.e.*, **end tutorial;** and **end tutorial_arch;**). To minimize confusion, the adopted convention would be to use **end entity;** and **end architecture;**.

```
architecture tutorial_arch of tutorial is
   signal net2, net1, net0 : STD_LOGIC;
begin
   net2 <= not a;
   net1 <= net2 or b;
   net0 <= b or c;
   z <= net1 and net0;
end architecture;
```

Although it is possible to implement the circuit in a single expression (without the use of signals), this is considered bad form. It is a nightmare to maintain and troubleshoot.

One last thing that deserves a mention..

> In VHDL, **AND** and **OR** operators have equal precedence, so the use of parentheses to preserve proper order of operations is a **must**.

C.3 Using Quartus Prime

This section will cover all aspects of development with the Intel Quartus software: creating a project, targeting the appropriate FPGA device, simulating the circuit, and programming the FPGA development board.

C.3.1 Creating a Project and Targeting the FPGA

1. Open Intel Quartus Prime and click on **New Project Wizard** in the *Home* tab. Click **Next** in the dialog window that appears (you can suppress future notifications by checking the *Don't show me this introduction again* checkbox).

2. Click the **[...]** button to browse to a folder on your computer, where the project will be stored, and name the project (**Fig. C.3**). Make sure to create a unique folder for your project, otherwise the project will be stored in the root folder. In this case, a folder named **tutorial** was created under the **cec220** folder. Click **Next**.

   Only alphanumeric characters and underscores can be used when naming the project. Spaces and special characters are not permitted in the file names!

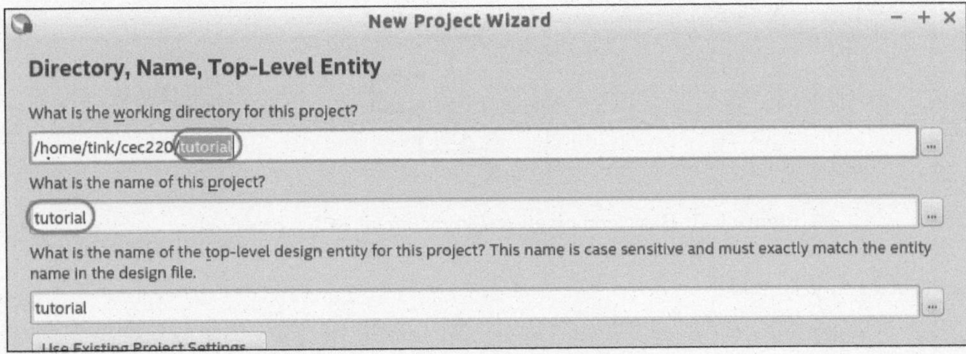

Figure C.3: New project creation dialog window.

3. Select **Empty project** and click **Next**. Skip through the *Add Files* dialog that follows by clicking **Next** again, unless some existing or already provided files need to be imported into the project.

4. Select the **MAX 10 (DA/DF/DC/SA/SC)** under *Family*, type in **10m50daf484c7g** into the *name filter* box, select the appropriate part (**Fig. C.4**), and click **Next**.

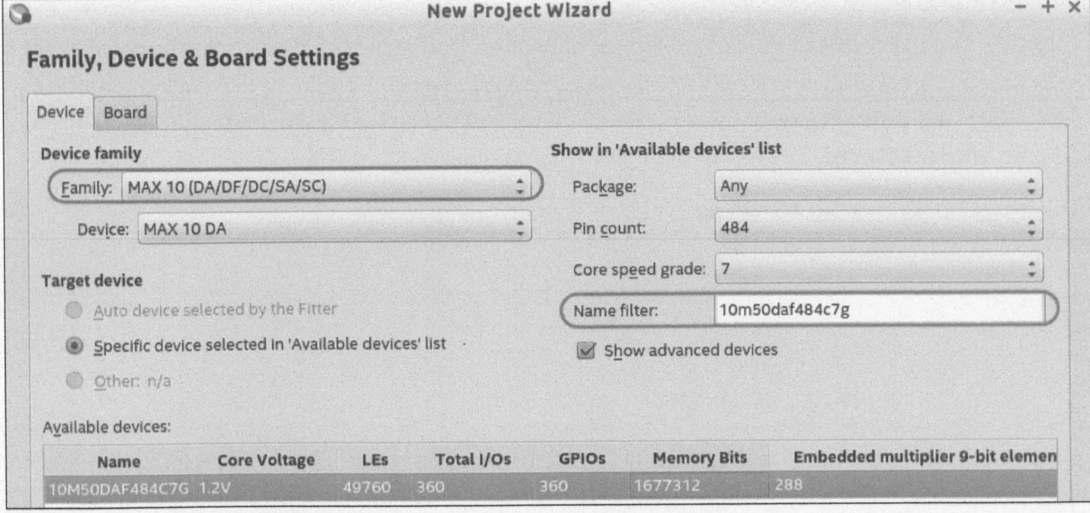

Figure C.4: Part selection dialog.

5. In the *EDA Tool Settings* window, pick **VHDL** as the *Simulator* format (**Fig. C.5**) and click **Next**, followed by **Finish**.

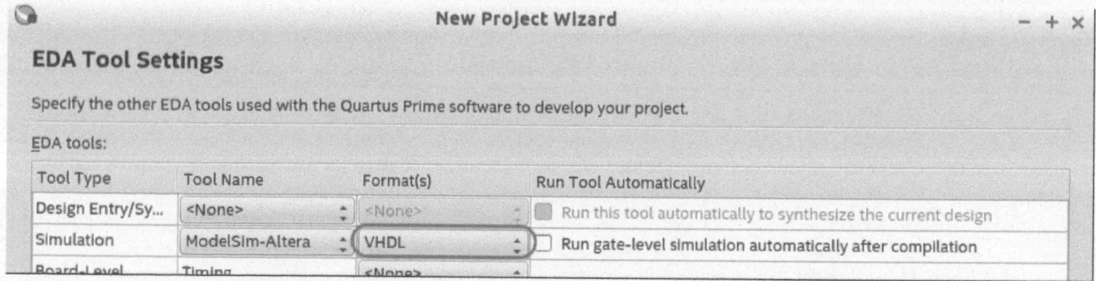

Figure C.5: Simulator format selection (EDA Tool Settings dialog).

C.3.2 Creating a New VHDL Source File

In order to write VHDL code, a VHDL source file will need to be added to the project.

1. Go to **File** > **New...** In the dialog window that appears, select **VHDL File** under *Design Files*. Click **OK**.

2. Add the *comments header* (required for all files you will be submitting), which consists of your identifying information, date, and a brief description of the entity. Comments in VHDL are denoted with a double-dash: **--**.

```
-- Akhan ALMAGAMBETOV (Sort no. 000)
-- CEC220.04PC Digital Circuit Design
-- 24 Apr 1990
-- Description: tutorial.vhd
-- Combinational logic circuit from tutorial.
```

3. Once the file is modified (*e.g.*, the comments are added), press **`Ctrl`** + **S** (or **File** > **Save**). Name the file (by default, it will be named with the top-level entity name that was specified during project creation) and click **Save**. **Make sure that the *Add file to current project* checkbox is checked and the file type is VHDL.**

4. Enter the code for your design under the header. Don't forget to include the libraries in addition to the entity and architecture. Periodically save your work (an ***** beside the filename indicates unsaved work).

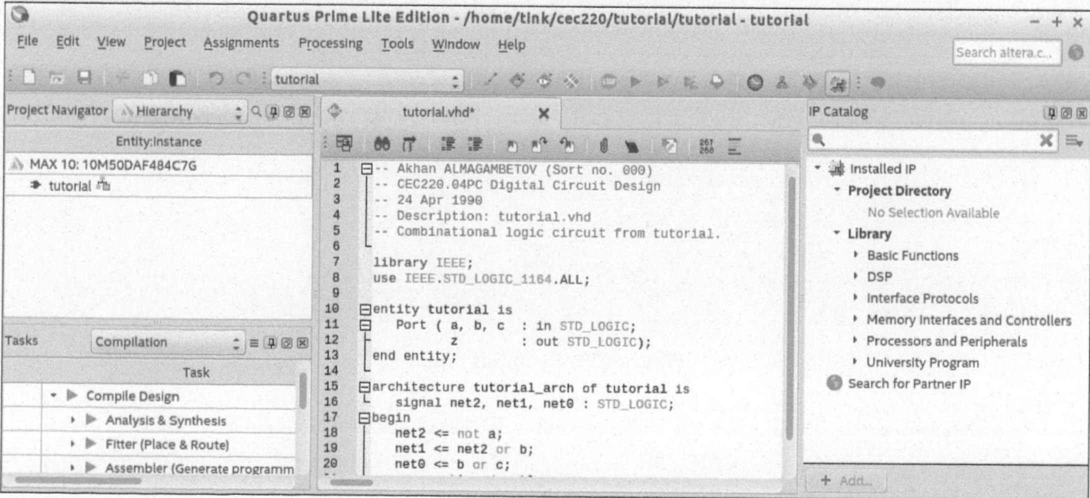

Figure C.6: Intel Quartus Prime user interface.

C.3.3 Synthesizing the Design

A typical FPGA design workflow is shown in **Fig. C.7**.

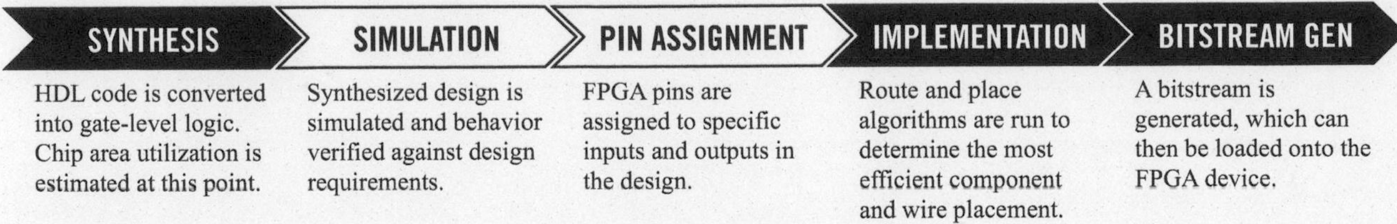

Figure C.7: Typical FPGA design workflow (steps in *white* must be completed by the user).

VHDL code must be synthesized down to gate-level logic. After synthesis, it will be possible to run a simulation and compare the output of the simulation to the design requirements.

Click on **Analysis and Synthesis** under *Tasks* on the left side of the window (**Fig. C.8**). Once synthesis is complete, a green checkmark should appear.

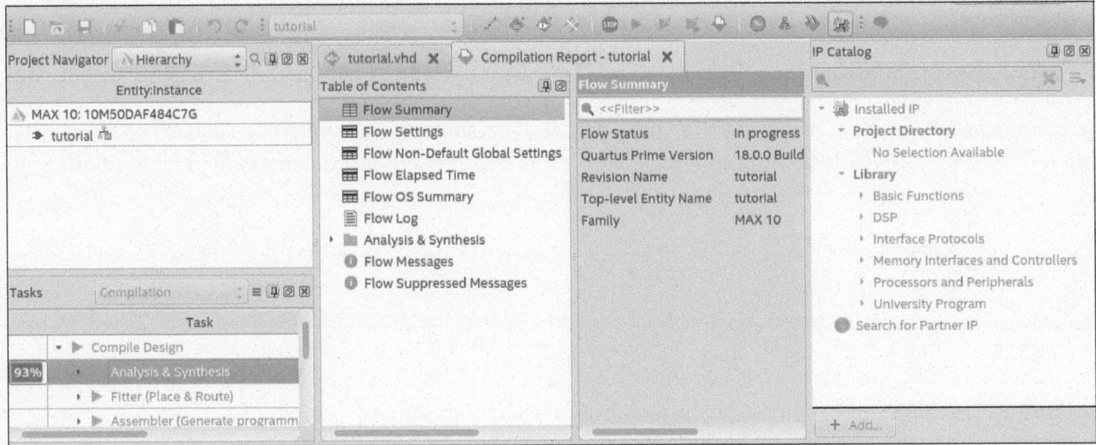

Figure C.8: *Analysis and Synthesis* selection.

If any errors are detected during synthesis, a red cross should appear by the *Analysis and Synthesis* entry. These error messages are viewable in the bottom of the window, under *Messages* (**Fig. C.9**). Filtering out all messages except critical errors can be accomplished by clicking on the button with the red cross, as shown in **Fig. C.10**.

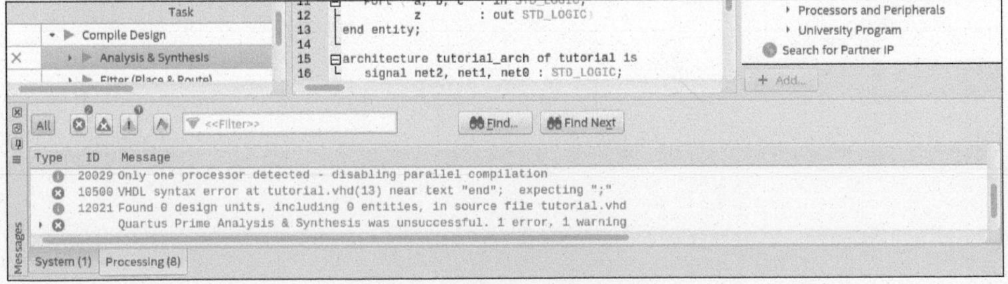

Figure C.9: Synthesis errors.

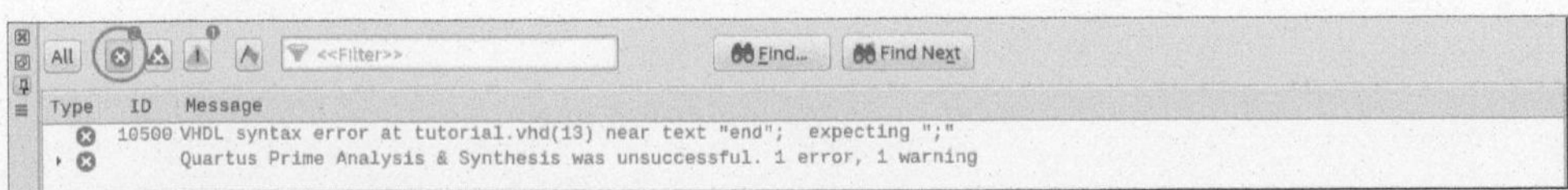

Figure C.10: Filtering of messages: critical errors only.

In most cases, VHDL errors are self-explanatory. The error typically occurs prior to the line referenced by the error (in this case, a semicolon was missing on line 12).

C.3.4 Simulating the Design with qsim

1. Once synthesis completes successfully, simulate the circuit using *qsim* by creating a new waveform file: go to **File** > **New...** In the dialog window that appears, select **University Program VWF** (vector waveform file) under *Verification/Debugging Files*. Click **OK**.

   Note that the simulation method described here uses the academic simulator called *qsim* (it is a light version of the simulator that comes bundled with Quartus). The full version of the simulator will be covered in class alongside self-checking test benches.

2. Right-click anywhere in the *Simulation Waveform Editor* and select **Insert Node or Bus...**, as shown in (**Fig. C.11**).

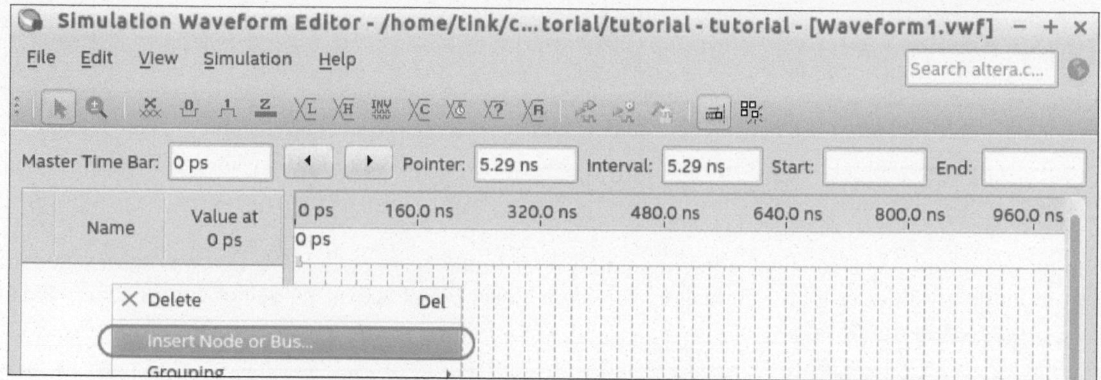

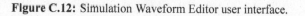

Figure C.11: Simulation Waveform Editor user interface.

3. In the *Insert Node or Bus* dialog that appears, click on **Node Finder...**. To list all available nodes, click **List**.
4. Click **>>** to add all ports to the simulation (**Fig. C.12**), followed by **OK** (twice).

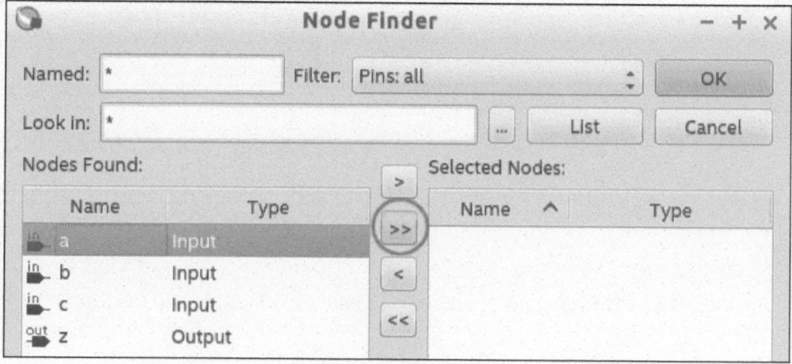

Figure C.12: Simulation Waveform Editor user interface.

NOTE

Once ports are added, it is possible to set signals to desired values using the top row of buttons in the menu bar. Some of the most common options that will be used are as follows (enabled when a signal or a portion of a signal is selected):

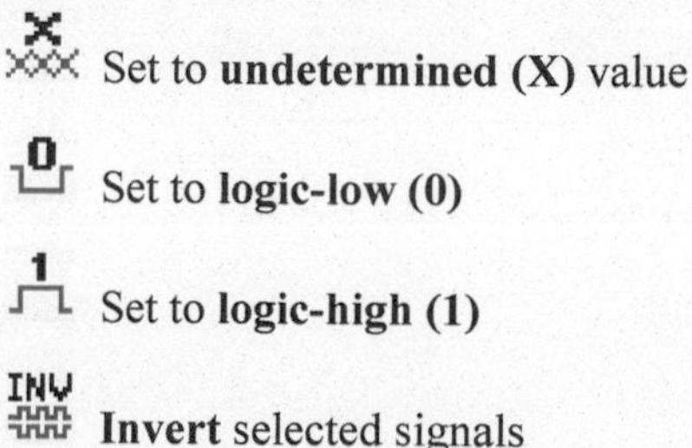

- Set to **undetermined (X)** value
- Set to **logic-low (0)**
- Set to **logic-high (1)**
- **Invert** selected signals
- Set signal(s) to a **count** value (*e.g.*, 2-bit signal means count `00`..`01`..`10`..`11`)
- **Force clock** on a signal (transition [0-to-1 and 1-to-0], duty cycle, and clock cycle period)

There exist three options for setting signal values:

(a) Clicking on and dragging across the signal to select certain regions, then forcing the selection to particular values (**Fig. C.13**).

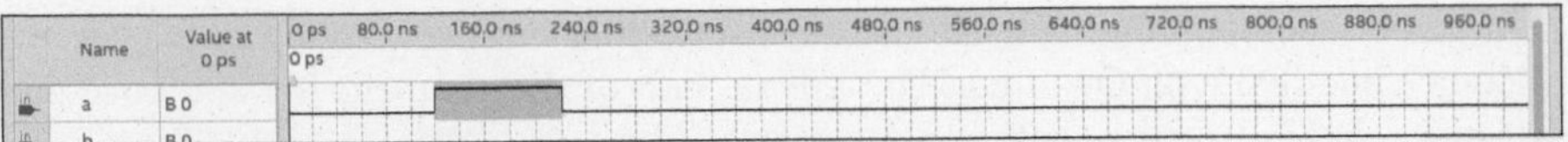

Figure C.13: *qsim*: Manual signal region selection.

(b) Selecting the entire signal by clicking on the signal name and using the menu buttons for forcing the values (as shown in **Fig. C.14**).

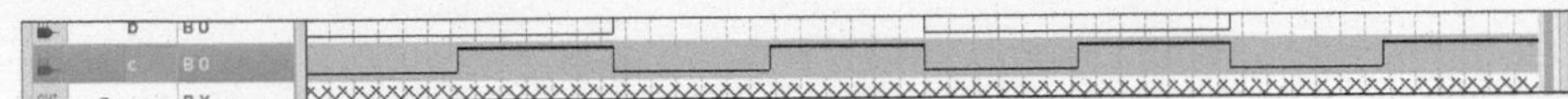

Figure C.14: *qsim*: Selection of the full signal.

(c) Grouping of multiple discrete signals into a single vector (multi-bit signal). This is the best way to simulate all input-output possibilities of a given circuit by forcing a binary count across the vector components. **This method will be discussed in detail below.**

---

4. Since this is a combinational logic circuit, simulating all of the input possibilities would prove its functionality and correctness (the results would be compared with a truth table).

   The easiest approach would be to group all of the individual inputs into a multi-bit vector and force a count from zero to the maximum possible binary number.

   Select all of the **input signals** by using **Shift** + click. Right-click on the selection and choose **Grouping** > **Group...** (**Fig. C.15**).

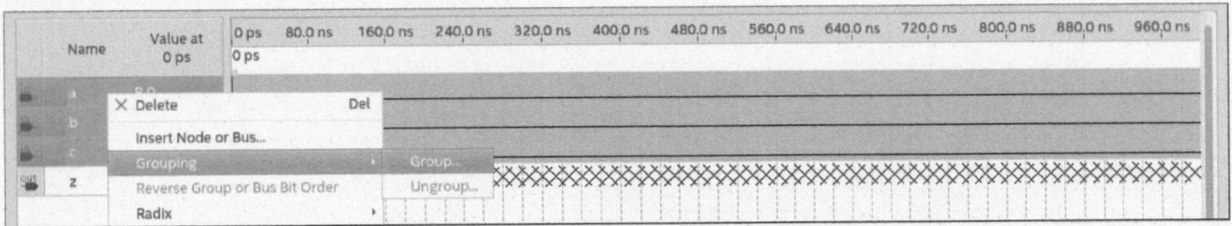

Figure C.15: Grouping of single-bit simulation signals into vectors.

5. The default simulation runtime is <u>*1000 ns*</u>. A 3-bit count would need 2^3 intervals, making the counter period $1000/2^3$ or **125 ns**.

   Set the *Count every* value to **125 ns** and click **OK** (**Fig. C.16**).

   The binary count will appear in the grouped vector (*i.e.*, **000**, **001** .. **111**).

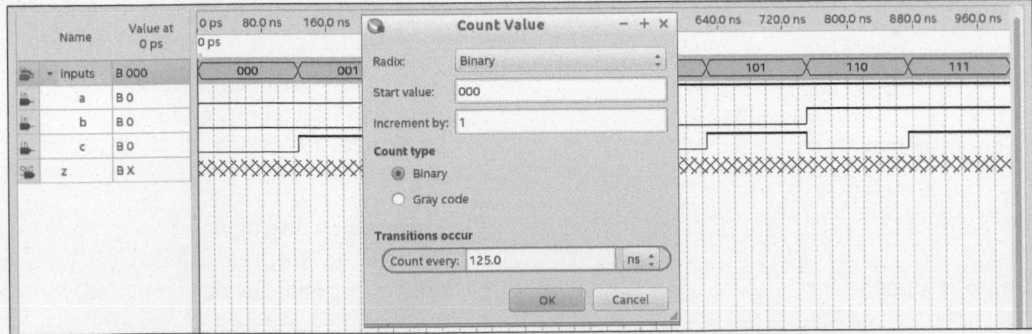

Figure C.16: *Force counter* options.

6. Once all of the input signal values are set (**do not set the output signal value!**), run the simulation by selecting **Simulation > Run Functional Simulation**. Another window will appear containing a read-only version of the simulation results (**Fig. C.17**).

   If asked to save, **do not modify the default filename** (*i.e.*, **Waveform.vwf**). Doing so may cause the simulation to fail with a file permissions error.

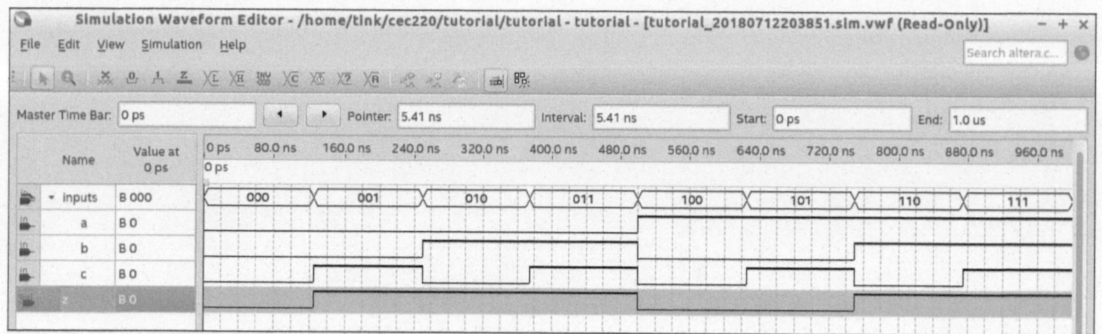

Figure C.17: Final simulation results.

7. Compare the simulation results with the original truth table. If there is a mismatch, troubleshoot the VHDL implementation of the circuit.

C.3.5 Manual Pin Assignment

Study the relevant hardware that will be used for input/output in **Appendix H**. In the case of the tutorial circuit, switches **SW2**, **SW1**, and **SW0** will be used for input (A, B, and C, respectively) and LED **LEDR0** will be used for the output (Z). The pin diagram is given in **Fig. C.18**

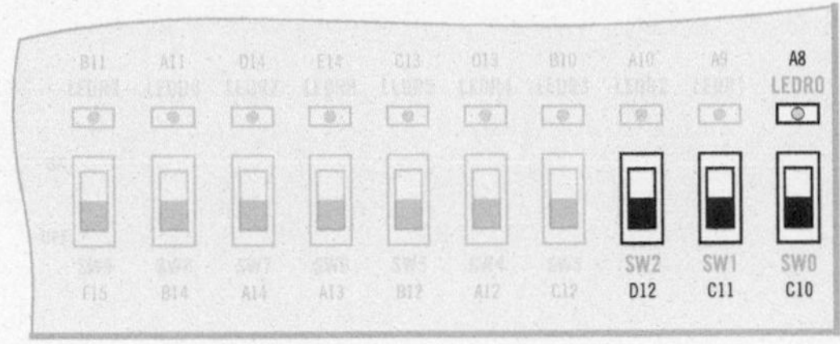

* Irrelevant parts have been grayed out.

Figure C.18: Pin diagram for switches **SW9..0** and LEDs **LEDR9..0**.

After determining pin locations of all I/O ports, assign them within the Quartus *Pin Planner*.

1. Within the main Quartus window, select **Assignments** > **Pin Planner**.
2. In the *Pin Planner* window that appears (**Fig. C.19**), populate the **Location** of each input and output port with the location from the pin diagram in **Fig. C.18**.

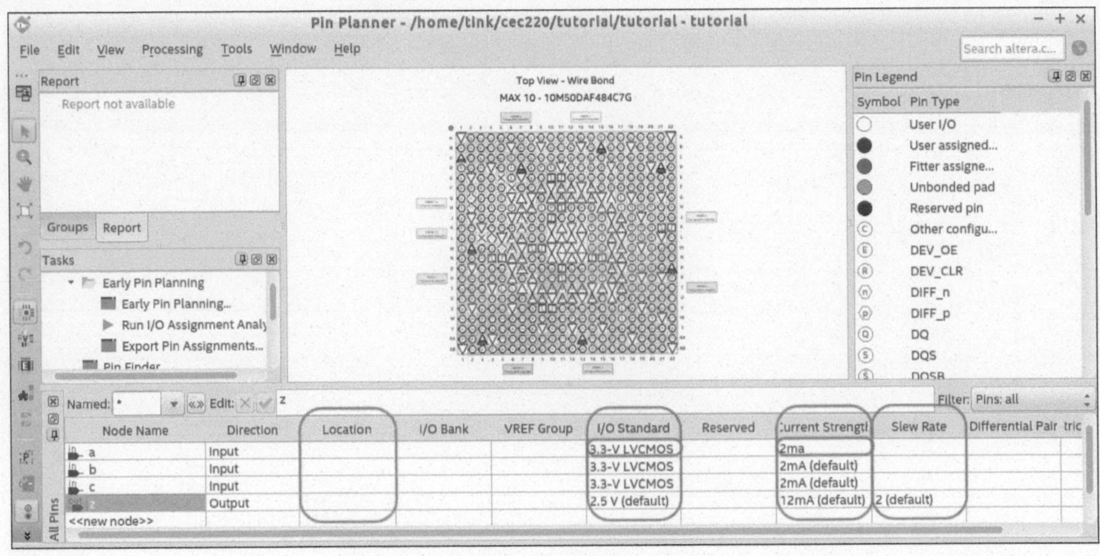

Figure C.19: *Pin Planner* interface.

Set the *I/O Standard* to **3.3-V LVCMOS**. The *Current Strength* and the *Slew Rate* of the output can be left as their *(default)* values (**2mA** and **2**, respectively), as shown in **Fig. C.20**. Close the *Pin Planner* window once done.

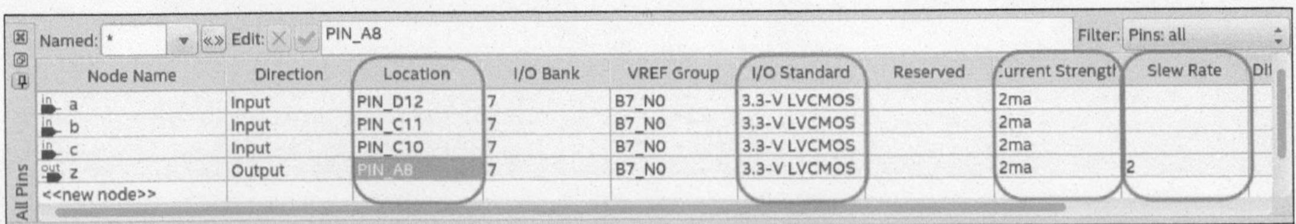

Figure C.20: Pin settings [do **not** leave any settings on *(default)*].

IMPORTANT: In older versions of Quartus, leaving pin settings as their **(default)** values will cause errors during implementation. This is designed as a safety measure.

3. It is strongly suggested to select all of the pins and set the *I/O Standard* at the same time. Otherwise, a lot of time and nerves would be wasted setting the signal level for each individual pin.

   To do this, select all of the pins and click on the drop-down menu that appears once the selection is made (**Fig. C.21**).

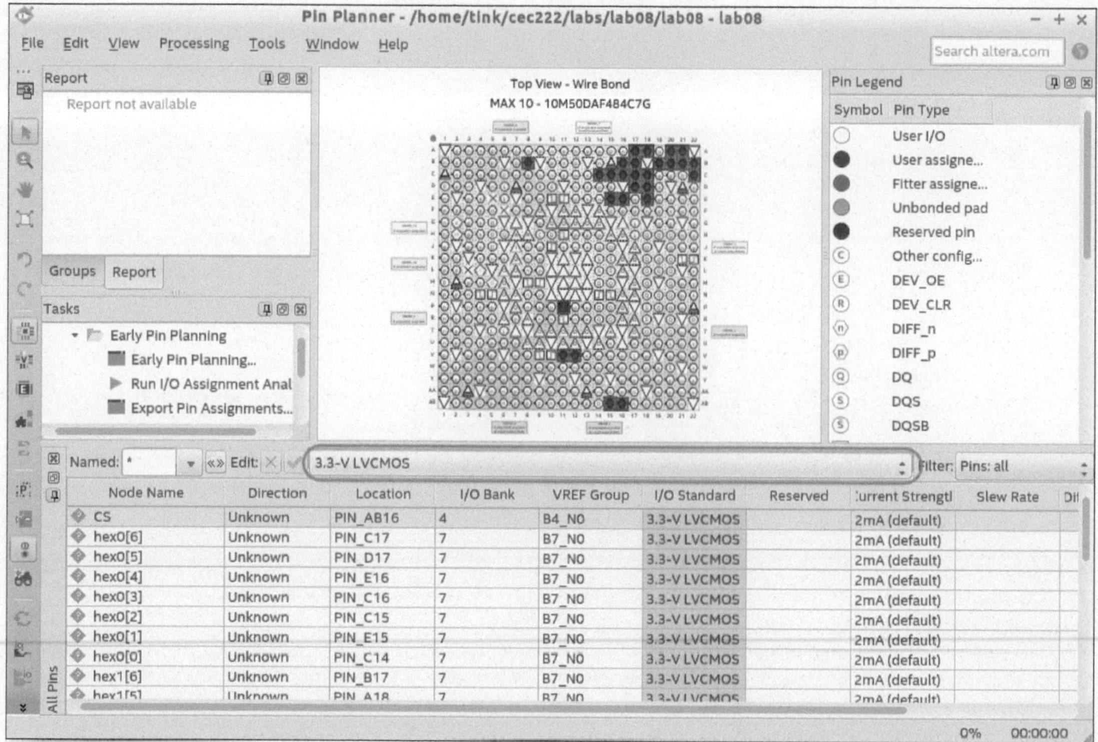

Figure C.21: Bulk assignment of voltage levels, once all pins are selected.

4. After all pin locations and voltage levels have been assigned, simply close the *Pin Planner* window. The pin assignments do not have to be saved.

C.3.6 Programming the Development Board

1. After assigning pins, recompile the project by clicking on the **Compile Design** item within the *Tasks* list on the left side of the main Quartus window (**Fig. C.22a**).

   This will take the project through synthesis, implementation, and bitstream generation.

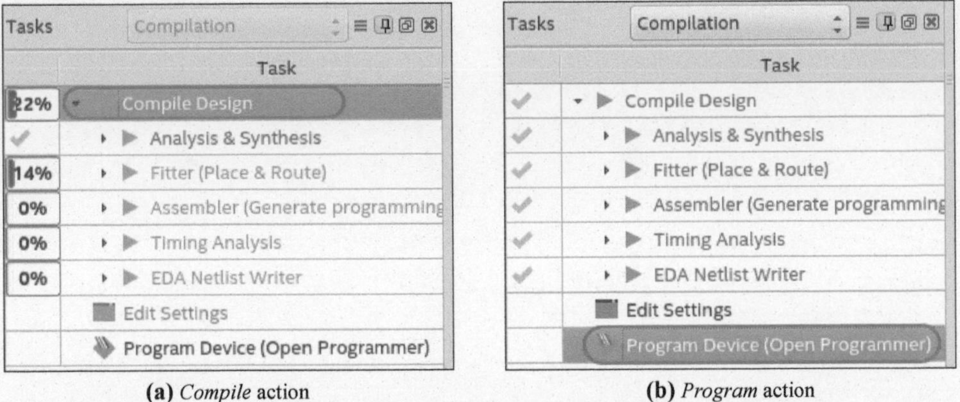

(a) *Compile* action **(b)** *Program* action

Figure C.22: Compiling the project files and programming the development board.

2. Once compilation has completed, click on **Program Device (Open Programmer)**, shown in **Fig. C.22b**. The *Programmer* window should open.

3. Click on **Hardware Setup**. Select **USB Blaster** from the dropdown menu and **Close** the *Hardware Setup* window. In the main *Programmer* window, click **Auto Detect**.

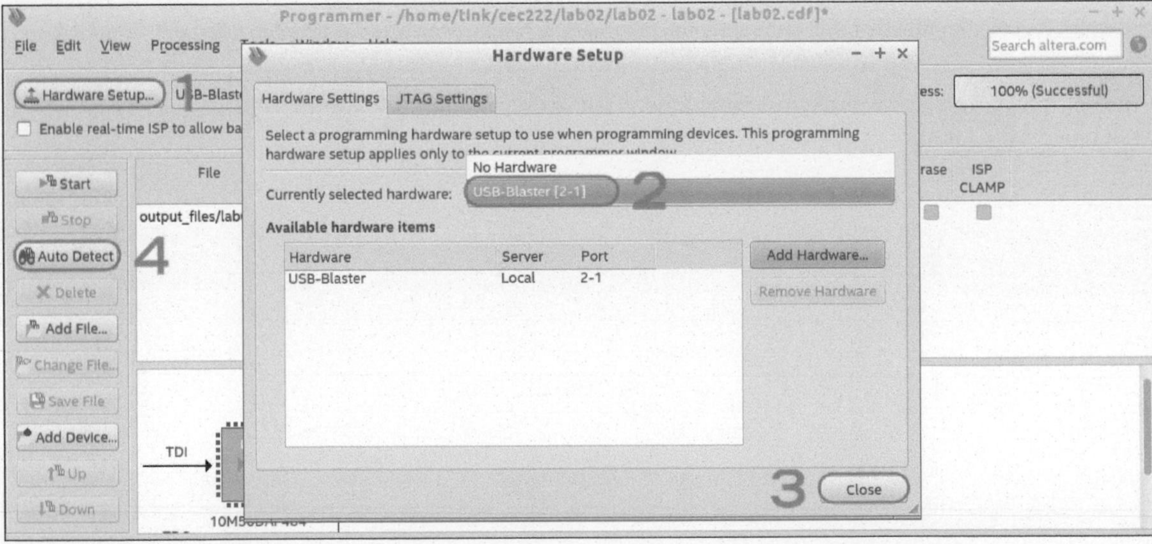

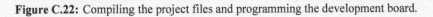

Figure C.23: Hardware setup dialog.

Note for Windows systems only: If the **USB Blaster** option does not appear in the dropdown menu, navigate to the Windows **Device Manager** and locate the unrecognized device ("USB Blaster" will have a yellow exclamation mark next to it).

Right-click on the unrecognized device and select **Update Driver**. In the subsequent dialog window, select **Browse my computer for driver software**.

Select the following directory and make sure that **Include subfolders** is checked.

```
C:\intelFPGA_lite\18.x\quartus
```

Click through the steps to install the driver.

4. To program the board, make sure that *USB Blaster* is displayed in the top right and click **Start**. Once the process completes, a green *100% (Successful)* progress indicator will appear in the top right corner of the window.

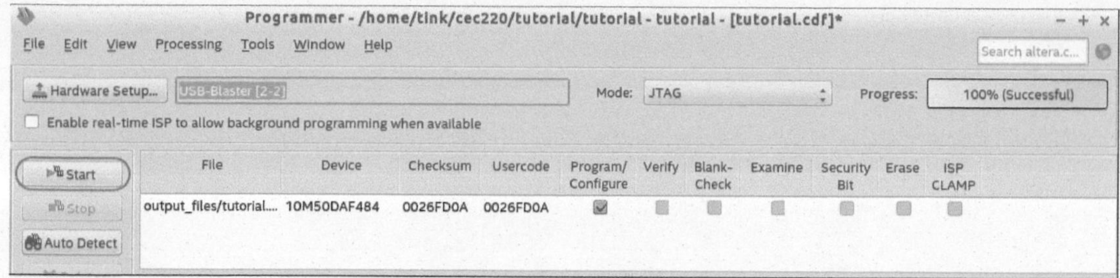

Figure C.24: Programmer UI.

C.4 Notes on Verifying the Result

Due to the way the LEDs are connected to the FPGA, unassigned LEDs will be at half-brightness. This makes the troubleshooting process easier, as you always know if a pin assignment error has occurred.

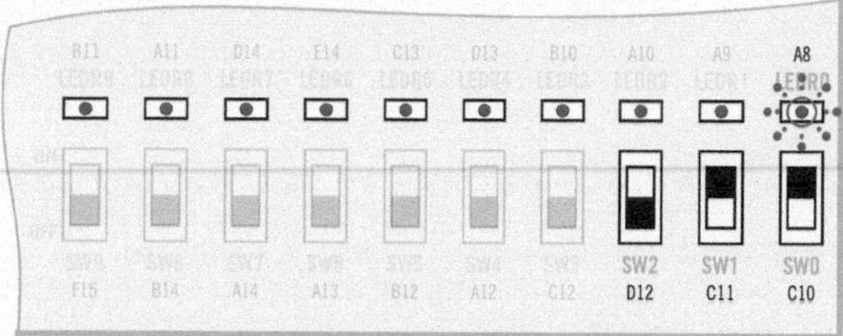

Figure C.25: Interpreting hardware results.

In **Fig. C.25**, the switches are set to a binary value of **`011`** (for inputs A, B, and C, respectively). Referencing the truth table in **Fig. C.1b**, the hardware results seem to be in line with the function of the circuit (**`LEDR0`** is on).

Using Symbolic Blocks in Intel Quartus

This tutorial focuses on using existing blocks (or symbols) in the *Primitives* library of Intel Quartus, such as logic gates. It is assumed that basic working knowledge of the Quartus workflow has been attained: starting a new project, targeting the FPGA, running synthesis and implementation, assigning pins, and using the *qsim* simulator for verifying your design.

Refer back to **Appendix C** for detailed steps on how to perform any of the above.

D.1 Objectives

After completing this tutorial, the student will be able to:

- Create a new block diagram (***.bdf**) within a Quartus project.
- Use the *Logic* blocks in the *Primitives* library of Intel Quartus.
- Create input and output ports in the block diagram, which can be mapped to FPGA pins.
- Correctly annotate the block diagram.
- Create (***.bsf**) block symbol files, which can be used in other projects.

D.2 Background

Block diagrams are a graphical representation of the underlying code—an abstraction. It is not possible to directly synthesize block diagrams. Instead, Quartus generates the required VHDL code from the graphical representation, which can then be synthesized.

In system design, block diagrams serve a useful purpose: it is far easier to convey the function of a system through a diagram of connected blocks, rather than annotating of explaining code. This is especially true on multi-disciplinary teams.

In this tutorial, the combinational logic circuit from **Appendix C.2** will be implemented using a block diagram. The circuit and its truth table are shown in **Fig. D.1**.

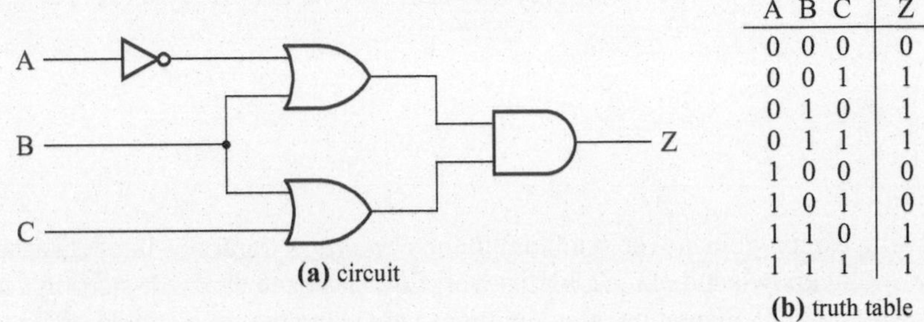

(a) circuit

A	B	C	Z
0	0	0	0
0	0	1	1
0	1	0	1
0	1	1	1
1	0	0	0
1	0	1	0
1	1	0	1
1	1	1	1

(b) truth table

Figure D.1: Basic logic circuit and truth table (from **Appendix C.2**, **Fig. C.1**).

Side Note Regarding IP blocks

Note that in industry, companies use something called *Intellectual Property (IP) blocks*. Essentially, they are blocks that cannot be reverse-engineered by a third-party and whose code is hidden from the user.

For example, when Qualcomm allows a manufacturer the use of their CDMA modem technology, they simply license an IP block containing all of the necessary implementation information. The manufacturer cannot reverse-engineer the IP and create their own modem.

Intel provides an IP block creation and management tool called *Platform Designer* (formerly *Qsys*, prior to Intel's acquisition of Altera Corporation in 2015 and subsequent changes). Platform Designer minimizes prototyping time by automatically generating HDL component interconnection logic.

For the purposes of this lab, Platform Designer is too advanced and requires a significant amount of training. You may choose to explore this tool on your own, since it is extensively used in industry.

D.3 Creating a Block Diagram

Create a new Quartus project and target the appropriate FPGA device.

1. Select **File** > **New...** > **Block Diagram / Schematic File** under *Design Files*. Click **OK**. An empty block diagram will appear (**Fig. D.2**).

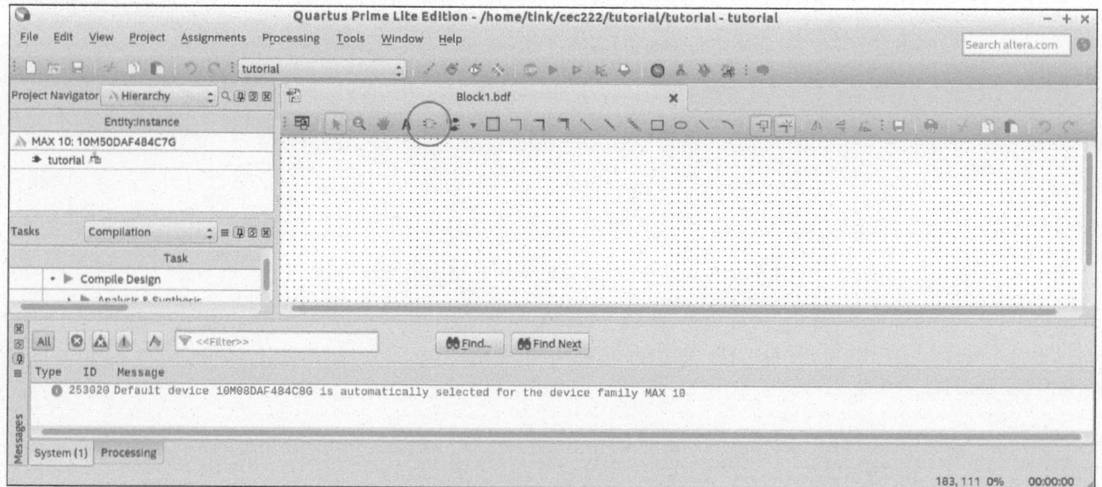

Figure D.2: New block diagram.

2. To place components, double click on the blank grid in the window or click the button in the menu. A component selection window will appear (**Fig. D.3**).

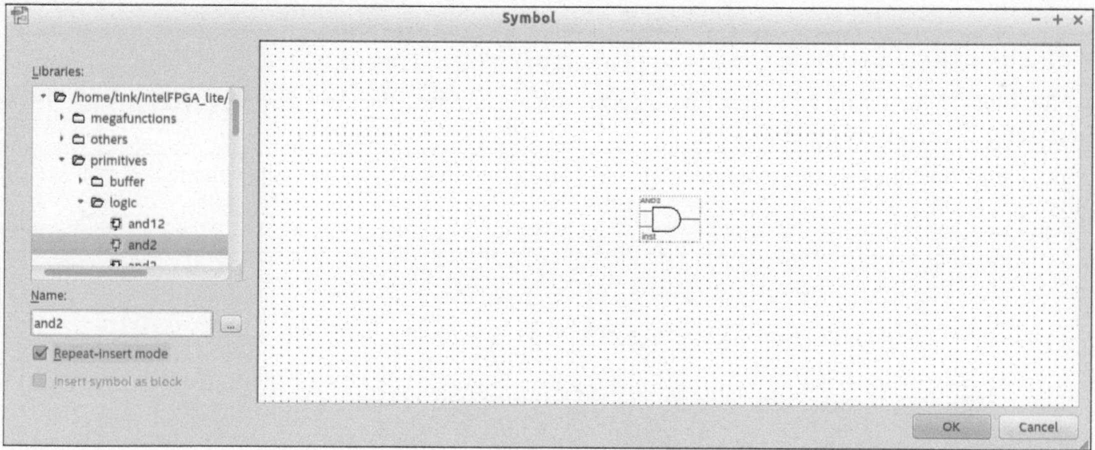

Figure D.3: Symbol insertion dialog.

Component names can either be typed into the **Name:** text box directly or can be chosen in the hierarchy under **primitives** > **logic**. If entering the name directly, the following components will be used:

- **not**—inverter
- **and2**—two-input AND gate
- **or2**—two-input OR gate (2x)

Click **OK** after selecting the appropriate component. If the **Repeat-insert mode** checkbox is checked, the component can be placed multiple times by simply clicking on the grid.

Press **ESC** on the keyboard to exit repeat-insert mode.

3. Once all of the components are placed, hover over one of the gate inputs or outputs. A crosshair cursor with a wire symbol (+⌝) should appear. Components can be connected by simply clicking and dragging the cursor.

4. Click on the dropdown to the right of the button to select the type of port being placed (**Fig. D.4**). The circuit in **Fig. D.1** has three input and one output ports. Place and wire the ports per the diagram.

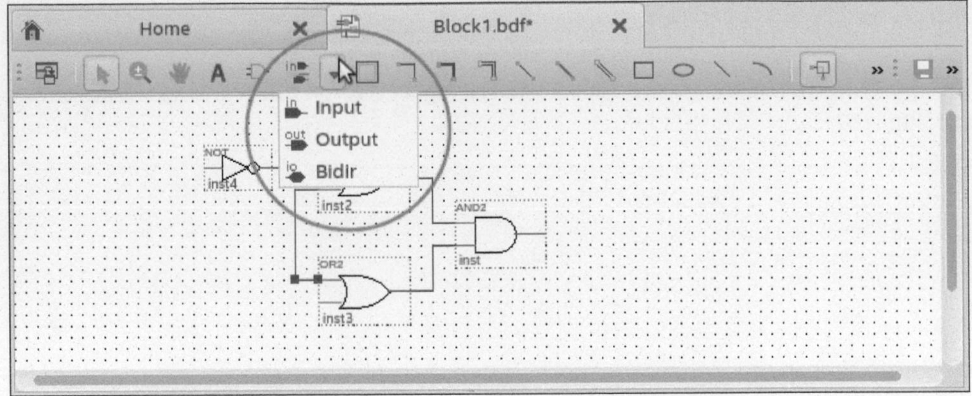

Figure D.4: Port type selection using the *Pin Tool*.

5. Ports can be named by double-clicking on the violet-colored port label. The completed block diagram should look similar to **Fig. D.5**.

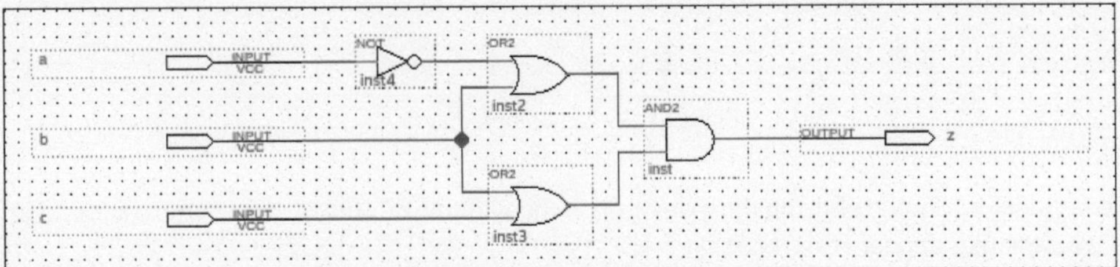

Figure D.5: Completed block diagram.

6. Save the block diagram by selecting **File** > **Save**. Make sure that the **Add file to current project** checkbox is selected and click **Save** (**Fig. D.6**).

   Do not change the block diagram name! It should correspond to the top-level entity name that you specified when creating the project.

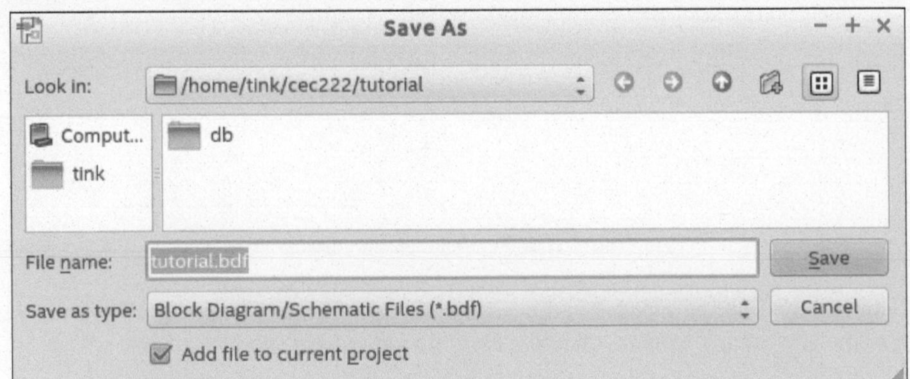

Figure D.6: Save dialog window.

7. To check for design errors, select **Processing** > **Analyze Current File**.

The design can now be synthesized, simulated, pin-assigned, and loaded onto the FPGA development board. See **Appendix C** for more details.

D.4 Proper Formatting for Deliverables

D.4.1 Component Placement and Wiring

When creating block diagrams, make sure to be as neat as possible. An example of a poorly-designed block diagram is given in **Fig. D.7**. Notice how the wires are placed randomly and it's generally very difficult to trace the connections.

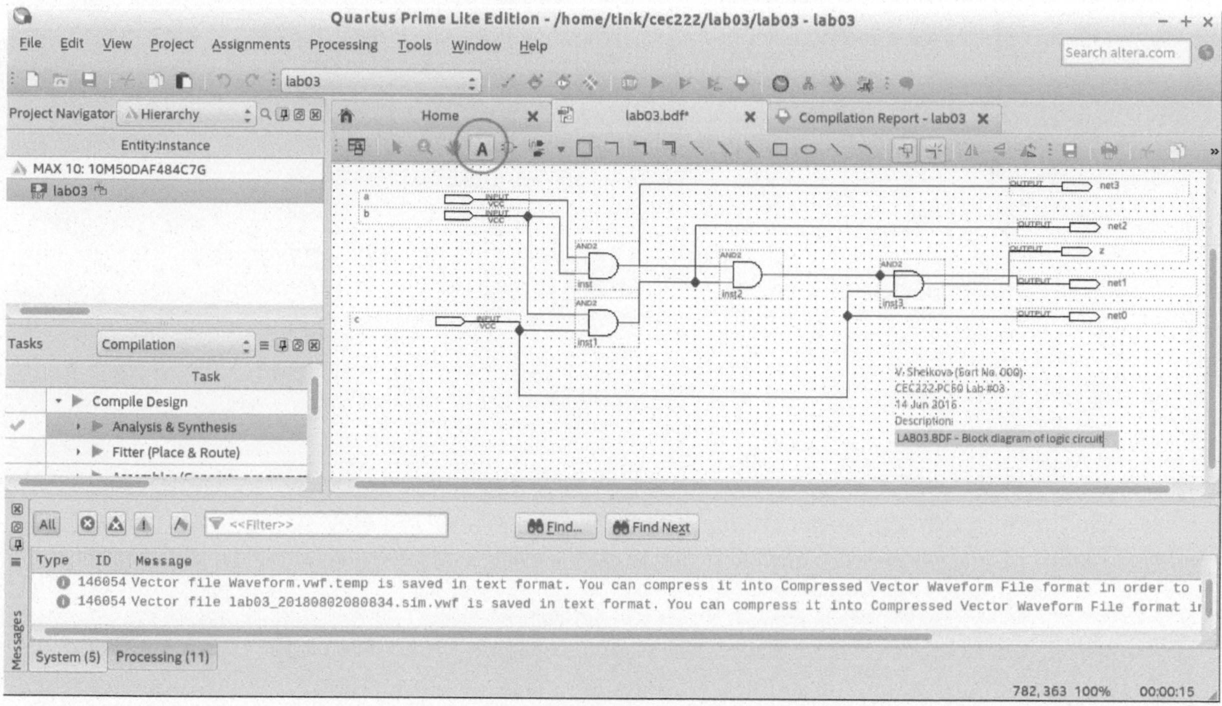

Figure D.7: An example of a poorly-designed block diagram.

An example of a well-designed diagram is shown in **Fig. D.5**. This block diagram represents the original circuit and is easy to understand.

D.4.2 Labeling

Every block diagram needs to have identifying information printed (via Quartus) in the lower right corner. Failure to do so may lead to grade penalties, as it is difficult to tell whether the diagram was original work or not.

The following information must be included:

- Full name
- Sort number (if assigned)
- Course number and section
- Laboratory number
- Date created
- A brief description of the diagram

D.5 Creating Custom Symbol Blocks from VHDL Files

This section will cover the creation of block symbol files (***.bsf**) from pure-VHDL files. Please do not read this section prior to reading **Appendices C.2 and E**. The first lab in the sequence to require this approach will be **Laboratory 6**.

Directory File Structure

Before beginning this part of the tutorial, make sure that all of the lab Quartus project files are stored in an accessible, easy-to-navigate directory structure. The required directory structure is given in (**Fig. D.8**).

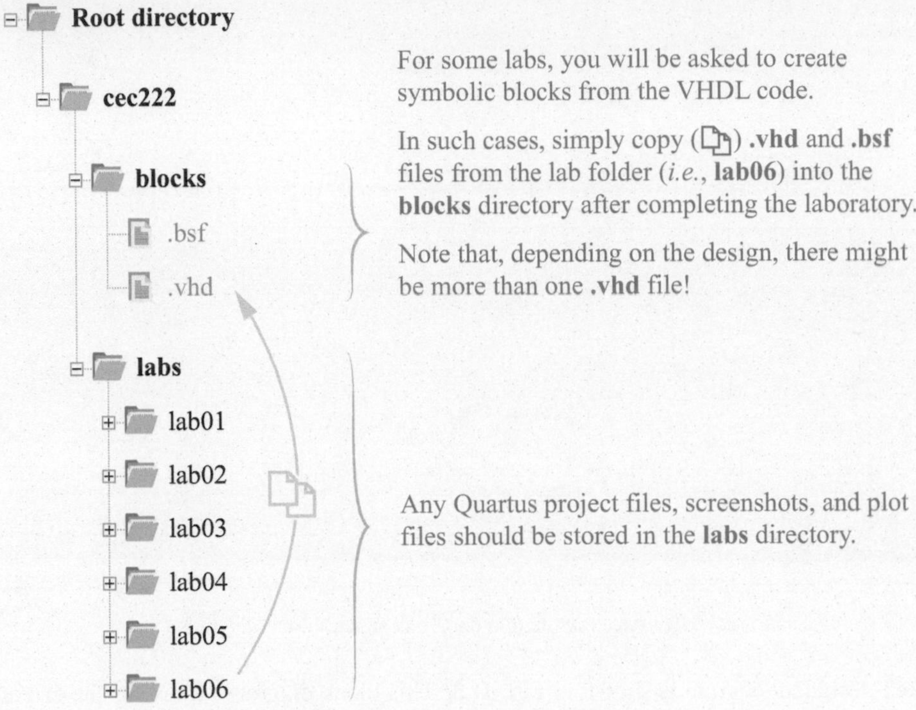
Root directory
cec222
blocks
.bsf
.vhd
labs
lab01
lab02
lab03
lab04
lab05
lab06
For some labs, you will be asked to create symbolic blocks from the VHDL code.
In such cases, simply copy ( ) .vhd and .bsf files from the lab folder (i.e., lab06) into the blocks directory after completing the laboratory.
Note that, depending on the design, there might be more than one .vhd file!
Any Quartus project files, screenshots, and plot files should be stored in the labs directory.

Figure D.8: Sample directory structure.

Note that not following these requirements will make subsequent labs an absolute nightmare to complete and maintain. Most of the code after **Laboratory 6** will be re-used for subsequent laboratories.

If your current directory structure is not neatly organized, please do so now. Make sure that your partner has a complete copy of both the **`labs`** and **`blocks`** directories at the end of each laboratory (in case partners are shuffled around or the drive is lost or corrupted). Even campus network drives have been known to get corrupted!

> **None of the folders or files can have spaces! Spaces will cause weird errors, which do not represent the actual error and are extremely difficult to troubleshoot.**
>
> For example, `/Documents and Settings/almagama/cec222/labs/lab06` would most likely cause an error. Despite there not being spaces in most folder names, `Documents and Settings` has spaces and would prevent some files from being accessed by Quartus.

D.5.1 Symbol Block Creation

In order to create a custom symbol block, open an existing Quartus project. For the purposes of this tutorial, code from the multiplexing device in **Appendix E** will be used.

1. Double-click on the top-level entity name in the *Project Navigator* (**Fig. D.9**).

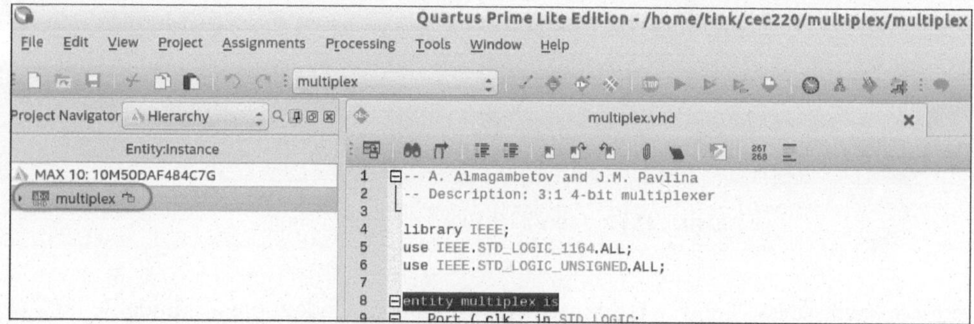

Figure D.9: Top-level module selection from the project hierarchy view.

2. Once the corresponding VHDL file is open, select **File** > **Create/Update** > **Create Symbol Files for Current File** from the main window menu.

   The messages window at the bottom should indicate that the symbol files have been created successfully (**Fig. D.10**).

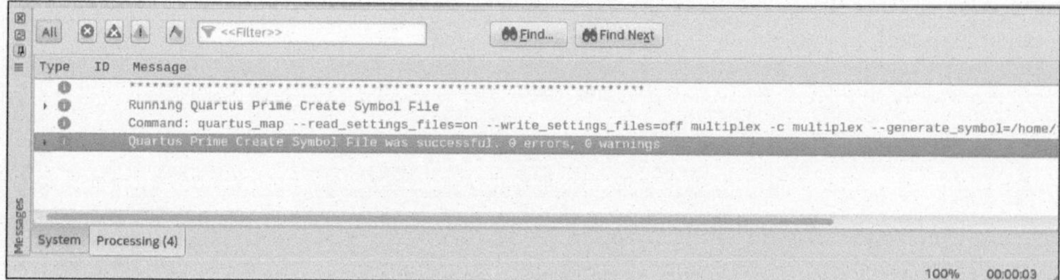

Figure D.10: Message to signal successful creation of symbol files.

The original project can now be closed. The symbol file is stored in the same directory as the Quartus project.

3. **Important!** Navigate to the Quartus project directory and copy all of the **.bsf** and **.vhd** files. Paste the files into the `/cec222/blocks` folder. Note that there might be multiple **.vhd** files, depending on the implemented design (**Fig. D.11**).

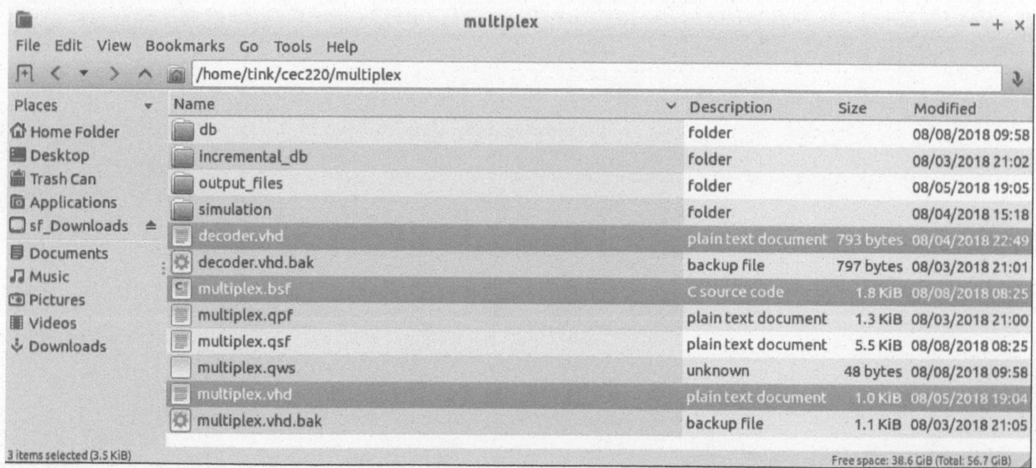

Figure D.11: Quartus project directory listing.

D.5.2 Using Custom Symbol Blocks

To use custom symbol blocks, create a new Quartus project and make a new block diagram. It is assumed that the **.bsf** and **.vhd** files have already been copied into the `/cec222/blocks` directory (**Fig. D.12**).

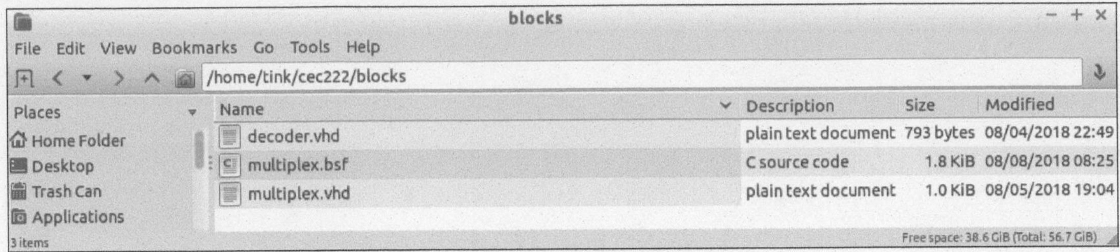

Figure D.12: `/cec222/blocks` directory listing.

1. With the project open, select **Tools** > **Options...** from the main window menu. Initially, the `/cec222/blocks` directory will have to be added as a *Global Library* and a *Project Library*.

2. In the *Options* window, click on **Libraries** (**Fig. D.13**).

   Click on the browse (**[...]**) symbol next to *Global library name*. Select `/cec222/blocks` folder (not the files inside!). Click **Add**. The folder path should be displayed in the libraries listing.

   Repeat the above procedure for *Project libraries*, but prior to selecting the folder, verify that the **Use project's relative path** checkbox is ticked. This is very important, as copying the files to another machine will likely render them unusable otherwise.

   Click **OK** when finished.

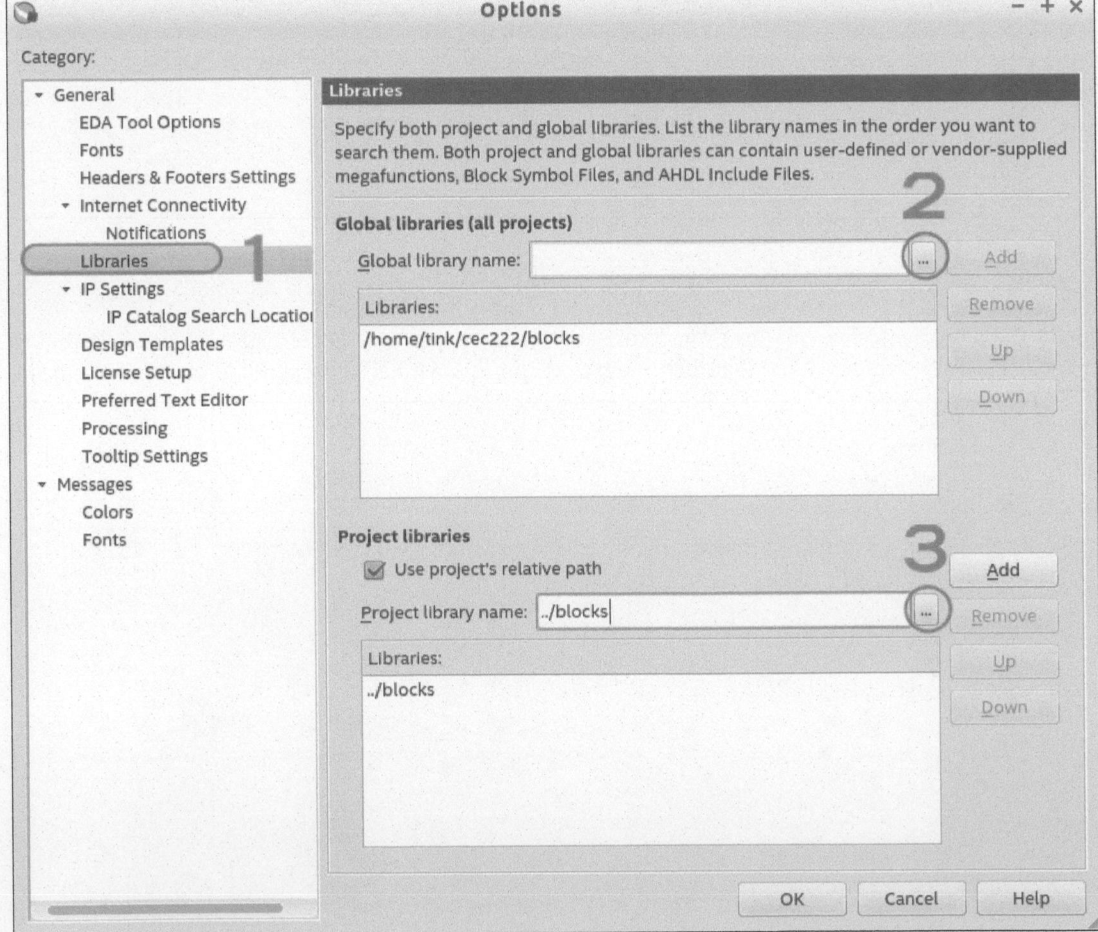

Figure D.13: *Options* window.

3. Double-click on the blank grid to bring up the **Symbol** selection window (**Fig. D.14**). All of the symbols stored in the `/cec222/blocks` directory should appear.

   Pick the **`multiplex`** symbol that has a relative (not full) path: `../blocks/`. Choosing this option will make it so Quartus is able to resolve all dependencies without errors.

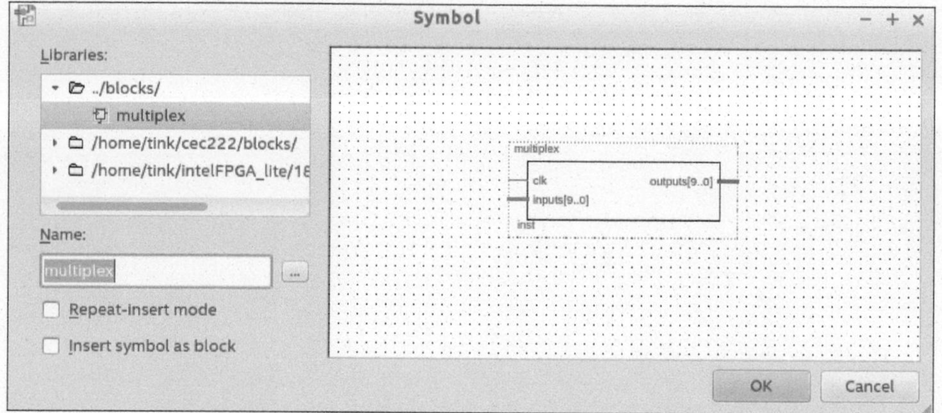

Figure D.14: *Symbol* selection window, with local project libraries.

Troubleshooting. If the following error appears during synthesis, the correct procedure was not followed and Quartus is unable to find **.vhd** file(s) associated with the **.bsf** files:

```
Error (12006): Node instance "inst" instantiates undefined entity "multiplex"
```

If an old project is opened and synthesis fails with the error above, Quartus has detected a directory structure change.

4. **IMPORTANT!** Since some of the component ports are buses with different widths, external ports **must** be generated by right-clicking the component and selecting **Generate Pins for Symbol Ports**. (**Fig. D.15**). If this is not followed, the ports will not have the appropriate width to accomodate the signal and will trigger an error during synthesis. Unneeded ports can be deleted.

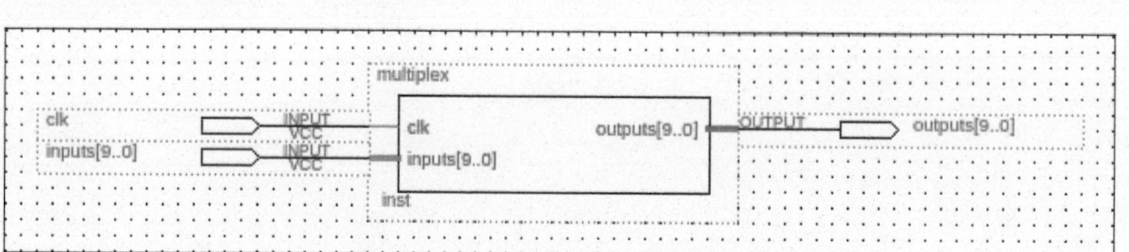

Figure D.15: Automatically-generated external ports.

5. Save the block diagram file. Make sure to verify the save location, as Quartus will (by default) attempt to save the diagram into the `/cec222/blocks` directory (**Fig. D.16**).

   Also verify that the **Add file to current project** checkbox is ticked.

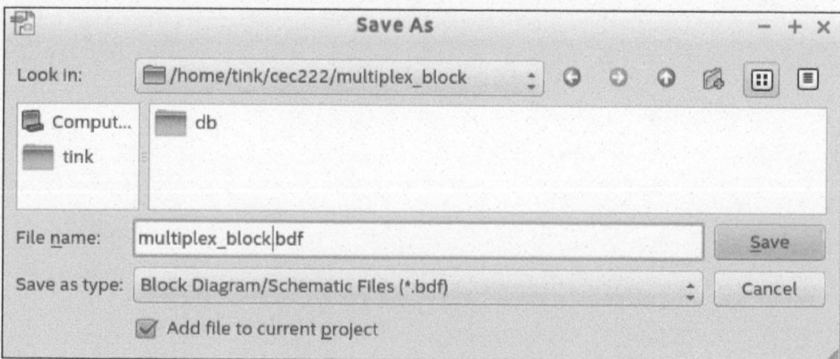

Figure D.16: Save As window—verify location.

Multiplexing

This tutorial covers the design and implementation of a 4:10 decoder and a frequency-scalable multiplexed circuit to accept data from three banks of switches.

Additional concepts included in this tutorial are:

- Multiplexers
- Buses (Vectors)
- Components and port maps
- Integers
- Sequential execution
- Conditional signal assignment

The circuit in this tutorial will be different from the circuit in lab. It is only designed to serve as an example.. All of the code (along with GitHub links) is given at the end of this appendix.

E.1 Objectives

After completing this tutorial, the student will be able to:

- Design a decoder circuit for arbitrary functions.
- Create a multiplexed circuit for displaying results.
- Use multiple linked VHDL files with a single project.
- Create a frequency-selectable counter.
- Add and instantiate components in VHDL files.

E.2 Introduction

The multiplexer/decoder combination that will be implemented as part of this tutorial is shown in **Fig. E.1**. The 2 pushbuttons **KEY1..0** and 10 slide switches **SW9..0** (padded with two leading zeros) provide the inputs to the multiplexer—three button/switch banks of four bits each. The decoder lights up one of the LEDs **LEDR9..0**, based on the four-bit binary number received at the input (*i.e.*, if decoder input is **0010**, **LEDR2** will be illuminated).

Note that the pushbuttons are inverted (normally closed), therefore their behavior is opposite to what is expected. They have to be depressed in order for the circuit to function correctly.

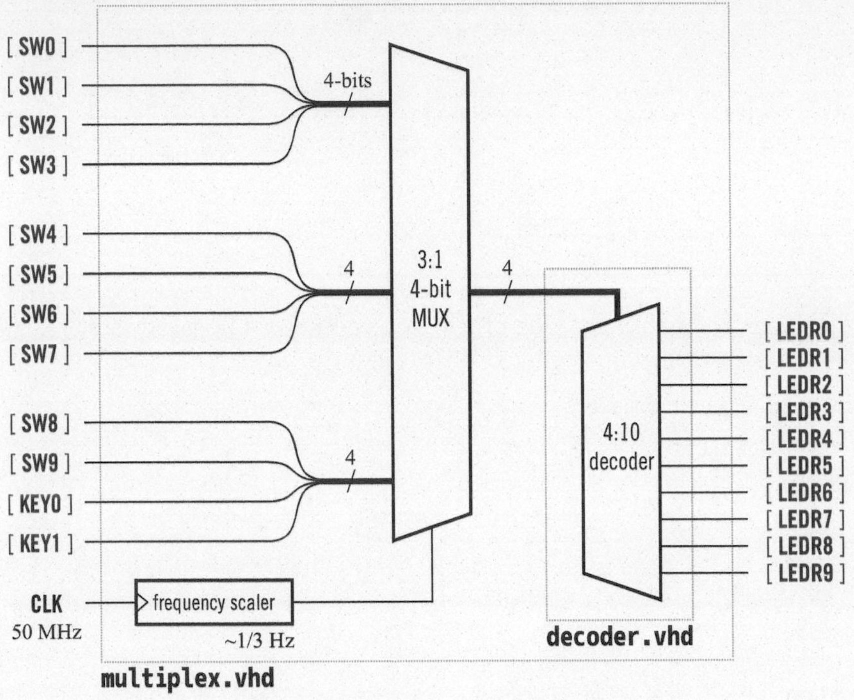

Figure E.1: Multiplexer/decoder circuit for displaying switch status.

A 50 MHz clock signal from the FPGA development board is scaled down and input to the control side of the multiplexer (MUX), causing the MUX to cycle through the three different banks of switches at a rate of approximately 1/3 Hz (three times per second). An example sequence of lights is illustrated in **Fig. E.2**. Note the positions of the slide switches and how these settings corresponds to the LEDs being illuminated.

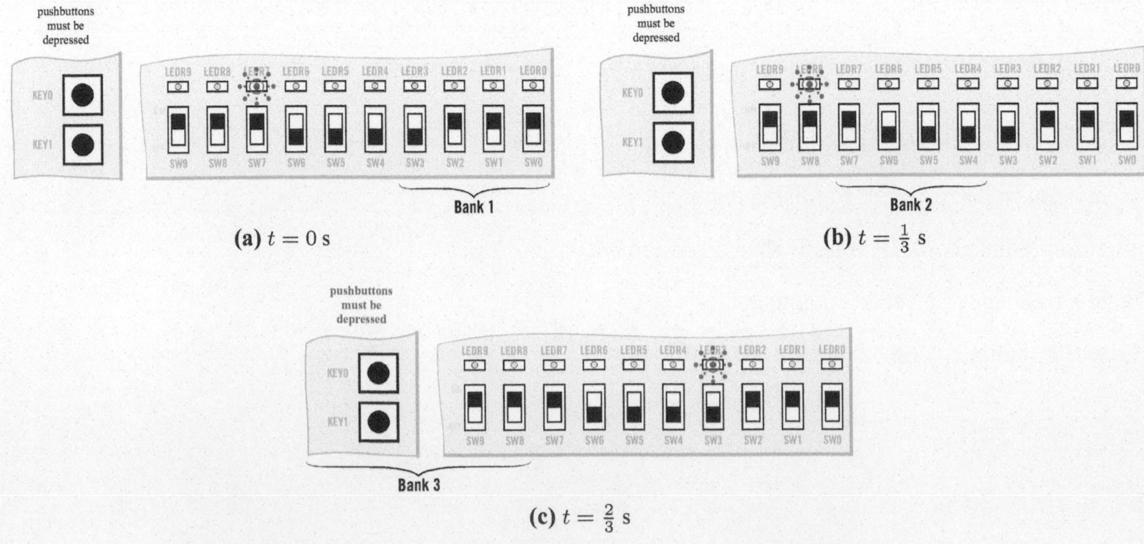

Figure E.2: Example light sequence and corresponding switch positions.

E.2.1 Multiplexers and Demultiplexers

A *multiplexer* is a device, which allows multiple signals to be sent over one transmission line with the use of control logic (**Fig. E.3**). Multiplexing is one way, for example, that RC aircraft controllers are able to send multiple PWM control signals over a limited number of channels (and why controllers with a greater number of channels cost more and work faster—direct control, no multiplexing).

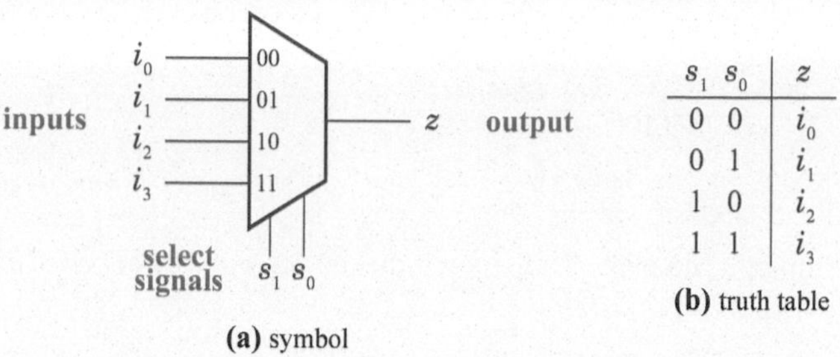

(a) symbol

s_1	s_0	z
0	0	i_0
0	1	i_1
1	0	i_2
1	1	i_3

(b) truth table

Figure E.3: 4:1 multiplexer and corresponding truth table.

In the basic example of a 4:1 multiplexer shown in the figure, only three lines are required to send four lines of data. With larger multiplexers, the advantage becomes even more apparent. **Eq. (E.1)** calculates the number of control bits (n_{control}) required to transmit n_{bits} using a multiplexer.

$$n_{\text{control}} = \log_2 (n_{\text{bits}}) \tag{E.1}$$

As can be seen from the truth table in **Fig. E.3**, a multiplexer switches between the input lines i_n and redirects them to the output z. The redirection is based on control signals (referred to as *select signals*) s_m. The operation of a basic multiplexer is illustrated in **Fig. E.4**.

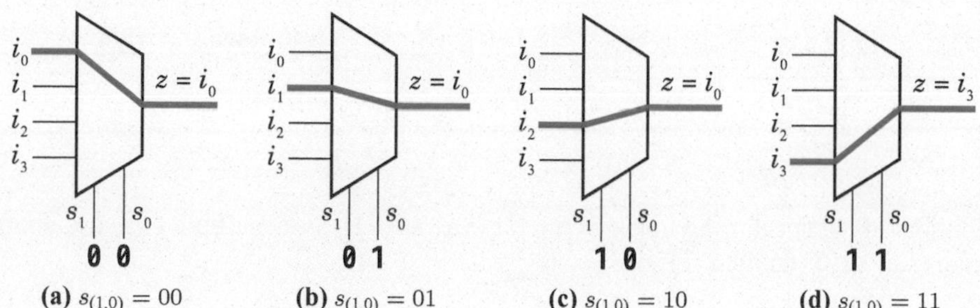

(a) $s_{(1,0)} = 00$ **(b)** $s_{(1,0)} = 01$ **(c)** $s_{(1,0)} = 10$ **(d)** $s_{(1,0)} = 11$

Figure E.4: Operation of a 4:1 multiplexer.

Demultiplexers (DEMUX) operate in the same way, but in reverse (**Fig. E.5**)

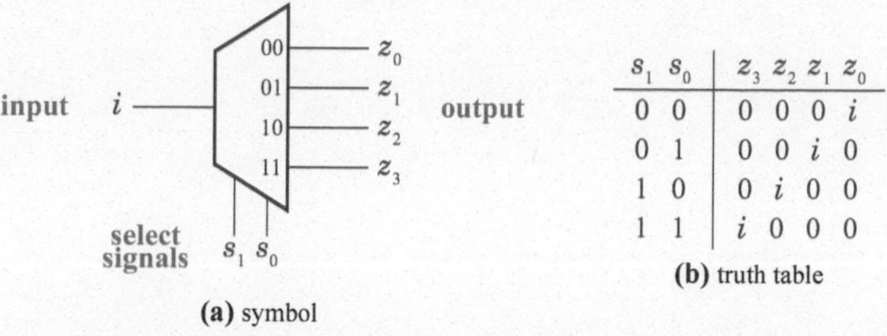

(a) symbol

s_1	s_0	z_3	z_2	z_1	z_0
0	0	0	0	0	i
0	1	0	0	i	0
1	0	0	i	0	0
1	1	i	0	0	0

(b) truth table

Figure E.5: 2:4 demultiplexer and corresponding truth table.

E.2.2 Buses (Vectors)

Buses (or Vectors) are signals that group a large number of individual nets together. For example, if there are four lines **sw3**, **sw2**, **sw1**, and **sw0**, it might be helpful to bundle these lines into a single bus **sw**—not only is it easier to pass a single bus between components, but there is also less chances for making an error.

A bus uses a **STD_LOGIC_VECTOR** data type in VHDL. The signal definitions for the input and output buses are placed inside the **entity** definition:

```
entity decoder is
   Port ( number : in STD_LOGIC_VECTOR (3 downto 0);
         segments : out STD_LOGIC_VECTOR (9 downto 0));
end entity;
```

The syntax for a bus is quite simple: **n downto 0**, where **n** indicates the number of wires contained within the bus, minus one. Indexing in VHDL starts with **0**.

Note that single quotes (**'**) are used for single-bit values (*i.e.*, **'0'**) and double quotes (**"**) are used for multi-bit values (*i.e.*, **"0000"**).

Operations with Buses

There are a number of things that can be done with buses. For the examples below, the following signals and values will be used (the **:=** operator is used for initial value assignment):

```
signal vector_a, vector_b : STD_LOGIC_VECTOR(4 downto 0) := "11111";
signal sw : STD_LOGIC_VECTOR(9 downto 0) := "0101010101";
signal a : STD_LOGIC := "1";
```

- **Assignment.**
  When assigning values to a bus, the number of bits being assigned has to equal the width of the bus.

  ```
  vector_a <= "00000";
  ```

- **Slicing.**
  To access individual bits, specify the index of the bit (*i.e.*, **sw(3)**). For multiple bits, use **downto** convention to indicate a range (*i.e.*, **sw(3 downto 1)**).

- **Concatenation.**
  Use the concatenation operator (**&**) for combining multiple signals. When assigning the concatenated result to a bus, make sure that the width of the result matches the width of the signal you are assigning to.

  ```
  vector_b <= vector_a(3 downto 1) & sw(3) & a;
  -- Result in vector_b: "11101"
  ```

E.2.3 Component Re-Use in VHDL

Component re-use is a very important aspect of design. In VHDL, even if a certain entity is stored in a different file, it can be used in the design by creating a *component*.

Components are like function declarations in programming: they indicate that a function with a certain set of inputs and outputs exists, but to look elsewhere for its definition.

Components need to be declared in the architecture (before the begin statement) and instantiated (below the begin statement).

Example

In the code snippet below, a component **decoder** is declared in the architecture, above the begin statement—prompting VHDL to look elsewhere for its definition. Note that the port definition should precisely match what is contained in the port definition of **decoder.vhd**.

Below the begin statement, a local instance of the component is created, labeled **dec_instance**. Any number of instances can be created. Think of it as putting ICs onto a breadboard. The **port map** statement ties the entity ports (pins of the IC) to local ports (other components on the breadboard).

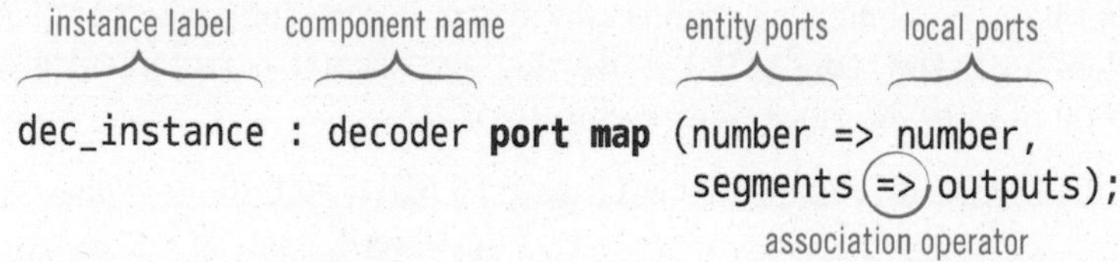


```
architecture multiplex_arch of multiplex is
   component decoder
   port (
      number : in STD_LOGIC_VECTOR (3 downto 0);
      segments : out STD_LOGIC_VECTOR (9 downto 0) );
   end component;
-- snip --
begin
   dec_instance : decoder port map (number => number,
                           segments => outputs);
-- snip --
end architecture;
```

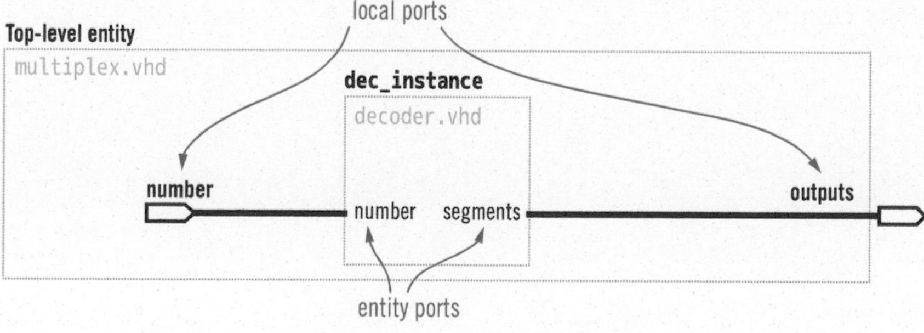

Figure E.6: Port map.

E.2.4 Sequential vs. Parallel Execution

As mentioned in previous tutorials, all VHDL code executes concurrently (at the same time), regardless of where lines of code are placed within the file... **except** when a certain section of the code is defined inside a **process**. Processes in VHDL are forced to run sequentially, executing the code line-by-line. This behavior is useful when implementing sequential logic, where the states change based on clocks or input signals.

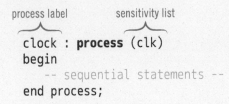

```
process label          sensitivity list
clock : process (clk)
begin
    -- sequential statements --
end process;
```

The process is triggered via a *sensitivity list*: a list of the signals that need to be observed for state changes. Although this is optional for a hardware implementation, there is no way to run a simulation, unless a sensitivity list has been specified.

Example: Integer Counter

In the example below, the process implements a counter (the syntax is very similar to MATLAB or other scripting/programming languages). When a **rising_edge(clk)** is detected, the counter is incremented by one. Once the counter reaches a count of 50,000,000 ticks of the clock, it is reset to zero.

Since the internal clock of the FPGA development board runs at 50 MHz, 50 million cycles represents 1 second of time.

This implementation uses an integer counter, so a signal of type **INTEGER** needs to be specified (with appropriate ranges). In addition, a special library needs to be used, which supports unsigned operations with integers.

```
use IEEE.STD_LOGIC_UNSIGNED.ALL;
```

```
architecture multiplex_arch of multiplex is
-- snip --
   signal counter : INTEGER RANGE 0 TO 50000000;
begin
-- snip --
   clock : process (clk)
   begin
      if rising_edge(clk) then
         if counter = 50000000 then
            counter <= 0;
         else
            counter <= counter + 1;
         end if;
      end if;
   end process;
-- snip --
end architecture;
```

E.3 Implementation

E.3.1 Decoder

The most important part of this device implementation is the *decoder*: it translates a four-bit binary input into an "on state" for one of the 10 LEDs **LEDR9..0**. The input to the decoder will therefore consist of four bits, while the output will consist of 10 bits.

In order to help visualize the operation of the decoder, a complete truth table for the circuit is given in **Table E.1**. Here, four-bit binary combinations are fed into the **number(3..0)** bus and a 10-bit output is generated on the **segments(9..0)** bus (each of the bits corresponds to the output of the 10 LEDs).

The goal of the decoder is to light a single LED, representing the selected binary-coded decimal (BCD) digit. Since BCD contains only numbers 0 through 9, anything other than these inputs should blank out the LEDs (all of them should be asserted low).

Table E.1: Truth table for the decoder.

number (3..0)	Decimal Value	segments(9) LEDR9	8	7	6	5	4	3	2	1	(0) LEDR0
0000	0	0	0	0	0	0	0	0	0	0	1
0001	1	0	0	0	0	0	0	0	0	1	0
0010	2	0	0	0	0	0	0	0	1	0	0
0011	3	0	0	0	0	0	0	1	0	0	0
0100	4	0	0	0	0	0	1	0	0	0	0
0101	5	0	0	0	0	1	0	0	0	0	0
0110	6	0	0	0	1	0	0	0	0	0	0
0111	7	0	0	1	0	0	0	0	0	0	0
1000	8	0	1	0	0	0	0	0	0	0	0
1001	9	1	0	0	0	0	0	0	0	0	0
others	—	0	0	0	0	0	0	0	0	0	0

The easiest way to implement this circuit is using *conditional signal assignment* in VHDL. Take a look at the following syntax for the **architecture** portion of the VHDL code—the syntax is pretty trivial:

```
architecture decoder_arch of decoder is
begin
    segments <= "0000000001" when number = "0000" else
             "0000000010" when number = "0001" else
             "0000000100" when number = "0010" else
             "0000001000" when number = "0011" else
             "0000010000" when number = "0100" else
             "0000100000" when number = "0101" else
             "0001000000" when number = "0110" else
             "0010000000" when number = "0111" else
             "0100000000" when number = "1000" else
             "1000000000" when number = "1001" else
             "0000000000";
end architecture;
```

At this point, you should be able to run synthesis and simulation. The results of the simulation are given in **Fig. E.7**.

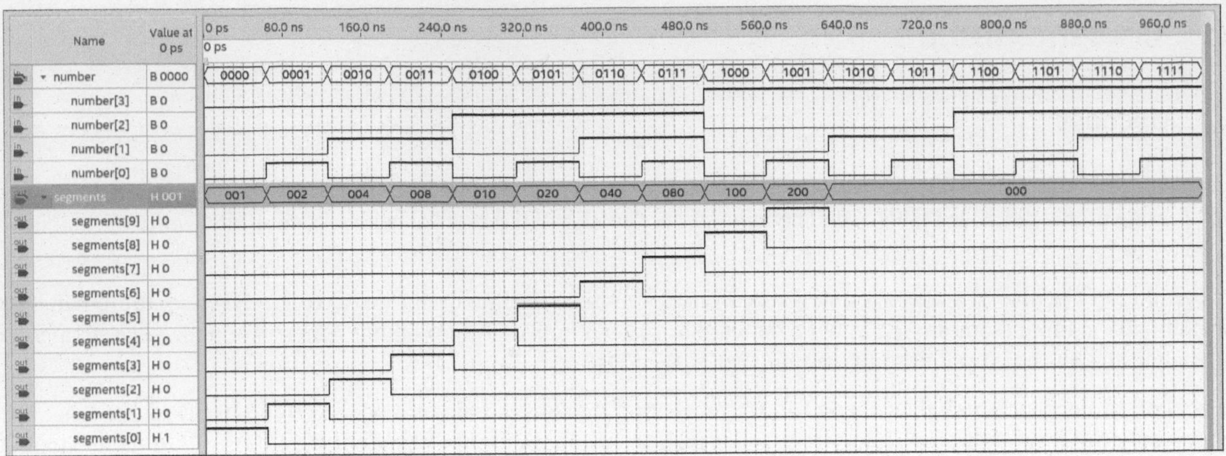

Figure E.7: Simulation results for a single decoder.

E.3.2 Multiplexing

Since the output of the decoder is directly connected to the LED outputs, only the input to the decoder needs to be multiplexed (refer back to **Fig. E.1**).

The code below uses *conditional signal assignment* and breaks the 50 million cycles of the counter into 3 approximately equal intervals (essentially implementing a 3:1 four-bit MUX):

- 0 to 17,000,000 cycles
- 17,000,001 to 34,000,000 cycles
- others (implied as 34,000,001 to 50,000,000 cycles)

During each of the three intervals, values for a different set of switches are passed to the decoder. For the first 1/3 sec, the first bank of switches **`inputs(3..0)`** is used. Subsequently, **`inputs(7..4)`** and **`inputs(11..8)`** are used.

Only 10 switches are available, so two slide switches **SW9** and **SW8** will be used for **`inputs(9..8)`**. The other two positions will be acquired from pushbuttons **KEY1** and **KEY0** [for **`inputs(11..10)`**]. The push buttons are normally closed / inverted (their behavior is opposite to what one would expect), so they have to be depressed to get the correct result.

```
number <= inputs(3 downto 0) when (counter < 17000001) else
   inputs(7 downto 4) when (counter > 17000000 and counter < 34000001) else
   inputs(11 downto 8);
```

E.4 VHDL Code: multiplex.vhd

```
-- A. Almagambetov and J.M. Pavlina
-- Description: 3:1 4-bit multiplexer

library IEEE;
use IEEE.STD_LOGIC_1164.ALL;
use IEEE.STD_LOGIC_UNSIGNED.ALL;

entity multiplex is
   Port ( clk : in STD_LOGIC;
         inputs : in STD_LOGIC_VECTOR (11 downto 0);
         outputs : out STD_LOGIC_VECTOR (9 downto 0));
end entity;

architecture multiplex_arch of multiplex is
   component decoder
   port (
      number : in STD_LOGIC_VECTOR (3 downto 0);
      segments : out STD_LOGIC_VECTOR (9 downto 0) );
   end component;

   signal number : STD_LOGIC_VECTOR(3 downto 0);
   signal counter : INTEGER RANGE 0 TO 50000000;
begin
   dec_instance : decoder port map (number => number,
                                    segments => outputs);

   clock : process (clk)
   begin
      if rising_edge(clk) then
         if counter = 50000000 then
            counter <= 0;
         else
            counter <= counter + 1;
         end if;
      end if;
   end process;

   number <= inputs(3 downto 0) when (counter < 17000001) else
      inputs(7 downto 4) when (counter > 17000000 and counter < 34000001) else
      inputs(11 downto 8);
end architecture;
```

Code available @ GitHub
https://git.io/fNX3N

E.5 VHDL Code: decoder.vhd

Code available @ GitHub
https://git.io/fNX3p

```
-- A. Almagambetov and J.M. Pavlina
-- Description: 4:10 decoder for LED patterns

library IEEE;
use IEEE.STD_LOGIC_1164.ALL;

entity decoder is
   Port ( number : in STD_LOGIC_VECTOR (3 downto 0);
          segments : out STD_LOGIC_VECTOR (9 downto 0));
end entity;

architecture decoder_arch of decoder is
begin
    segments <= "0000000001" when number = "0000" else
                "0000000010" when number = "0001" else
                "0000000100" when number = "0010" else
                "0000001000" when number = "0011" else
                "0000010000" when number = "0100" else
                "0000100000" when number = "0101" else
                "0001000000" when number = "0110" else
                "0010000000" when number = "0111" else
                "0100000000" when number = "1000" else
                "1000000000" when number = "1001" else
                "0000000000";
end architecture;
```

Pulse Width Modulation (PWM)

This tutorial will cover the design and implementation of a digital dimmer for light emitting diodes (LEDs) using a technique called pulse width modulation (PWM). All of the circuits will be implemented on the FPGA development board using VHDL.

F.1 Objectives

After completing this tutorial, the student will be able to:

- Design a circuit for generating PWM signals using VHDL.
- Create integer counters, which are able to count to arbitrary values and reset.
- Perform conversions from base-2 to base-10, leveraging the functions contained in the VHDL standard.

F.2 Introduction

Pulse width modulation (PWM) is a technique for encoding a message into a periodic pulsed signal. PWM is generally used for the control of motors and lights, as it has the capability of varying the power delivered to the load without changing the operating voltage (which is difficult, if not impossible, to do with inexpensive digital circuitry).

PWM is particularly useful when it comes to the digital domain, as dimming (or motor control) can be accomplished by simply varying the frequency of the signal (**Fig. F.1**).

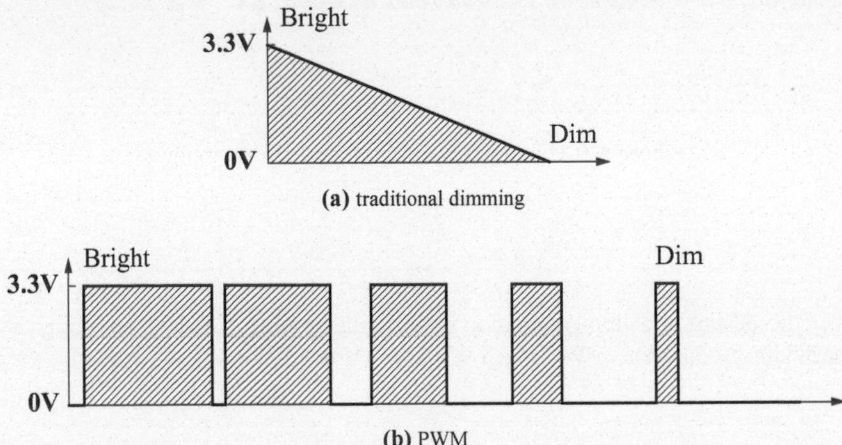

(a) traditional dimming

(b) PWM

Figure F.1: Traditional dimming (voltage reduction) vs. PWM (pulse width reduction).

The voltage in the latter approach (PWM) is maintained either at 0 or 3.3V (there are no intermediate values), yet this technique achieves the same outcome as the traditional voltage reduction dimming. Since digital signals consist only of logic-high and logic-low values, it is easy to implement PWM using digital circuits (counters and other sequential logic).

F.2.1 Duty Cycle

Prior to covering more advanced topics, the concept of a *duty cycle* needs to be introduced. As PWM is a pulsed signal with a varying width, there are two regions of interest (**Fig. F.2**): t_{on} and t_{off}. When added together, these two intervals comprise the period of the waveform T. The duty cycle is computed based on the "on" region as it relates to the period, **Eq. (F.1)**:

$$\text{duty cycle} = \frac{t_{\text{on}}}{T} \tag{F.1}$$

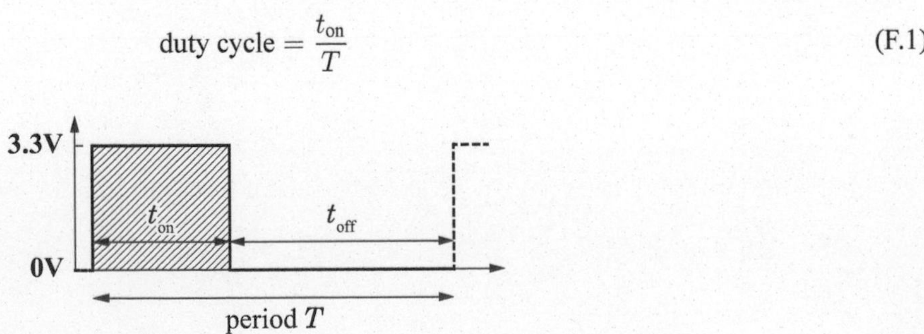

Figure F.2: Duty cycle definitions.

If less power needs to be delivered to the load, then the t_{off} region must be much larger than t_{on}. For more power to be delivered to the load, the reverse is true.

Note that for a true PWM signal, the t_{on} and t_{off} intervals **can never be zero or 100%**! Otherwise, no period information will be available.

F.3 Dimming LEDs

In this section, a circuit for dimming LED **LEDR0** will be designed. The dimming will occur from 95% to 5% power. This is a simplified version of the circuit that is used for dimming common household LED fixtures (notice how "dimmable" LED bulbs cost significantly more than non-dimmable ones). A diagram of the inputs and outputs is given in **Fig. F.3**.

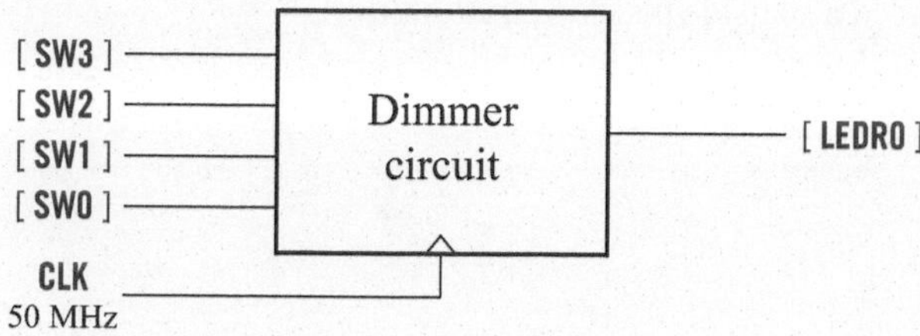

Figure F.3: High-level diagram of the dimmer circuit.

Four switches **SW3..0** (**inputs** bus in the VHDL implementation) will be used to adjust the LED dimming level. Switch combination **0000** will be assigned to the lowest dimming setting (5%) and **1001** to the highest level (95%).

The LED will be pulsed with a frequency of 100 Hz (10 ms), in order to use persistence of vision and make the flicker imperceptible to the naked eye. Since the system clock on the FPGA development board runs at 50 MHz, this would mean that each period of the waveform would have the following number of clock cycles, **Eq. (F.2)**:

$$\text{clock cycles per period} = \frac{50\text{ MHz}}{100\text{ Hz}} = 500,000 \tag{F.2}$$

This information can be expressed in table form (**Table F.1**).

Table F.1: PWM characteristics (select levels are given).

SW3..0	Duty cycle	Timing	Clock cycles
0000	5%	0.5 ms / 10 ms	25,000
0010	25%	2.5 ms / 10 ms	125,000
0100	45%	4.5 ms / 10 ms	225,000
0110	65%	6.5 ms / 10 ms	325,000
1000	85%	8.5 ms / 10 ms	425,000

Since there are 9 discrete dimming levels (not including zero) and the duty cycle should be no less than 5% (or 25,000 cycles), the following formula can be used for calculating the number of cycles required for the t_{on} period, **Eq. (F.3)**. $\texttt{inputs}_{10}$ is the decimal representation of the binary switch input.

This is similar to finding the function of a line (y-intercept is 25,000 and the slope the rise over run).

$$t_{\text{on,cycles}} = \frac{\texttt{inputs}_{10} \times (475,000 - 25,000)}{9 - 0} + 25,000 \tag{F.3}$$

F.4 VHDL Implementation

To make clock cycle calculations easier to implement, the binary number received from switches **SW3..0** will be converted to a decimal (base-10) integer.

In order to use any functions relating to algebraic operations (which includes converting from binary to decimal), an additional library should be included alongside the standard libraries:

```
use IEEE.STD_LOGIC_UNSIGNED.ALL;
```

F.4.1 Entity

The **clk** port will need to be interfaced to the appropriate pin on the FPGA development board that would provide a 50 MHz clock signal (see **Appendix H**). **inputs** will be connected to switches **SW3..0** and **pwm** will be linked to the output LED **LEDR0**.

```
entity pwmDimmer is
    Port ( clk : in STD_LOGIC;
           inputs : in STD_LOGIC_VECTOR (3 downto 0);
           pwm : out STD_LOGIC);
end pwmDimmer;
```

F.4.2 Architecture

Within the architecture for **dimmer**, two signals of type **INTEGER** are present:

- **counter**, which will count to the maximum number of clock cycles within 1 period of the PWM waveform, after which it will reset.

```
signal counter : INTEGER RANGE 0 to 500000;
```

- **transition** signal, which will determine the clock cycle when the PWM signal should switch from a logic-HIGH to a logic-LOW (**Fig. F.4**).

```
signal transition : INTEGER;
```

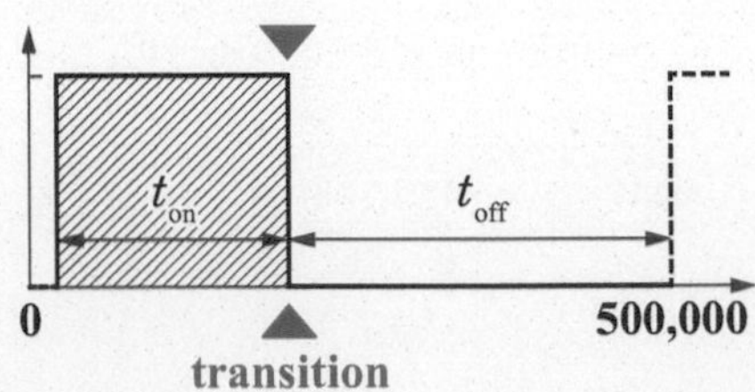

Figure F.4: Cycle count, determining the transition between t_{on} and t_{off}.

To determine the transition clock cycle, **Eq. (F.3)** needs to be implemented in the **begin** section of **dimmer_arch**. This calculation will convert from a dimming level (0..9, set by **SW3..0**) to a clock cycle for the transition between t_{on} and t_{off} (**Table F.1**).

```
transition <= CONV_INTEGER(level) * (475000 - 25000) / 9 + 50000;
```

The same type of counter designed during the multiplexer tutorial will be implemented here. In this case, the period of the counter must equal the full period of the PWM waveform (500,000 cycles).

```
clock : process (clk)
begin
   if RISING_EDGE(clk) then
      if (counter = 500000) then
         counter <= 0;
      else
         counter <= counter + 1;
      end if;
   end if;
end process;
```

The transition can be implemented as a concurrent logic statement:

```
pwm <= '1' when (counter < transition) else '0';
```

F.5 Simulation and Hardware Testing

Synthesize, assign pins, and run implementation. After programming the FPGA development board, the brightness of LED **LEDR0** can be controlled using the four switches **SW3..0**. The output of the PWM circuit is shown in **Fig. F.5**.

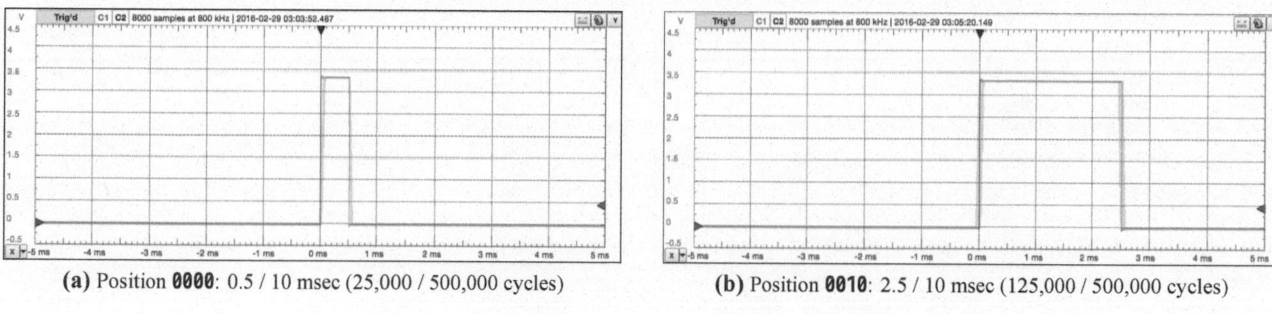

(a) Position **0000**: 0.5 / 10 msec (25,000 / 500,000 cycles)

(b) Position **0010**: 2.5 / 10 msec (125,000 / 500,000 cycles)

Figure F.5: Waveform captures for select positions of **SW3..0**.

The Quartus simulator (*qsim*) is not designed for running lengthy simulations (the maximum simulation time is 100 μs—a hundred times less than a single period of the PWM waveform in this tutorial).

To simulate this circuit, an alternative simulator called *ModelSim* needs to be used. It is an industry-standard tool that is used across many manufacturers and for many applications. **Appendix G** covers the simulation of this circuit.

ModelSim generates a slightly uglier simulation than *qsim* (**Fig. F.6**), but it's more powerful than the Quartus simulator.

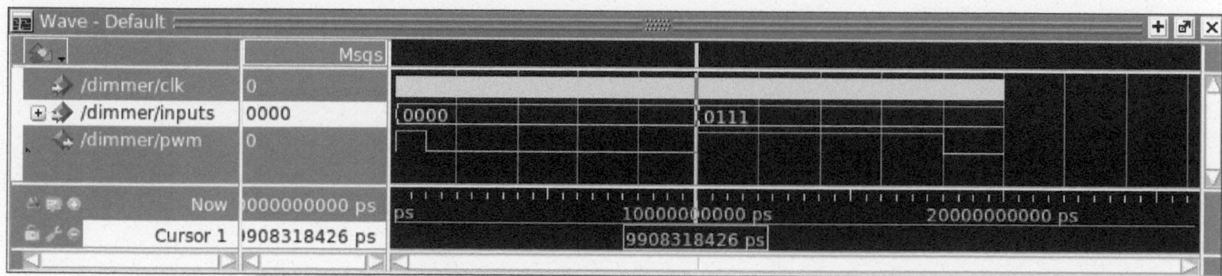

Figure F.6: ModelSim simulation of switch combinations **0000** and **0111**.

F.6 VHDL Code: dimmer.vhd

Code available @ GitHub
https://git.io/fNyLT

```
-- A. Almagambetov and J.M. Pavlina
-- Description: LED PWM dimmer

library IEEE;
use IEEE.STD_LOGIC_1164.ALL;
use IEEE.STD_LOGIC_UNSIGNED.ALL;

entity dimmer is
   Port ( clk : in STD_LOGIC;
          inputs : in STD_LOGIC_VECTOR (3 downto 0);
          pwm : out STD_LOGIC);
end entity;

architecture dimmer_arch of dimmer is
   signal counter : INTEGER RANGE 0 to 500000;
   signal transition : INTEGER;
begin
   transition <= CONV_INTEGER(inputs) * (475000 - 25000) / 9 + 25000;

clock : process (clk)
begin
   if RISING_EDGE(clk) then
      if (counter = 500000) then
         counter <= 0;
      else
         counter <= counter + 1;
      end if;
   end if;
end process;

pwm <= '1' when (counter < transition) else '0';

end architecture;
```

Functional Simulation using ModelSim

This tutorial will introduce *ModelSim*—a powerful multi-language simulator for HDLs. While the built-in Quartus simulator (*qsim*) is more than adequate for simple combinational circuits, its lack of certain important features makes it a bottleneck in the troubleshooting process.

ModelSim is a third-party simulator produced by Mentor Graphics. It comes bundled with HDL development tools, such as Intel Quartus and Xilinx Vivado.

G.1 Objectives

After completing this tutorial, the student will be able to:

- Simulate complex circuits using the ModelSim simulation tool.
- Create new projects within ModelSim.
- Adjust simulation runtimes and signal display parameters.
- Manually simulate circuits by forcing clock signals and constants.

G.2 Simulating an Existing Design

Due to the fact that ModelSim is a third-party tool, the project workflow is not as smooth as using the built-in simulation tool in Quartus: a separate project needs to be created within ModelSim and the `.vhd` files have to be imported into ModelSim manually.

G.2.1 Creating a New ModelSim Project and Importing Files

1. Start ModelSim within the Quartus project window by selecting **Tools** > **Run Simulation Tool** > **RTL Simulation**. The ModelSim user interface should appear (**Fig. G.1**)

Figure G.1: ModelSim user interface (new project selection).

Note for Windows systems only: If ModelSim fails to launch, navigate to **Tools** > **Options** > **EDA Tool Options** > **ModelSim-Altera** (last option). Browse and select the following path. Click **OK** to confirm selection.

```
C:\intelFPGA_lite\18.x\modelsim_ase\win32aloem
```

2. In the ModelSim UI, select **File** > **New** > **Project...**. In the *Create Project* dialog window that appears, do not modify anything except the project name. Make sure that it matches your top-level entity name.

   Since the entity being simulated is the LED dimming device from **`dimmer.vhd`** in **Appendix F**, type in **`dimmer`** into the *Project Name* box. Click **OK**.

3. In the *Add items to the Project* window, click the **Add Existing File** button.

4. **Important!** A selection dialog (**Fig. G.2**) will appear. It would seem that clicking OK would be in order, however the selected file would be incorrect (it is a **`.vho`** file, not a **`.vhd`**). The simulation would still run, but would take close to fifteen minutes to complete.

   Instead, navigate to the project root directory and select the actual **`dimmer.vhd`** file.

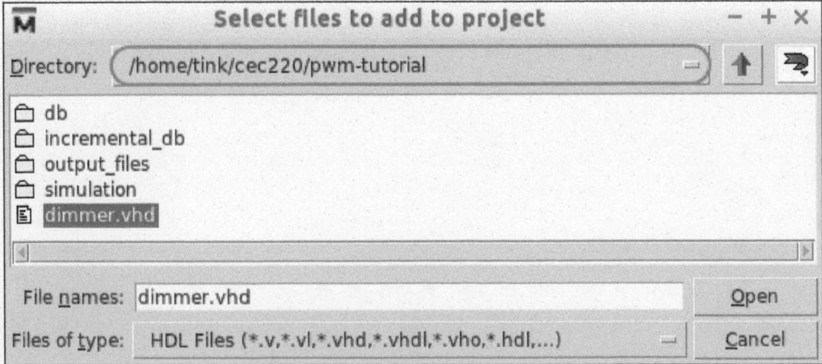

Figure G.2: File selection window.

5. Verify that the **Reference from current location** radio button is selected in the subsequent *Add file to Project* window—this allows any changes to the file outside of the ModelSim environment to be reflected in the simulations. Click **OK**.

G.2.2 Compiling and Simulating the Design

6. The imported VHDL file should now be visible in the project hierarchy.

   In the ModelSim main window, select **Compile > Compile All** from the menu. After the project files are compiled, a green check mark should be displayed by the **`dimmer.vhd`** file (**Fig. G.3**).

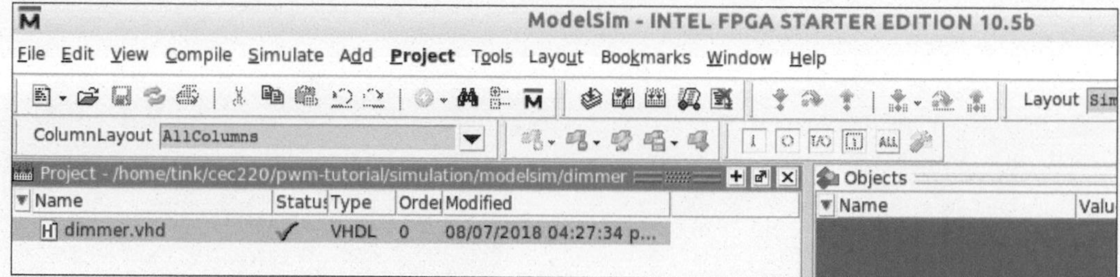

Figure G.3: Project hierarchy, indicating that all files have been compiled.

7. To start the simulator, select **Simulate > Start Simulation...** from the main window menu.

8. If during project creation, the default library name was not changed, select the **`dimmer`** entity under the **work** library in the *Start Simulation* dialog (**Fig. G.4**). Click **OK**.

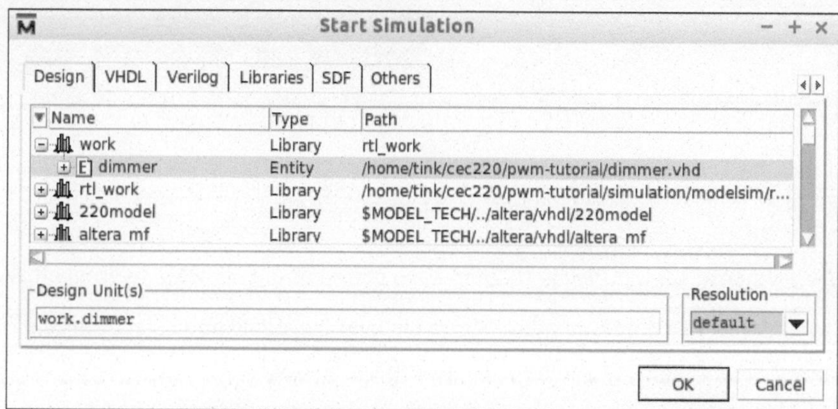

Figure G.4: *Start Simulation* entity selection.

9. The *Objects* window should populate with ports and signals from the entity. Select the signals of interest, right-click, and **Add to > Wave > Selected Signals** (**Fig. G.5**).

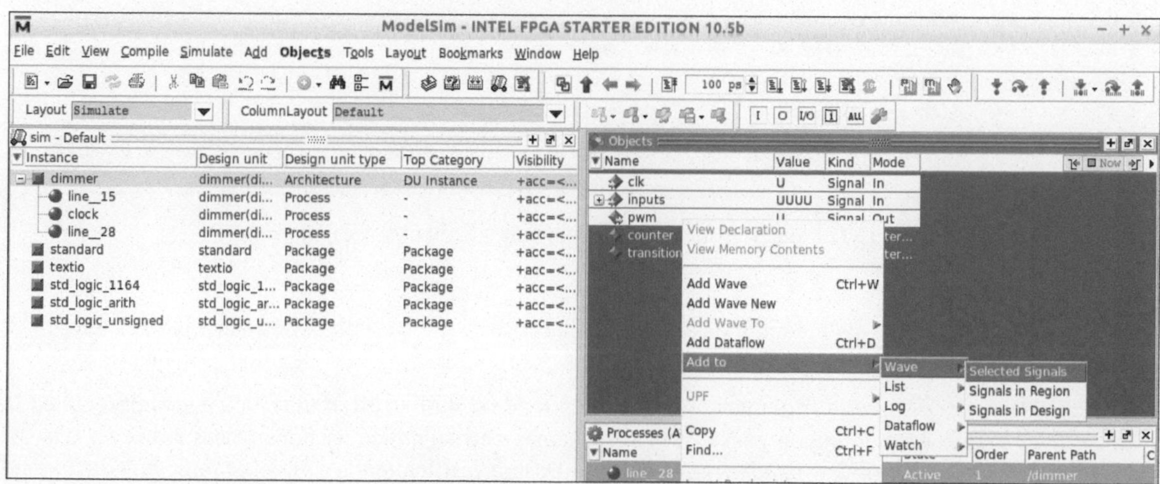

Figure G.5: Adding signals to a Wave file.

10. A *Wave* window should appear, containing all of the added signals. It is possible to manually force the values of the signals to either be clocks or constants (**Fig. G.6**).

    Initially, force the **`clk`** signal to be a clock. Right-click on the signal and select **Clock...**

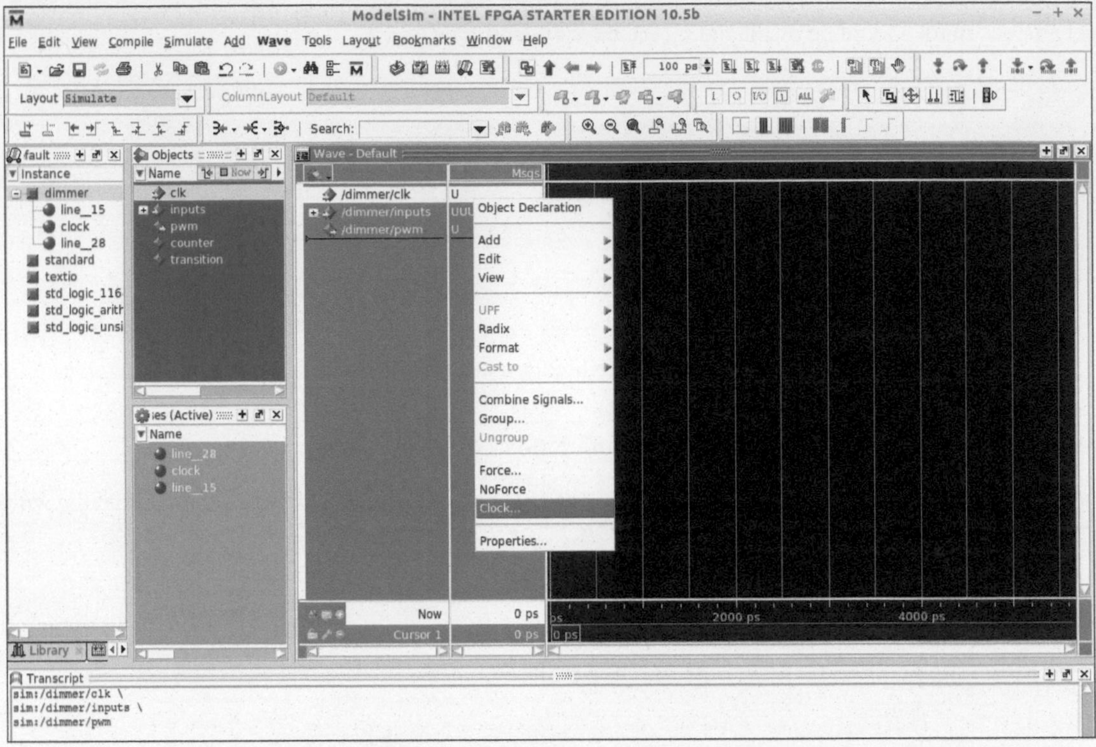

Figure G.6: *Wave* window user interface.

In the *Define Clock* window, set the *Period* to **`20ns`**—the period of the 50 MHz internal clock. Click **`OK`**.

11. Next, force the **`inputs`** bus to a constant value. Right-click on the signal and select **Force...**

    In the *Force Selected Signal* window, set the *Value* to **`0000`**. Click **`OK`**.

12. Change the *Run Length* (simulation period) of the simulation to the period of the PWM waveform—**`10ms`**—and click on the **Run** button (**Fig. G.7**).

    Generally, signals should be simulated one period at a time. This way, it is easy to see whether or not their behavior deviates from the design requirements.

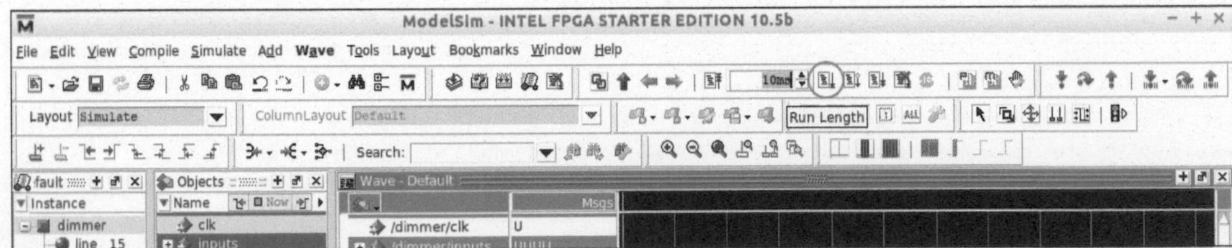

Figure G.7: Modifying the simulation runtime and running the simulation.

Side note. Forcing all of the signals manually is a rather tedious process, especially when this involves a lot of signals or multiple code or revisions.

Industry specialists use *test benches*—files that automatically provide stimuli to all of the simulated entity (called *Design Under Test, or DUT*) ports. Depending on your instructor, you may or may not cover this in class, however it is strongly recommended that you brush up on *test benches* on your own. Design verification is a very big topic in industry and very few of the recent graduates know how to verify digital circuit designs.

As a step up, there exist *self-checking VHDL test benches*, which automatically verify whether or not the DUT is fulfilling design requirements.

13. Initially, the results of the simulation might not look like much—this is because they are focusing in on the last few nanoseconds of the simulation (**Fig. G.8**).

    Use the **Zoom Full (F)** button to view the entire simulation period (**Fig. G.9**).

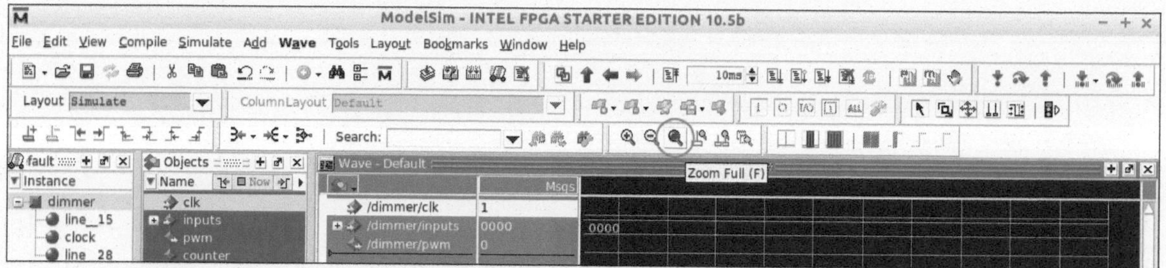

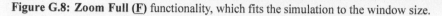

Figure G.8: Zoom Full (F) functionality, which fits the simulation to the window size.

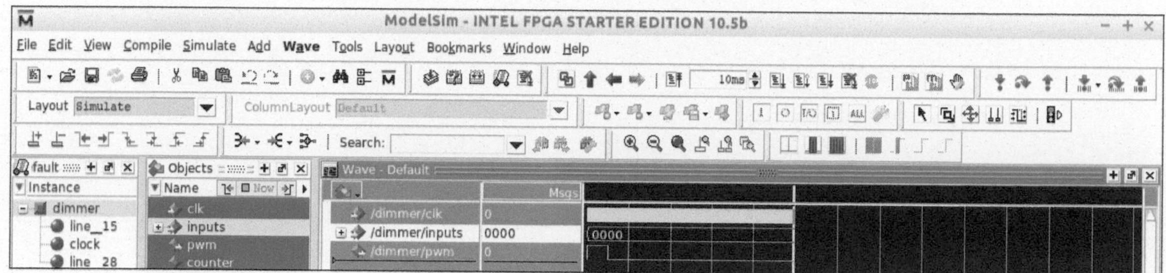

Figure G.9: Full simulation period.

14. To fully test device functionality, simulate it for another period after forcing **`inputs`** to **`0111`** (**Fig. G.10**).

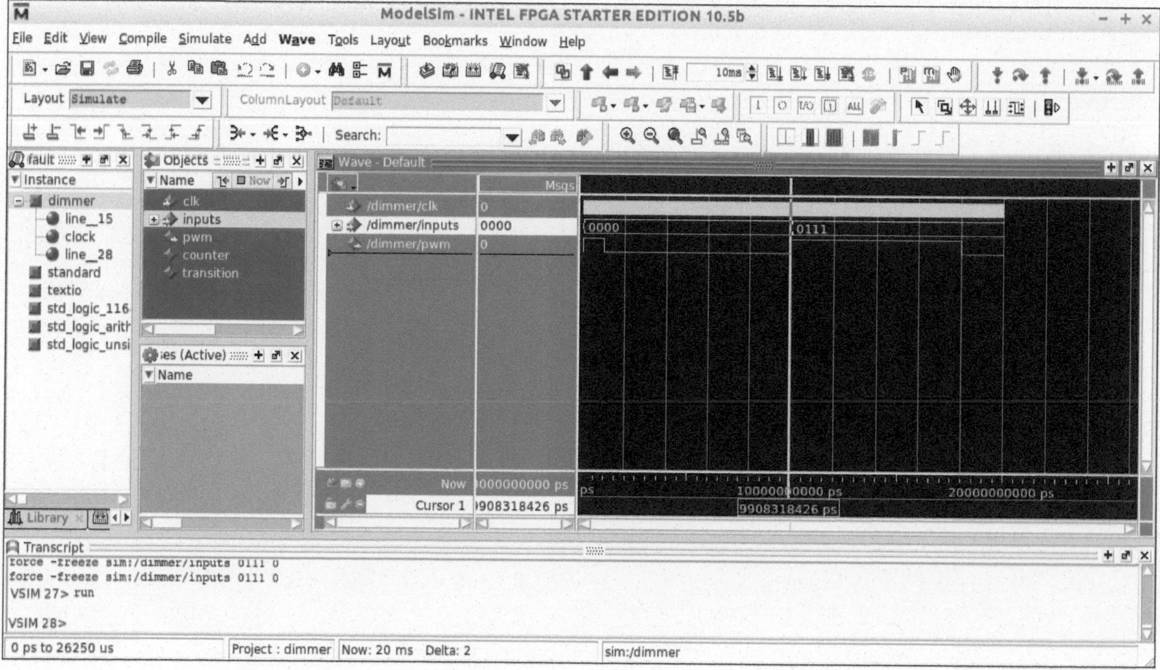

Figure G.10: Two full simulation periods with inputs forced to **`0000`** and **`0111`**.

Development Board Pin Listings

This appendix contains all of the pin diagrams for Intel's DE10-Lite FPGA development board. As of this printing date, the DE10-Lite board is populated with the Intel MAX 10 FPGA, part no. **10M50DAF484C7G**.

A simplified development board diagram is given in **Fig. H.1**. The following interfaces will be used in the laboratory (**USB BLASTER** connector **J3** will be used for connecting the FPGA board to a computer):

- **Internal 50 MHz clock** (on pins **P11** and **N14**) ⟸ **IMPORTANT!**
- Debounced pushbuttons **KEY1** and **KEY0**
- Switches **SW9..0** and LEDs **LEDR9..0**
- Seven segment displays **HEX5..0**
- ADXL345 3-axis Accelerometer
- GPIO connector **JP1**

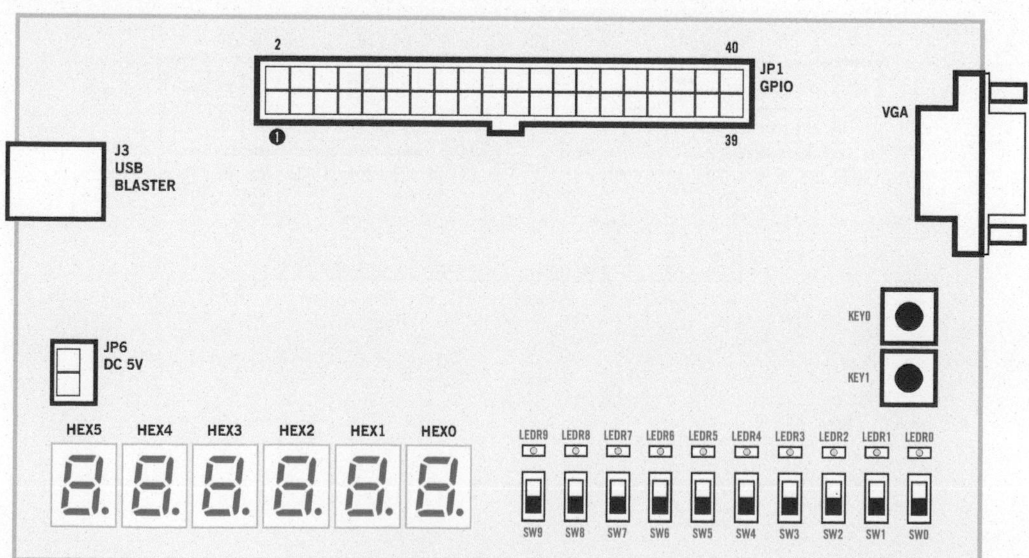

Figure H.1: Intel FPGA development board interfaces.

H.1 LEDs and Switches

Fig. H.2 contains the pin locations for the 10 switches **SW9..0** and 10 LEDs **LEDR9..0**. Note that unassigned LEDs will glow at half-brightness, making it easier to troubleshoot incorrect pin assignments.

The pin settings should be set to the following (slew rate is not set for inputs):

- **Logic Level**: 3.3-V LVCMOS
- **Current Strength**: 2 mA *
- **Slew Rate** (for outputs only): 2 *

* These settings can be left as their *(default)* values. No modifications are necessary.

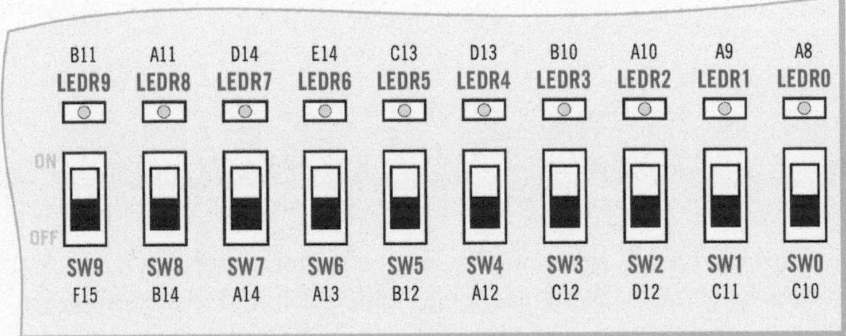

Figure H.2: Pin diagram for switches **SW9..0** and LEDs **LEDR9..0**.

H.2 GPIO Connector

The GPIO connector (**JP1**) will be used whenever the FPGA development board needs to be interfaced to external hardware, such as servo motors or motor driver circuitry. **Fig. H.3** contains the pin locations for the GPIO connector.

Pin settings from **Section H.1** should be used in the Pin Planner.

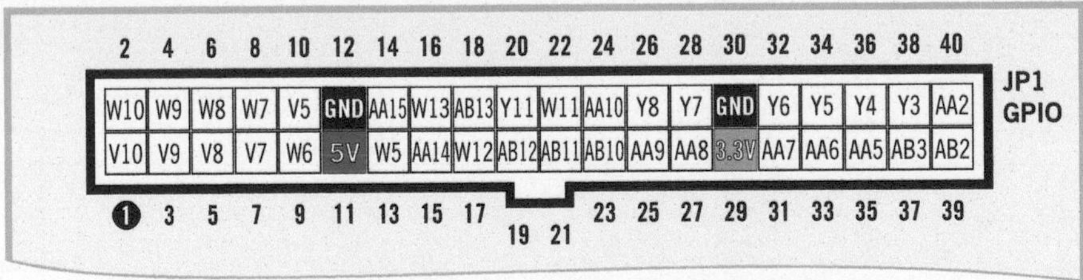

Figure H.3: Pin diagram for GPIO connector **JP1**.

H.3 Seven Segment Displays

The FPGA development board contains six seven-segment LED displays. Each display has a common anode and is directly connected to a pin on the FPGA. **Fig. H.2** contains a graphical representation of the pin locations for the displays, while **Table H.1** contains a listing of all pin locations, arranged by segment number.

Pin settings from **Section H.1** should be used in the Pin Planner.

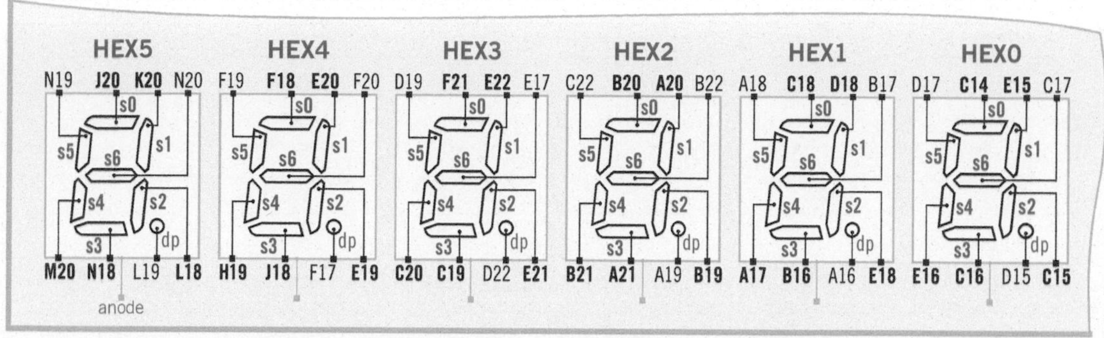

Figure H.4: Pin diagram for seven segment displays **HEX5..0**.

Example: In order to display a "7" on the seven-segment display, segments **s0**, **s1**, and **s2** have to be powered.

H.3.1 Active-LOW Logic Levels

Due to the way the transistor logic works on this FPGA development board, the displays use "active-LOW" logic—when the signal is a logic-**0**, the segment is powered. Remember this when designing the decoder circuits.

In the example above (displaying a number "7"), segments **s0**, **s1**, and **s2** have to be driven with a logic-**0** signal, whereas the remaining segments have to be driven with a logic-**1** signal.

Table H.1: Pin locations for the seven segment displays.

Segment	**Display**						**Pin Settings**		
	HEX5	**HEX4**	**HEX3**	**HEX2**	**HEX1**	**HEX0**	**Logic Level**	**Current Strength**	**Slew Rate**
s6	N20	F20	E17	B22	B17	C17			
s5	N19	F19	D19	C22	A18	D17			
s4	M20	H19	C20	B21	A17	E16			
s3	N18	J18	C19	A21	B16	C16	**3.3-V LVCMOS**	2 mA	2
s2	L18	E19	E21	B19	E18	C15			
s1	K20	E20	E22	A20	D18	E15			
s0	J20	F18	F21	B20	C18	C14			
dp	L19	F17	D22	A19	A16	D15			

H.4 Debounced Pushbuttons

There are two debounced pushbuttons available on the development board. A Schmitt trigger (a comparator circuit with hysteresis) is implemented to process pushbutton input and provide a clean transition for every state change.

Note that the pushbuttons are normally closed (NC), therefore their behavior is opposite to what one would expect.

Fig. H.5 contains pin locations for the two pushbuttons and **Fig. H.6** demonstrates the operation of the Schmitt trigger circuit for eliminating electromechanical bounce from the input. Pin settings from **Section H.1** should be used in the Pin Planner.

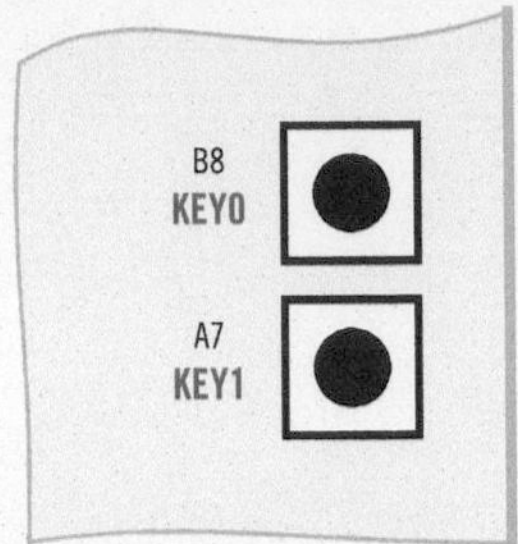

Figure H.5: Pin diagram pushbuttons **KEY1** and **KEY0**.

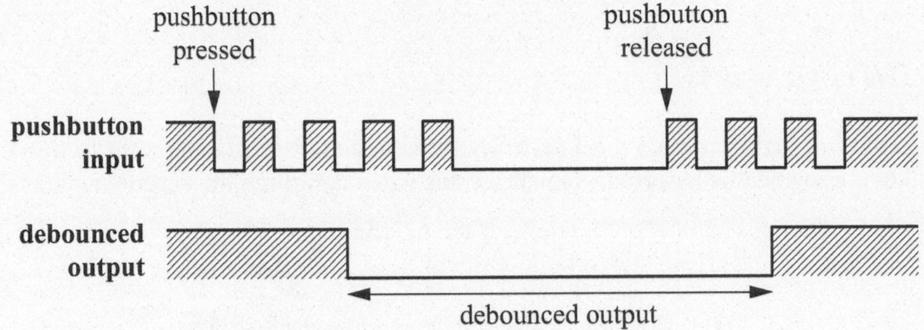

Figure H.6: Debounced pushbutton output.

H.5 Accelerometer

The FPGA development board contains an Analog Devices ADXL345 3-axis microelectromechanical system (MEMS) *accelerometer*, sometimes referred to as the *G-sensor*. **Fig. H.7** provides the pinouts for including the accelerometer in the design. Pin settings from **Section H.1** should be used in the Pin Planner. A detailed data sheet of the ADXL345 IC is given in **Appendix J**.

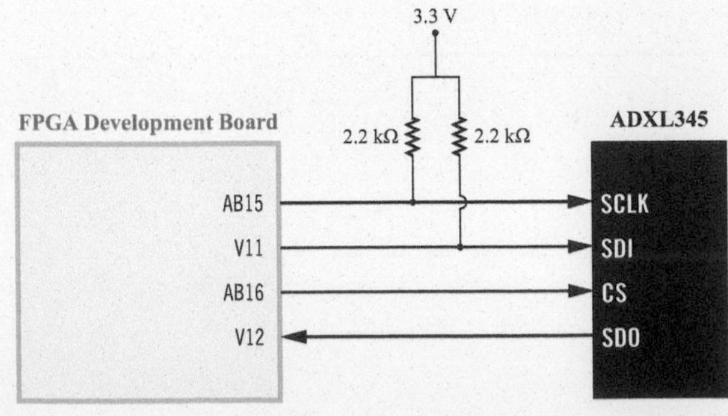

Figure H.7: Connections to the ADXL345 accelerometer IC.

APPENDIX I

VHDL Source Code Listing

All of the required code from this laboratory will be given in this section.

Note that every source code listing will have a short url link to the original code repository or code gist (hosted on GitHub). If required, the code can be downloaded or copied-and-pasted directly into a new project.

Do not retype this code!

The code in this section is provided for reference purposes only or in the rare case that the short links are dead after this laboratory manual has been sent to the publisher.

The GitHub box in the margins will provide the path (or short url link) to files being used in the lab (an example is given on the right).

Code available @ GitHub
`https://git.io/url`

I.1 Laboratory 2

I.1.1 lab02.vhd : Code for driving a four-bit R-2R DAC

Code available @ GitHub
https://git.io/fNlr7

```
-- CEC222 Lab 02 code
-- A. Almagambetov and J.M. Pavlina
-- Description: Code for driving a four-bit R-2R DAC

library IEEE;
use IEEE.STD_LOGIC_1164.ALL;

entity lab02 is
    Port ( sw   : in STD_LOGIC_VECTOR (3 downto 0);
           ledr : out STD_LOGIC_VECTOR (3 downto 0);
           gpio_4, gpio_3, gpio_2, gpio_1 : out STD_LOGIC);
end entity;

architecture lab02_arch of lab02 is
   signal temp : STD_LOGIC_VECTOR (3 downto 0);
begin
    temp <= sw;

    ledr <= temp;

    gpio_4 <= temp(0);
    gpio_3 <= temp(1);
    gpio_2 <= temp(2);
    gpio_1 <= temp(3);

end architecture;
```

I.1.2 `lab02_plot.m` : Code for generating a plot in MATLAB

```
% CEC222 Lab 02 MATLAB plot
% A. Almagambetov and J.M. Pavlina
% Description: Code to generate a MATLAB plot from lab data

clear; clc; close all;

set(0,'defaultAxesFontName','Times');
set(0,'defaultAxesFontSize',12);
set(0,'defaultTextFontName','Times');
set(0,'defaultTextFontSize',12);

dec_val = (0:15)';
Vin = [0.04 0.19 0.402 0.610 0.830 1.027 1.230 1.450 1.640 1.850 2.05 2.27 2.48 2.68 2.89 3.14];
Vout = [3.312 3.210 3.20 3.15 3.18 3.19 3.15 3.14 1.53 0.08 0.02 0.00 0.04 0.07 0.09 0.10];

figure(1);

plot(dec_val,Vin,'k-*')
grid on;
hold on;
plot(dec_val,Vout,'k--o')

legend('V_{in}','V_{out}');
title('V_{in} and V_{out} vs. Decimal Levels from testing the 74HC04 IC');
xlabel('Decimal Value (Base-10)');
ylabel('Voltage (V)');
```

Code available @ GitHub
https://git.io/fNloR

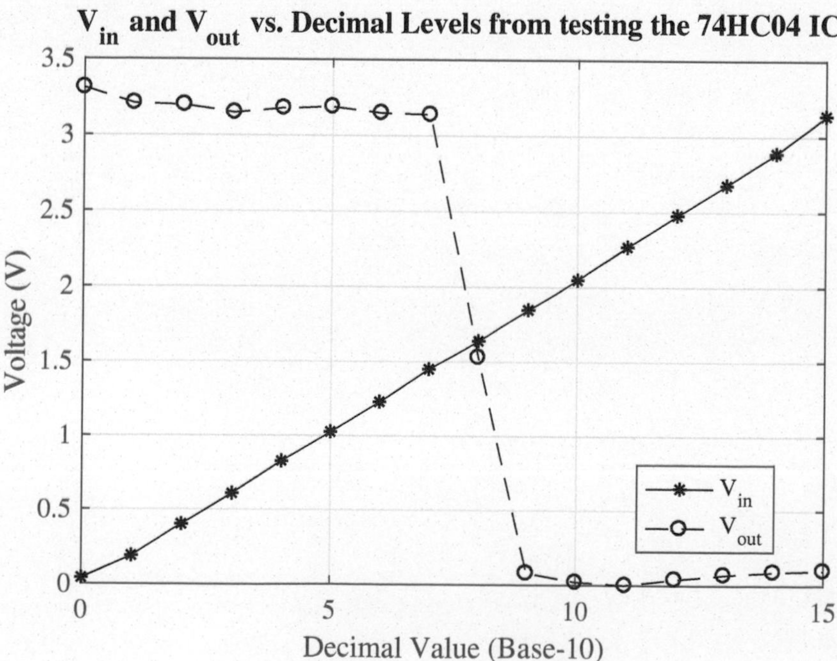

Figure I.1: Sample plot of measured values.

I.2 Counter for Multiplexed Displays (2-bit 1 kHz)

I.2.1 `counter_1kHz.bsf` : Block symbol file for the `counter_1kHz.vhd` file

Figure I.2: Counter block symbol.

Code available @ GitHub
https://git.io/fpSB5

```
/*
A. Almagambetov and J.M. Pavlina
Description: counter_1kHz.bsf block symbol file
*/
(header "symbol" (version "1.1"))
(symbol
   (rect 16 16 200 96)
   (text "counter_1kHz" (rect 5 0 59 12)(font "Arial" ))
   (text "inst" (rect 8 64 20 76)(font "Arial" ))
   (port
      (pt 0 32)
      (input)
      (text "clk_in" (rect 0 0 22 12)(font "Arial" ))
      (text "clk_in" (rect 21 27 43 39)(font "Arial" ))
      (line (pt 0 32)(pt 16 32)(line_width 1))
   )
   (port
      (pt 184 32)
      (output)
      (text "count_out[1..0]" (rect 0 0 57 12)(font "Arial" ))
      (text "count_out[1..0]" (rect 106 27 163 39)(font "Arial" ))
      (line (pt 184 32)(pt 168 32)(line_width 3))
   )
   (drawing
      (rectangle (rect 16 16 168 64)(line_width 1))
   )
)
```

I.2.2 counter_1kHz.vhd : Top-level entity

```
-- A. Almagambetov and J.M. Pavlina
-- Description: 1 kHz 2-bit counter for display multiplexing

library IEEE;
use IEEE.STD_LOGIC_1164.ALL;
use IEEE.STD_LOGIC_UNSIGNED.ALL;

entity counter_1kHz is
   Port ( clk_in : in STD_LOGIC;
          count_out : out STD_LOGIC_VECTOR(1 downto 0) );
end entity;

architecture counter_1kHz_arch of counter_1kHz is
   signal counter : INTEGER RANGE 0 TO 25000 := 0;
   signal counter_2bit : STD_LOGIC_VECTOR(1 downto 0) := "00";
begin
   count_out <= counter_2bit;

   clock : process (clk_in)
   begin
      if rising_edge(clk_in) then
         if counter = 25000 then
            counter <= 0;
            counter_2bit <= counter_2bit + 1;
         else
            counter <= counter + 1;
         end if;
      end if;
   end process;
end architecture;
```

Code available @ GitHub
https://git.io/fpSBN

I.3 Port Breakout Module for Multiplexed Displays

I.3.1 `port_breakout.bsf` : Block symbol file for the `port_breakout.vhd` file

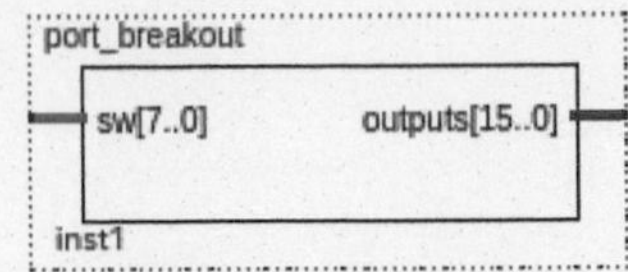

Figure I.3: Port breakout module block symbol.

Code available @ GitHub **https://git.io/fpSBp**

```
/*
A. Almagambetov and J.M. Pavlina
Description: port_breakout.bsf block symbol file
*/
(header "symbol" (version "1.1"))
(symbol
   (rect 16 16 200 96)
   (text "port_breakout" (rect 5 0 60 12)(font "Arial" ))
   (text "inst" (rect 8 64 20 76)(font "Arial" ))
   (port
      (pt 0 32)
      (input)
      (text "sw[7..0]" (rect 0 0 30 12)(font "Arial" ))
      (text "sw[7..0]" (rect 21 27 51 39)(font "Arial" ))
      (line (pt 0 32)(pt 16 32)(line_width 3))
   )
   (port
      (pt 184 32)
      (output)
      (text "outputs[15..0]" (rect 0 0 51 12)(font "Arial" ))
      (text "outputs[15..0]" (rect 112 27 163 39)(font "Arial" ))
      (line (pt 184 32)(pt 168 32)(line_width 3))
   )
   (drawing
      (rectangle (rect 16 16 168 64)(line_width 1))
   )
)
```

I.3.2 `port_breakout.vhd` : Top-level entity

Code available @ GitHub **https://git.io/fpSRe**

```
-- A. Almagambetov and J.M. Pavlina
-- Description: Port breakout block for display multiplexing lab
library IEEE;
use IEEE.STD_LOGIC_1164.ALL;

entity port_breakout is
   Port ( sw : in STD_LOGIC_VECTOR(7 downto 0);
          outputs : out STD_LOGIC_VECTOR(15 downto 0) );
end entity;

architecture port_breakout_arch of port_breakout is
begin
   outputs <= "00000000" & sw;
end architecture;
```

I.4 Binary to BCD Decoder (10-bit to 12-bit)

I.4.1 `bcd_decoder.bsf` : Block symbol file for the `bcd_decoder.vhd` file

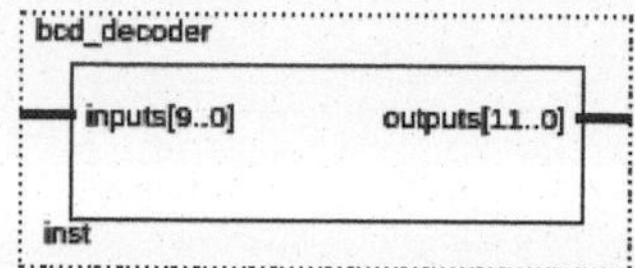

Figure I.4: Binary to BCD decoder block symbol.

```
/*
A. Almagambetov and J.M. Pavlina
Description: bcd_decoder.bsf block symbol file
Required file: bcd_decoder.vhd
*/
(header "symbol" (version "1.2"))
(symbol
   (rect 16 16 208 96)
   (text "bcd_decoder" (rect 5 0 56 12)(font "Arial" ))
   (text "inst" (rect 8 64 20 76)(font "Arial" ))
   (port
      (pt 0 32)
      (input)
      (text "inputs[9..0]" (rect 0 0 42 12)(font "Arial" ))
      (text "inputs[9..0]" (rect 21 27 63 39)(font "Arial" ))
      (line (pt 0 32)(pt 16 32)(line_width 3))
   )
   (port
      (pt 192 32)
      (output)
      (text "outputs[15..0]" (rect 0 0 50 12)(font "Arial" ))
      (text "outputs[15..0]" (rect 121 27 171 39)(font "Arial" ))
      (line (pt 192 32)(pt 176 32)(line_width 3))
   )
   (drawing
      (rectangle (rect 16 16 176 64)(line_width 1))
   )
)
```

Code available @ GitHub
https://git.io/fNHPh

I.4.2 bcd_decoder.vhd : Top-level entity

Code available @ GitHub
https://git.io/fNHXc

```
-- A. Almagambetov and J.M. Pavlina
-- Description: Binary-to-BCD decoder (supports 0-2048)

library IEEE;
use IEEE.STD_LOGIC_1164.ALL;
use IEEE.STD_LOGIC_UNSIGNED.ALL;
use IEEE.STD_LOGIC_ARITH.ALL;

entity bcd_decoder is
   Port ( inputs : in STD_LOGIC_VECTOR (9 downto 0);
          outputs : out STD_LOGIC_VECTOR (15 downto 0));
end entity;

architecture bcd_decoder_arch of bcd_decoder is
   signal decimal : INTEGER RANGE 0 TO 2048 := 0;
   signal thousands, hundreds, tens, ones : INTEGER RANGE 0 TO 9 := 0;
   signal thousands_bus, hundreds_bus, tens_bus, ones_bus : STD_LOGIC_VECTOR(3 downto 0) := X"0";
begin
   decimal <= CONV_INTEGER(inputs);

   thousands <= decimal / 1000;
   hundreds <= (decimal - thousands * 1000) / 100;
   tens <= (decimal - thousands * 1000 - hundreds * 100) / 10;
   ones <= (decimal - thousands * 1000 - hundreds * 100 - tens * 10);

   thousands_bus <= CONV_STD_LOGIC_VECTOR(thousands,4);
   hundreds_bus <= CONV_STD_LOGIC_VECTOR(hundreds,4);
   tens_bus <= CONV_STD_LOGIC_VECTOR(tens,4);
   ones_bus <= CONV_STD_LOGIC_VECTOR(ones,4);

   outputs <= thousands_bus & hundreds_bus & tens_bus & ones_bus;
end architecture;
```

I.5 SPI Accelerometer Interface

I.5.1 `spi_axl.bsf` : Block symbol file for the `spi_axl` interface

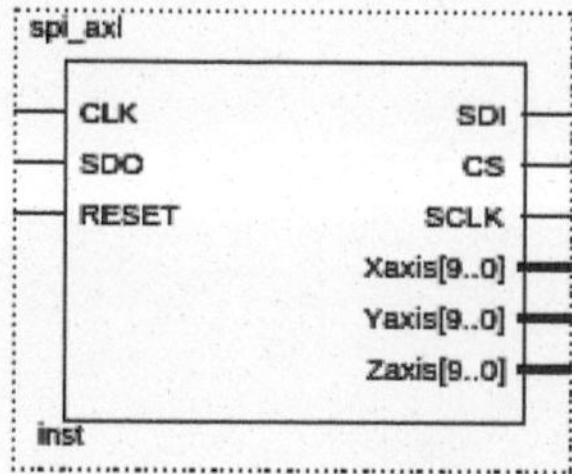

Figure I.5: SPI accelerometer interface block symbol.

```
/*
-- A. Almagambetov and J.M. Pavlina
-- Description: spi_axl.bsf block symbol file
-- Required files: spi_axl.vhd, spi_interface.vhd, spi_master.vhd
*/
(header "symbol" (version "1.2"))
(symbol
   (rect 16 16 192 160)
   (text "spi_axl" (rect 5 0 32 12)(font "Arial" ))
   (text "inst" (rect 8 128 20 140)(font "Arial" ))
   (port
      (pt 0 32)
      (input)
      (text "CLK" (rect 0 0 20 12)(font "Arial" ))
      (text "CLK" (rect 21 27 41 39)(font "Arial" ))
      (line (pt 0 32)(pt 16 32)(line_width 1))
   )
   (port
      (pt 0 48)
      (input)
      (text "SDO" (rect 0 0 20 12)(font "Arial" ))
      (text "SDO" (rect 21 43 41 55)(font "Arial" ))
      (line (pt 0 48)(pt 16 48)(line_width 1))
   )
   (port
      (pt 0 64)
      (input)
      (text "RESET" (rect 0 0 34 12)(font "Arial" ))
      (text "RESET" (rect 21 59 55 71)(font "Arial" ))
      (line (pt 0 64)(pt 16 64)(line_width 1))
   )
   (port
      (pt 176 32)
      (output)
      (text "SDI" (rect 0 0 15 12)(font "Arial" ))
      (text "SDI" (rect 140 27 155 39)(font "Arial" ))
      (line (pt 176 32)(pt 160 32)(line_width 1))
   )
   (port
      (pt 176 48)
      (output)
      (text "CS" (rect 0 0 12 12)(font "Arial" ))
      (text "CS" (rect 143 43 155 55)(font "Arial" ))
      (line (pt 176 48)(pt 160 48)(line_width 1))
   )
   (port
      (pt 176 64)
```

Code available @ GitHub
https://git.io/fNH6o

```
      (output)
      (text "SCLK" (rect 0 0 25 12)(font "Arial" ))
      (text "SCLK" (rect 130 59 155 71)(font "Arial" ))
      (line (pt 176 64)(pt 160 64)(line_width 1))
   )
   (port
      (pt 176 80)
      (output)
      (text "Xaxis[9..0]" (rect 0 0 41 12)(font "Arial" ))
      (text "Xaxis[9..0]" (rect 114 75 155 87)(font "Arial" ))
      (line (pt 176 80)(pt 160 80)(line_width 3))
   )
   (port
      (pt 176 96)
      (output)
      (text "Yaxis[9..0]" (rect 0 0 42 12)(font "Arial" ))
      (text "Yaxis[9..0]" (rect 113 91 155 103)(font "Arial" ))
      (line (pt 176 96)(pt 160 96)(line_width 3))
   )
   (port
      (pt 176 112)
      (output)
      (text "Zaxis[9..0]" (rect 0 0 42 12)(font "Arial" ))
      (text "Zaxis[9..0]" (rect 113 107 155 119)(font "Arial" ))
      (line (pt 176 112)(pt 160 112)(line_width 3))
   )
   (drawing
      (rectangle (rect 16 16 160 128)(line_width 1))
   )
)
```

I.5.2 spi_axl.vhd : Top-level entity

Code available @ GitHub
https://git.io/fNH65

```
-- A. Almagambetov and J.M. Pavlina
-- Description: SPI ADXL345 interface

library IEEE;
use IEEE.STD_LOGIC_1164.ALL;

entity spi_axl is
   Port ( CLK, SDO, RESET : in  STD_LOGIC;
          SDI, CS, SCLK : out  STD_LOGIC;
          Xaxis, Yaxis, Zaxis : out STD_LOGIC_VECTOR(9 downto 0));
end entity;

architecture spi_axl_arch of spi_axl is
   component spi_interface
   Port( txbuffer : in STD_LOGIC_VECTOR (15 downto 0);
         rxbuffer : out STD_LOGIC_VECTOR (7 downto 0);
         transmit, miso, reset, clk : in STD_LOGIC;
         done_out, mosi, sclk : out STD_LOGIC);
   end component;

   component spi_master
   Port ( clk, clk_5hz, reset, done : in STD_LOGIC;
          transmit : out STD_LOGIC;
          txdata : out STD_LOGIC_VECTOR(15 downto 0);
          rxdata : in STD_LOGIC_VECTOR(7 downto 0);
          x_axis_data, y_axis_data, z_axis_data : out STD_LOGIC_VECTOR(9 downto 0));
   end component;

```

```
    signal TxBuffer : STD_LOGIC_VECTOR(15 downto 0);
    signal RxBuffer : STD_LOGIC_VECTOR(7 downto 0);
    signal doneConfigure, done, transmit : STD_LOGIC;

    signal clk_5hz : STD_LOGIC := '0';
    signal counter : INTEGER RANGE 0 TO 5000000;

    signal xAxis_data_local, yAxis_data_local, zAxis_data_local : STD_LOGIC_VECTOR(9 downto 0);

 begin
    xAxis <= xAxis_data_local(9 downto 0);
    yAxis <= yAxis_data_local(9 downto 0);
    zAxis <= zAxis_data_local(9 downto 0);

    -- 5 Hz clock generator to determine capture rate
    clock_5Hz_instance : process (clk)
    begin
       if rising_edge(clk) then
          if counter = 5000000 then counter <= 0;
             clk_5hz <= not clk_5hz;
          else counter <= counter + 1;
          end if;
       end if;
    end process;

    spi_control : process (clk)       -- CS 0 (enabled), 1 (disabled)
    begin
       if rising_edge( clk ) then
          if reset = '1' then cs <= '1';
          elsif transmit = '1' then cs <= '0';
          elsif done = '1' then cs <= '1';
          end if;
       end if;
    end process;

    -- SPI interface control, data storage, send data control
    spi_master_instance: spi_master port map ( RESET => RESET,
                                 CLK_5HZ => CLK_5HZ,
                                 CLK => CLK,
                                 transmit => transmit,
                                 TxData => txBuffer,
                                 RxData => RxBuffer,
                                 done => done,
                                 x_axis_data => xAxis_data_local,
                                 y_axis_data => yAxis_data_local,
                                 z_axis_data => zAxis_data_local);

    -- Timing data generation, AXL data read/write
    spi_interface_instance: spi_interface port map ( MISO => SDO,
                                 MOSI => SDI,
                                 RESET => RESET,
                                 CLK => CLK,
                                 SCLK => SCLK,
                                 TxBuffer => TxBuffer,
                                 RxBuffer => RxBuffer,
                                 done_out => done,
                                 transmit => transmit);
 end architecture;
```

I.5.3 spi_interface.vhd : Timing data generator, ADXL read/write

Code available @ GitHub
https://git.io/fNHin

```
-- Copyright (c) 2012, A. Skreen, J. Sackos, Digilent, Inc.
-- Modified 9 Aug 2018 by A. Almagambetov

library IEEE;
use IEEE.STD_LOGIC_1164.ALL;
use IEEE.STD_LOGIC_ARITH.ALL;
use IEEE.STD_LOGIC_UNSIGNED.ALL;

entity spi_interface is
   Port( txbuffer : in STD_LOGIC_VECTOR (15 downto 0);
         rxbuffer : out STD_LOGIC_VECTOR (7 downto 0);
         transmit, miso, reset, clk : in STD_LOGIC;
         done_out, mosi, sclk : out STD_LOGIC);
end entity;

architecture spi_interface_arch of spi_interface is
   constant CLKDIVIDER : STD_LOGIC_VECTOR(7 downto 0) := X"FF"; -- 100/50 kHz
   signal clk_count : STD_LOGIC_VECTOR(7 downto 0);
   signal clk_edge_buffer, sck_previous, sck_buffer, done : STD_LOGIC;
   signal tx_shift_register : STD_LOGIC_VECTOR(15 downto 0);
   signal rx_shift_register : STD_LOGIC_VECTOR(7 downto 0);
   signal tx_count, rx_count : STD_LOGIC_VECTOR(3 downto 0);

   type TxType is (IDLE, TXG);
   signal TxSTATE : TxType;

   type RxType is (IDLE, RXG);
   signal RxSTATE : RxType;

   type SCLKType is (IDLE, RUN);
   signal SCLKSTATE : SCLKType;
begin
   sclk <= sck_buffer;
   rxbuffer <= rx_shift_register;
   done_out <= done;

   TxProcess : process (clk)
   begin
      if rising_edge(clk) then
         if reset = '1' then
            tx_shift_register <= (others => '0');
            tx_count <= (others => '0');
            mosi <= '1';
            TxSTATE <= IDLE;
         else
            case TxSTATE is
               when IDLE =>
                  tx_shift_register <= txbuffer;
                  if transmit = '1' then
                     TxSTATE <= TXG;
                  elsif done = '1' then
                     mosi <= '1';
                  end if;
               when TXG =>
                  if (sck_previous = '1' and sck_buffer = '0') then
                     if tx_count = "1111" then
                        TxSTATE <= IDLE;
                        tx_count <= (others => '0');
                        mosi <= tx_shift_register(15);
                     else
                        tx_count<= tx_count + "0001";
```

```
                    mosi<= tx_shift_register(15);
                    tx_shift_register<= tx_shift_register( 14 downto 0 ) & '0';
                  end if;
                end if;
              when others => null;
            end case;
          end if;
        end if;
      end process;

      RxProcess : process (clk)
      begin
        if rising_edge(clk) then
          if reset = '1' then
            rx_shift_register <= (others => '0');
            rx_count <= (others => '0');
            done <= '0';
          else
            case RxSTATE is
              when IDLE =>
                if transmit = '1' then
                  RxSTATE<= RXG;
                  rx_shift_register <= (others => '0');
                elsif SCLKSTATE = IDLE then done <= '0';
                end if;
              when RXG =>
                if (sck_previous = '0' and sck_buffer = '1') then
                  if rx_count = "1111" then
                    RxSTATE <= IDLE;
                    rx_count <= (others => '0');
                    rx_shift_register <= rx_shift_register (6 downto 0) & miso;
                    done <= '1';
                  else
                    rx_count<= rx_count + "0001";
                    rx_shift_register<= rx_shift_register ( 6 downto 0 ) & miso;
                  end if;
                end if;
              when others => null;
            end case;
          end if;
        end if;
      end process;

      sclk_generator : process (clk)
      begin
        if rising_edge(clk) then
          if reset = '1' then
            clk_count <= (others => '0');
            SCLKSTATE <= IDLE;
            sck_previous <= '1';
            sck_buffer <= '1';
          else
            case SCLKSTATE is
              when IDLE =>
                sck_previous <= '1';
                sck_buffer <='1';
                if transmit = '1' then
                  SCLKSTATE <= RUN;
                  clk_count <= (others => '0');
                  clk_edge_buffer <= '0';
                  sck_previous <= '1';
                  sck_buffer <= '1';
                end if;
              when RUN =>
```

```
                    if done = '1' then SCLKSTATE <= IDLE;
                    elsif clk_count = CLKDIVIDER then
                        if clk_edge_buffer = '0' then
                            sck_buffer <= '1';
                            clk_edge_buffer <= '1';
                        else
                            sck_buffer <= not sck_buffer;
                            clk_count <= (others => '0');
                        end if;
                    else
                        sck_previous<= sck_buffer;
                        clk_count<= clk_count + 1;
                    end if;
                when others => null;
            end case;
        end if;
    end if;
  end process;
end architecture;
```

I.5.4 spi_master.vhd : SPI interface control, data storage

Code available @ GitHub
https://git.io/fNHiK

```
-- Copyright (c) 2012, A. Skreen, J. Sackos, Digilent, Inc.
-- Modified 9 Aug 2018 by A. Almagambetov

library IEEE;
use IEEE.STD_LOGIC_1164.ALL;
use IEEE.STD_LOGIC_ARITH.ALL;
use IEEE.STD_LOGIC_UNSIGNED.ALL;

entity spi_master is
   Port ( clk, clk_5hz, reset, done : in STD_LOGIC;
          transmit : out STD_LOGIC;
          txdata : out STD_LOGIC_VECTOR(15 downto 0);
          rxdata : in STD_LOGIC_VECTOR(7 downto 0);
          x_axis_data, y_axis_data, z_axis_data : out STD_LOGIC_VECTOR(9 downto 0));
end entity;

architecture spi_master_arch of spi_master is
   type state_type is (IDLE, CONF, TXG, RXG, FIN, BRK, HOLD);
   signal STATE : state_type;

   type data_type is (x_axis, y_axis, z_axis);
   signal DATA : data_type;

   type CONF_type is (powerCtl , bwRate , dataFormat);
   signal CONFsel : CONF_type;

   -- Configuration registers
   constant POWER_CTL : STD_LOGIC_VECTOR(15 downto 0) := X"2D08";
   constant BW_RATE : STD_LOGIC_VECTOR(15 downto 0) := X"2C08";
   constant DATA_FORMAT : STD_LOGIC_VECTOR(15 downto 0) := X"3100";

   -- Read only for axis registers, single-byte increments
   constant XAXIS0 : STD_LOGIC_VECTOR(15 downto 0) := X"B200"; --10110010;
   constant XAXIS1 : STD_LOGIC_VECTOR(15 downto 0) := X"B300"; --10110011;
   constant YAXIS0 : STD_LOGIC_VECTOR(15 downto 0) := X"B400"; --10110100;
   constant YAXIS1 : STD_LOGIC_VECTOR(15 downto 0) := X"B500"; --10110101;
   constant ZAXIS0 : STD_LOGIC_VECTOR(15 downto 0) := X"B600"; --10110110;
   constant ZAXIS1 : STD_LOGIC_VECTOR(15 downto 0) := X"B700"; --10110111;

```

```
    signal BRK_count : STD_LOGIC_VECTOR(11 downto 0);
    signal hold_count : STD_LOGIC_VECTOR(20 downto 0);
    signal end_CONF : STD_LOGIC;
    signal done_CONF : STD_LOGIC;
    signal register_select : STD_LOGIC;
    signal finish : STD_LOGIC;
    signal sample_done : STD_LOGIC;
    signal prevstart : STD_LOGIC_VECTOR(3 downto 0);

begin

   spi_masterProcess : process (clk)
   begin
      if rising_edge(clk) then
         prevstart <= prevstart(2 downto 0) & clk_5hz;     -- Debounce start button
         if reset = '1' then
            transmit <= '0';
            STATE <= IDLE;
            DATA <= x_axis;
            BRK_count <= (others => '0');
            hold_count <= (others => '0');
            done_CONF <= '0';
            CONFsel <= powerCtl;
            txdata <= (others => '0');
            register_select <= '0';
            sample_done <= '0';
            finish <= '0';
            x_axis_data <= (others => '0');
            y_axis_data <= (others => '0');
            z_axis_data <= (others => '0');
            end_CONF <= '0';
         else
            case STATE is
               when IDLE =>
                  if done_CONF = '0' then
                     STATE <= CONF;
                     txdata <= POWER_CTL;
                     Transmit <= '1';
                  elsif (prevstart = "0011" and clk_5hz = '1' and done_CONF = '1') then
                     STATE <= TXG;
                     finish <= '0';
                     txdata <= xAxis0;
                     sample_done <= '0';
                  end if;
               when CONF =>
                  case CONFsel is
                     when powerCtl =>
                        STATE <= FIN;
                        CONFsel <= bwRate;
                        transmit <= '1';
                     when bwRate =>
                        txdata <= BW_RATE;
                        STATE <= FIN;
                        CONFsel <= dataFormat;
                        transmit <= '1';
                     when dataFormat =>
                        txdata <= DATA_FORMAT;
                        STATE <= FIN;
                        transmit <= '1';
                        finish <= '1';
                        end_CONF <= '1';
                     when others => null;
                  end case;
               when TXG =>
```

```
            case DATA is
               when x_axis =>
                  transmit <= '1';
                  STATE <= RXG;
               when y_axis =>
                  transmit <= '1';
                  STATE <= RXG;
               when z_axis =>
                  transmit <= '1';
                  STATE <= RXG;
               when others => null;
            end case;
         when RXG =>
            case DATA is
               when x_axis =>
                  case register_select is
                     when '0' =>
                        transmit <= '0';
                           if done = '1' then
                              txdata <= xAxis1;
                              x_axis_data(7 downto 0) <= rxdata(7 downto 0);
                              STATE <= FIN;
                              register_select <= '1';
                           end if;
                     when others =>
                        transmit <= '0';
                        if done = '1' then
                           txdata <= yAxis0;
                           x_axis_data(9 downto 8) <= rxdata(1 downto 0);
                           txdata <= yAxis0;
                           register_select <= '0';
                           DATA <= y_axis;
                           STATE <= FIN;
                        end if;
                  end case;
               when y_axis =>
                  case register_select is
                     when '0' =>
                        transmit <= '0';
                        if done = '1' then
                           txdata <= yAxis1;
                           y_axis_data(7 downto 0) <= rxdata(7 downto 0);
                           txdata <= yAxis1;
                           register_select <='1';
                           STATE <= FIN;
                        end if;
                     when others =>
                        transmit <= '0';
                        if done = '1' then
                           txdata <= zAxis0;
                           y_axis_data(9 downto 8) <= rxdata(1 downto 0);
                           txdata <= zAxis0;
                           register_select <= '0';
                           DATA <= z_axis;
                           STATE <= FIN;
                        end if;
                  end case;
               when z_axis =>
                  case register_select is
                     when '0' =>
                        transmit <= '0';
                        if done = '1' then
                           txdata <= zAxis1;
                           z_axis_data(7 downto 0) <= rxdata(7 downto 0);
```

```
                                 txdata <= zAxis1;
                                 register_select <='1';
                                 STATE <= FIN;
                              end if;
                           when others =>
                              transmit<= '0';
                              if done = '1' then
                                 txdata <= xAxis0;
                                 z_axis_data(9 downto 8) <= rxdata(1 downto 0);
                                 txdata <= xAxis0;
                                 register_select <= '0';
                                 DATA <= x_axis;
                                 STATE <= FIN;
                                 sample_done <= '1';
                              end if;
                        end case;
                     when others => null;
                  end case;
               when FIN =>
                  transmit<= '0';
                  if done = '1' then
                     STATE <= BRK;
                     if end_CONF = '1' then done_CONF <='1';
                     end if;
                  end if;
               when BRK =>
                  if BRK_count = X"FFF" then
                     BRK_count<= ( others => '0' );
                     if (finish = '1' or sample_done = '1') and clk_5hz = '0' then
                        STATE <= IDLE;
                        txdata <= xAxis0;
                     elsif (sample_done = '1' and clk_5hz = '1') then
                        STATE <= HOLD;
                     elsif (done_CONF = '1' and sample_done = '0') then
                        STATE <= TXG;
                        transmit <= '1';
                     elsif done_CONF = '0' then
                        STATE <= CONF;
                     end if;
                  else BRK_count <= BRK_count + 1;
                  end if;
               when HOLD =>
                  if hold_count = X"1FFFFF" then
                     hold_count <= (others => '0');
                     STATE <= TXG;
                     sample_done <= '0';
                  elsif clk_5hz <= '0' then
                     STATE <= IDLE;
                     hold_count <= (others => '0');
                  else hold_count <= hold_count + 1;
                  end if;
               when others => null;
            end case;
         end if;
      end if;
   end process;
end architecture;
```

I.6 Frequency Scaler (50 MHz to 2 ms period)

I.6.1 `clk_2ms.bsf` : Block symbol file for the `clk_2ms.vhd` file

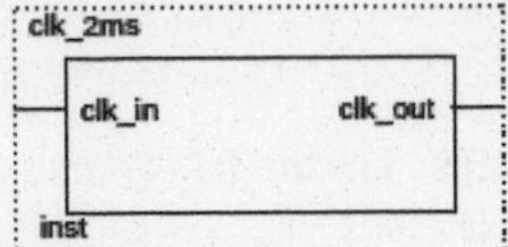

Figure I.6: Frequency scaler block symbol.

Code available @ GitHub
https://git.io/fN5HK

```
/*
A. Almagambetov and J.M. Pavlina
Description: clk_2ms.bsf block symbol file
Required files: clk_2ms.bsf
*/
(header "symbol" (version "1.1"))
(symbol
   (rect 16 16 168 96)
   (text "clk_2ms" (rect 5 0 39 12)(font "Arial" ))
   (text "inst" (rect 8 64 20 76)(font "Arial" ))
   (port
      (pt 0 32)
      (input)
      (text "clk_in" (rect 0 0 22 12)(font "Arial" ))
      (text "clk_in" (rect 21 27 43 39)(font "Arial" ))
      (line (pt 0 32)(pt 16 32)(line_width 1))
   )
   (port
      (pt 152 32)
      (output)
      (text "clk_out" (rect 0 0 28 12)(font "Arial" ))
      (text "clk_out" (rect 103 27 131 39)(font "Arial" ))
      (line (pt 152 32)(pt 136 32)(line_width 1))
   )
   (drawing
      (rectangle (rect 16 16 136 64)(line_width 1))
   )
)
```

I.6.2 clk_2ms.vhd : Top-level entity

```
-- A. Almagambetov and J.M. Pavlina
-- Description: Clock scaler 50 MHz to 2ms period

library IEEE;
use IEEE.STD_LOGIC_1164.ALL;
use IEEE.STD_LOGIC_UNSIGNED.ALL;

entity clk_2ms is
   Port ( clk_in : in STD_LOGIC;
          clk_out : out STD_LOGIC );
end entity;

architecture clk_2ms_arch of clk_2ms is
   signal counter : INTEGER RANGE 0 TO 50000 := 0;
   signal clk_buf : STD_LOGIC := '0';
begin
   clk_out <= clk_buf;

   clock : process (clk_in)
   begin
      if rising_edge(clk_in) then
         if counter = 50000 then
            counter <= 0;
            clk_buf <= not clk_buf;
         else
            counter <= counter + 1;
         end if;
      end if;
   end process;

end architecture;
```

Code available @ GitHub
https://git.io/fN5Hi

Device Data Sheets

This section contains the following device data sheets, which will be used in this laboratory:

- **7400**: Quad 2-input NAND gates
- **7402**: Quad 2-input NOR gates
- **7404**: Hex inverter (NOT gate)
- **7408**: Quad 2-input AND gates
- **7432**: Quad 2-input OR gates
- **7447**: BCD-to-seven-segment decoder
- **7486**: Quad 2-input exclusive-OR (XOR) gates
- **54153**: Dual 4-line to 1-line data selector/multiplexer
- **54590**: 8-bit binary counter with 3-state output registers
- **TIP122**: Complementary silicon power Darlington transistors
- **ADXL345**: Analog Devices 3-axis MEMS accelerometer
- **Series 206/208**: Through-hole DIP switch
- **5161A**: Single-digit numeric LED display

SN74LS00

Quad 2-Input NAND Gate

- ESD > 3500 Volts

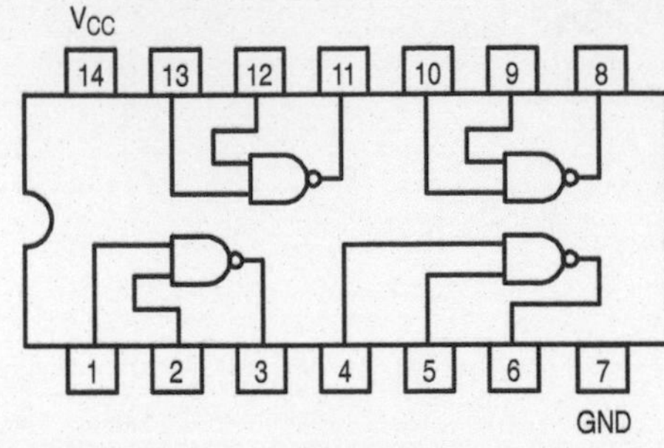

GUARANTEED OPERATING RANGES

Symbol	Parameter	Min	Typ	Max	Unit
V_{CC}	Supply Voltage	4.75	5.0	5.25	V
T_A	Operating Ambient Temperature Range	0	25	70	°C
I_{OH}	Output Current – High			–0.4	mA
I_{OL}	Output Current – Low			8.0	mA

ON Semiconductor

Formerly a Division of Motorola

http://onsemi.com

LOW POWER SCHOTTKY

PLASTIC
N SUFFIX
CASE 646

SOIC
D SUFFIX
CASE 751A

ORDERING INFORMATION

Device	Package	Shipping
SN74LS00N	14 Pin DIP	2000 Units/Box
SN74LS00D	14 Pin	2500/Tape & Reel

December, 1999 – Rev. 6

Publication Order Number:
SN74LS00/D

DC CHARACTERISTICS OVER OPERATING TEMPERATURE RANGE (unless otherwise specified)

Symbol	Parameter	Limits			Unit	Test Conditions
		Min	Typ	Max		
V_{IH}	Input HIGH Voltage	2.0			V	Guaranteed Input HIGH Voltage for All Inputs
V_{IL}	Input LOW Voltage			0.8	V	Guaranteed Input LOW Voltage for All Inputs
V_{IK}	Input Clamp Diode Voltage		−0.65	−1.5	V	V_{CC} = MIN, I_{IN} = −18 mA
V_{OH}	Output HIGH Voltage	2.7	3.5		V	V_{CC} = MIN, I_{OH} = MAX, V_{IN} = V_{IH} or V_{IL} per Truth Table
V_{OL}	Output LOW Voltage		0.25	0.4	V	I_{OL} = 4.0 mA; V_{CC} = V_{CC} MIN, V_{IN} = V_{IL} or V_{IH} per Truth Table
			0.35	0.5	V	I_{OL} = 8.0 mA; V_{CC} = V_{CC} MIN, V_{IN} = V_{IL} or V_{IH} per Truth Table
I_{IH}	Input HIGH Current			20	µA	V_{CC} = MAX, V_{IN} = 2.7 V
				0.1	mA	V_{CC} = MAX, V_{IN} = 7.0 V
I_{IL}	Input LOW Current			−0.4	mA	V_{CC} = MAX, V_{IN} = 0.4 V
I_{OS}	Short Circuit Current (Note 1)	−20		−100	mA	V_{CC} = MAX
I_{CC}	Power Supply Current				mA	V_{CC} = MAX
	Total, Output HIGH			1.6		
	Total, Output LOW			4.4		

Note 1: Not more than one output should be shorted at a time, nor for more than 1 second.

AC CHARACTERISTICS (T_A = 25°C)

Symbol	Parameter	Limits			Unit	Test Conditions
		Min	Typ	Max		
t_{PLH}	Turn–Off Delay, Input to Output		9.0	15	ns	V_{CC} = 5.0 V, C_L = 15 pF
t_{PHL}	Turn–On Delay, Input to Output		10	15	ns	

August 1986
Revised February 2000

DM7402
Quad 2-Input NOR Gates

General Description

This device contains four independent gates each of which performs the logic NOR function.

Ordering Code:

Order Number	Package Number	Package Description
DM7402N	N14A	14-Lead Plastic Dual-In-Line Package (PDIP), JEDEC MS-001, 0.300 Wide

Connection Diagram

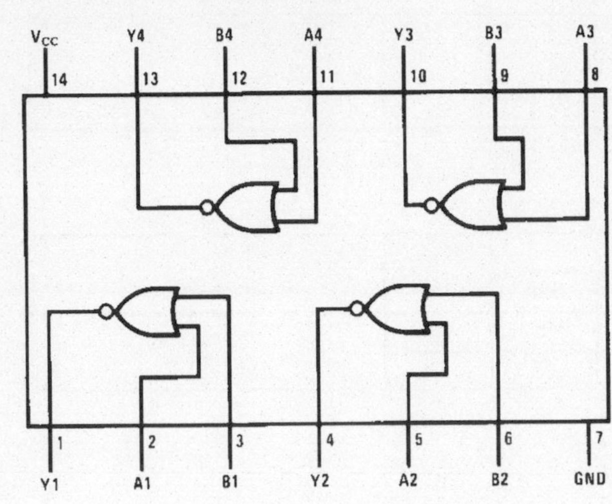

Function Table

$$Y = \overline{A + B}$$

Inputs		Output
A	B	Y
L	L	H
L	H	L
H	L	L
H	H	L

H = HIGH Logic Level
L = LOW Logic Level

Absolute Maximum Ratings (Note 1)

Supply Voltage	7V
Input Voltage	5.5V
Operating Free Air Temperature Range	0°C to +70°C
Storage Temperature Range	−65°C to +150°C

Note 1: The "Absolute Maximum Ratings" are those values beyond which the safety of the device cannot be guaranteed. The device should not be operated at these limits. The parametric values defined in the Electrical Characteristics tables are not guaranteed at the absolute maximum ratings. The "Recommended Operating Conditions" table will define the conditions for actual device operation.

Recommended Operating Conditions

Symbol	Parameter	Min	Nom	Max	Units
V_{CC}	Supply Voltage	4.75	5	5.25	V
V_{IH}	HIGH Level Input Voltage	2			V
V_{IL}	LOW Level Input Voltage			0.8	V
I_{OH}	HIGH Level Output Current			−0.4	mA
I_{OL}	LOW Level Output Current			16	mA
T_A	Free Air Operating Temperature	0		70	°C

Electrical Characteristics

over recommended operating free air temperature range (unless otherwise noted)

Symbol	Parameter	Conditions	Min	Typ (Note 2)	Max	Units
V_I	Input Clamp Voltage	V_{CC} = Min, I_I = −12 mA			−1.5	V
V_{OH}	HIGH Level Output Voltage	V_{CC} = Min, I_{OH} = Max V_{IL} = Max	2.4	3.4		V
V_{OL}	LOW Level Output Voltage	V_{CC} = Min, I_{OL} = Max V_{IH} = Min		0.2	0.4	V
I_I	Input Current @ Max Input Voltage	V_{CC} = Max, V_I = 5.5V			1	mA
I_{IH}	HIGH Level Input Current	V_{CC} = Max, V_I = 2.4V			40	μA
I_{IL}	LOW Level Input Current	V_{CC} = Max, V_I = 0.4V			−1.6	mA
I_{OS}	Short Circuit Output Current	V_{CC} = Max (Note 3)	−18		−55	mA
I_{CCH}	Supply Current with Outputs HIGH	V_{CC} = Max		8	16	mA
I_{CCL}	Supply Current with Outputs Low	V_{CC} = Max		14	27	mA

Note 2: All typicals are at V_{CC} = 5V, T_A = 25°C.

Note 3: Not more than one output should be shorted at a time.

Switching Characteristics

at V_{CC} = 5V and T_A = 25°C

Symbol	Parameter	Conditions	Min	Max	Units
t_{PLH}	Propagation Delay Time LOW-to-HIGH Level Output	C_L = 15 pF R_L = 400Ω		22	ns
t_{PHL}	Propagation Delay Time HIGH-to-LOW Level Output			15	ns

MC74HC04A

Hex Inverter

High–Performance Silicon–Gate CMOS

The MC74HC04A is identical in pinout to the LS04 and the MC14069. The device inputs are compatible with Standard CMOS outputs; with pullup resistors, they are compatible with LSTTL outputs.

The device consists of six three–stage inverters.

- Output Drive Capability: 10 LSTTL Loads
- Outputs Directly Interface to CMOS, NMOS and TTL
- Operating Voltage Range: 2 to 6V
- Low Input Current: 1μA
- High Noise Immunity Characteristic of CMOS Devices
- In Compliance With the JEDEC Standard No. 7A Requirements
- Chip Complexity: 36 FETs or 9 Equivalent Gates

LOGIC DIAGRAM

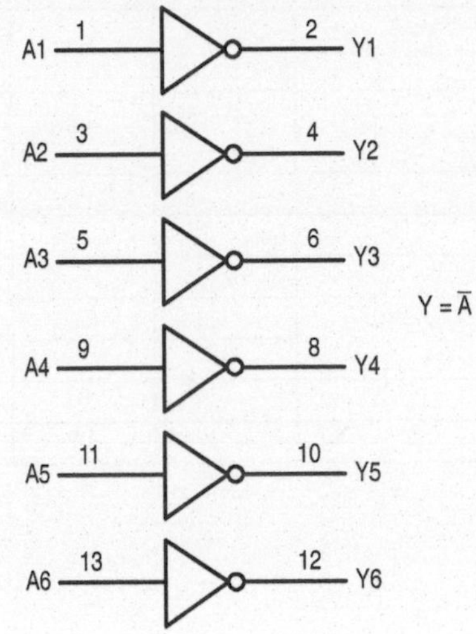

Pinout: 14–Lead Packages (Top View)

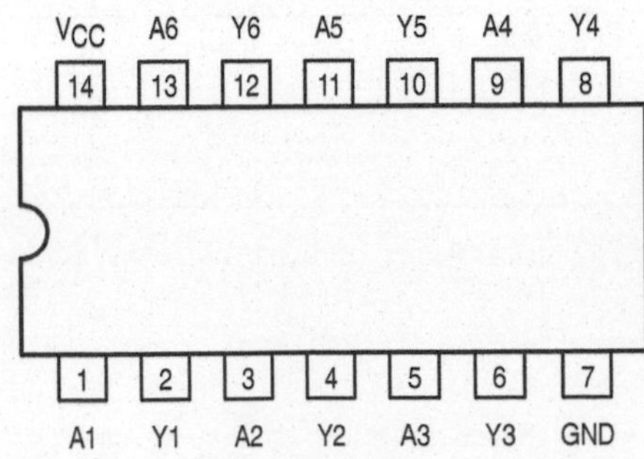

ON Semiconductor

http://onsemi.com

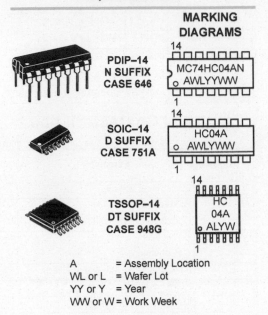

MARKING DIAGRAMS

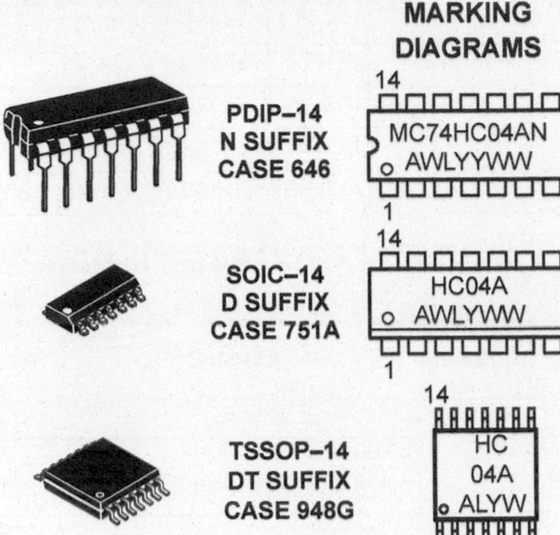

A = Assembly Location
WL or L = Wafer Lot
YY or Y = Year
WW or W = Work Week

FUNCTION TABLE

Inputs	Outputs
A	Y
L	H
H	L

ORDERING INFORMATION

Device	Package	Shipping
MC74HC04AN	PDIP–14	2000 / Box
MC74HC04AD	SOIC–14	55 / Rail
MC74HC04ADR2	SOIC–14	2500 / Reel
MC74HC04ADT	TSSOP–14	96 / Rail
MC74HC04ADTR2	TSSOP–14	2500 / Reel

MAXIMUM RATINGS*

Symbol	Parameter	Value	Unit
V_{CC}	DC Supply Voltage (Referenced to GND)	– 0.5 to + 7.0	V
V_{in}	DC Input Voltage (Referenced to GND)	– 0.5 to V_{CC} + 0.5	V
V_{out}	DC Output Voltage (Referenced to GND)	– 0.5 to V_{CC} + 0.5	V
I_{in}	DC Input Current, per Pin	± 20	mA
I_{out}	DC Output Current, per Pin	± 25	mA
I_{CC}	DC Supply Current, V_{CC} and GND Pins	± 50	mA
P_D	Power Dissipation in Still Air, Plastic DIP† SOIC Package† TSSOP Package†	750 500 450	mW
T_{stg}	Storage Temperature	– 65 to + 150	°C
T_L	Lead Temperature, 1 mm from Case for 10 Seconds Plastic DIP, SOIC or TSSOP Package	260	°C

*Maximum Ratings are those values beyond which damage to the device may occur.
Functional operation should be restricted to the Recommended Operating Conditions.

†Derating — Plastic DIP: – 10 mW/°C from 65° to 125°C
SOIC Package: – 7 mW/°C from 65° to 125°C
TSSOP Package: – 6.1 mW/°C from 65° to 125°C

For high frequency or heavy load considerations, see Chapter 2 of the ON Semiconductor High–Speed CMOS Data Book (DL129/D).

This device contains protection circuitry to guard against damage due to high static voltages or electric fields. However, precautions must be taken to avoid applications of any voltage higher than maximum rated voltages to this high–impedance circuit. For proper operation, V_{in} and V_{out} should be constrained to the range GND ≤ (V_{in} or V_{out}) ≤ V_{CC}.

Unused inputs must always be tied to an appropriate logic voltage level (e.g., either GND or V_{CC}). Unused outputs must be left open.

RECOMMENDED OPERATING CONDITIONS

Symbol	Parameter	Min	Max	Unit
V_{CC}	DC Supply Voltage (Referenced to GND)	2.0	6.0	V
V_{in}, V_{out}	DC Input Voltage, Output Voltage (Referenced to GND)	0	V_{CC}	V
T_A	Operating Temperature, All Package Types	– 55	+ 125	°C
t_r, t_f	Input Rise and Fall Time (Figure 1) V_{CC} = 2.0 V V_{CC} = 4.5 V V_{CC} = 6.0 V	0 0 0	1000 500 400	ns

DC CHARACTERISTICS (Voltages Referenced to GND)

Symbol	Parameter	Condition	V_{CC} V	Guaranteed Limit –55 to 25°C	385°C	3125°C	Unit
V_{IH}	Minimum High–Level Input Voltage	V_{out} = 0.1V or V_{CC} –0.1V $\|I_{out}\|$ 3 20μA	2.0 3.0 4.5 6.0	1.50 2.10 3.15 4.20	1.50 2.10 3.15 4.20	1.50 2.10 3.15 4.20	V
V_{IL}	Maximum Low–Level Input Voltage	V_{out} = 0.1V or V_{CC} – 0.1V $\|I_{out}\|$ 3 20μA	2.0 3.0 4.5 6.0	0.50 0.90 1.35 1.80	0.50 0.90 1.35 1.80	0.50 0.90 1.35 1.80	V
V_{OH}	Minimum High–Level Output Voltage	V_{in} = V_{IH} or V_{IL} $\|I_{out}\|$ 3 20μA	2.0 4.5 6.0	1.9 4.4 5.9	1.9 4.4 5.9	1.9 4.4 5.9	V
		V_{in} =V_{IH} or V_{IL} $\|I_{out}\|$ 3 2.4mA $\|I_{out}\|$ 3 4.0mA $\|I_{out}\|$ 3 5.2mA	3.0 4.5 6.0	2.48 3.98 5.48	2.34 3.84 5.34	2.20 3.70 5.20	
V_{OL}	Maximum Low–Level Output Voltage	V_{in} = V_{IH} or V_{IL} $\|I_{out}\|$ 3 20μA	2.0 4.5 6.0	0.1 0.1 0.1	0.1 0.1 0.1	0.1 0.1 0.1	V
		V_{in} = V_{IH} or V_{IL} $\|I_{out}\|$ 3 2.4mA $\|I_{out}\|$ 3 4.0mA $\|I_{out}\|$ 3 5.2mA	3.0 4.5 6.0	0.26 0.26 0.26	0.33 0.33 0.33	0.40 0.40 0.40	
I_{in}	Maximum Input Leakage Current	V_{in} = V_{CC} or GND	6.0	± 0.1	± 1.0	± 1.0	μA
I_{CC}	Maximum Quiescent Supply Current (per Package)	V_{in} = V_{CC} or GND I_{out} = 0μA	6.0	1.0	10	40	μA

NOTE: Information on typical parametric values can be found in Chapter 2 of the ON Semiconductor High–Speed CMOS Data Book (DL129/D).

AC CHARACTERISTICS (C_L = 50pF, Input t_r = t_f = 6ns)

Symbol	Parameter	V_{CC} V	Guaranteed Limit –55 to 25°C	385°C	3125°C	Unit
t_{PLH}, t_{PHL}	Maximum Propagation Delay, Input A or B to Output Y (Figures 1 and 2)	2.0 3.0 4.5 6.0	75 30 15 13	95 40 19 16	110 55 22 19	ns
t_{TLH}, t_{THL}	Maximum Output Transition Time, Any Output (Figures 1 and 2)	2.0 3.0 4.5 6.0	75 27 15 13	95 32 19 16	110 36 22 19	ns
C_{in}	Maximum Input Capacitance		10	10	10	pF

NOTE: For propagation delays with loads other than 50 pF, and information on typical parametric values, see Chapter 2 of the ON Semiconductor High–Speed CMOS Data Book (DL129/D).

		Typical @ 25°C, V_{CC} = 5.0 V	
C_{PD}	Power Dissipation Capacitance (Per Inverter)*	20	pF

* Used to determine the no–load dynamic power consumption: $P_D = C_{PD} V_{CC}^2 f + I_{CC} V_{CC}$. For load considerations, see Chapter 2 of the ON Semiconductor High–Speed CMOS Data Book (DL129/D).

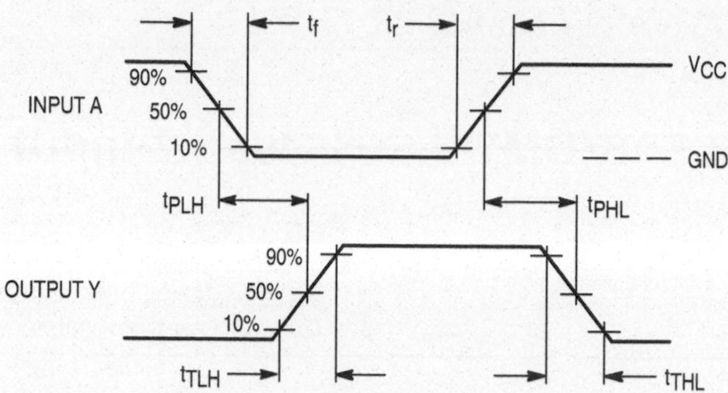

Figure 1. Switching Waveforms

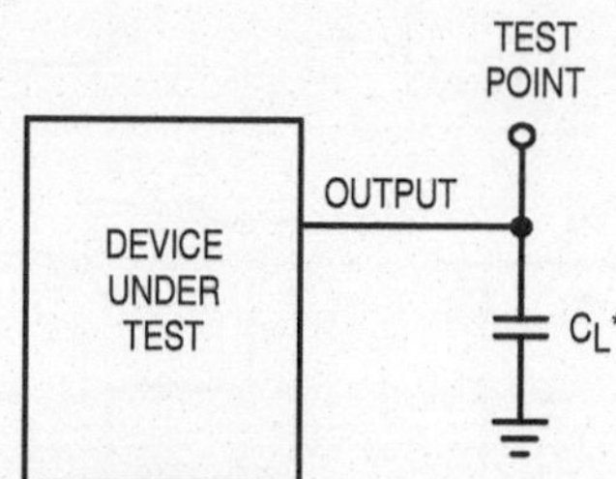

*Includes all probe and jig capacitance

Figure 2. Test Circuit

Figure 3. Expanded Logic Diagram
(1/6 of the Device Shown)

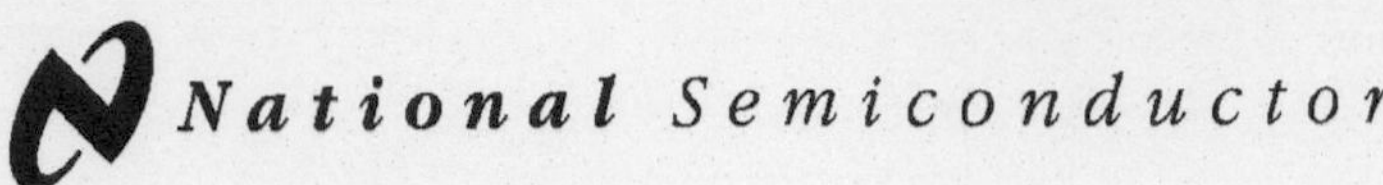

54LS08/DM54LS08/DM74LS08 Quad 2-Input AND Gates

General Description

This device contains four independent gates each of which performs the logic AND function.

Features

- Alternate Military/Aerospace device (54LS08) is available. Contact a National Semiconductor Sales Office/Distributor for specifications.

Connection Diagram

Dual-In-Line Package

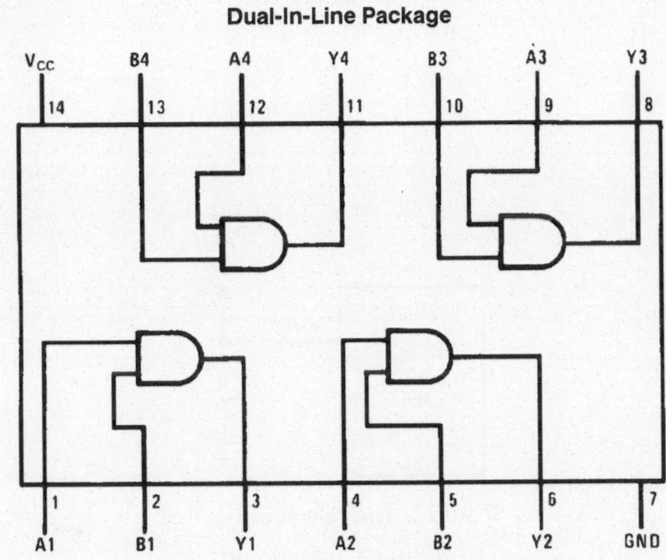

TL/F/6347–1

Order Number 54LS08DMQB, 54LS08FMQB, 54LS08LMQB, DM54LS08J, DM54LS08W, DM74LS08M or DM74LS08N
See NS Package Number E20A, J14A, M14A, N14A or W14B

Function Table

Y = AB

Inputs		Output
A	B	Y
L	L	L
L	H	L
H	L	L
H	H	H

H = High Logic Level
L = Low Logic Level

Absolute Maximum Ratings (Note)

If Military/Aerospace specified devices are required, please contact the National Semiconductor Sales Office/Distributors for availability and specifications.

Supply Voltage	7V
Input Voltage	7V
Operating Free Air Temperature Range	
DM54LS and 54LS	−55°C to +125°C
DM74LS	0°C to +70°C
Storage Temperature Range	−65°C to +150°C

Note: *The "Absolute Maximum Ratings" are those values beyond which the safety of the device cannot be guaranteed. The device should not be operated at these limits. The parametric values defined in the "Electrical Characteristics" table are not guaranteed at the absolute maximum ratings. The "Recommended Operating Conditions" table will define the conditions for actual device operation.*

Recommended Operating Conditions

June 1989

Symbol	Parameter	DM54LS08			DM74LS08			Units
		Min	Nom	Max	Min	Nom	Max	
V_{CC}	Supply Voltage	4.5	5	5.5	4.75	5	5.25	V
V_{IH}	High Level Input Voltage	2			2			V
V_{IL}	Low Level Input Voltage			0.7			0.8	V
I_{OH}	High Level Output Current			−0.4			−0.4	mA
I_{OL}	Low Level Output Current			4			8	mA
T_A	Free Air Operating Temperature	−55		125	0		70	°C

Electrical Characteristics over recommended operating free air temperature range (unless otherwise noted)

Symbol	Parameter	Conditions		Min	Typ (Note 1)	Max	Units
V_I	Input Clamp Voltage	V_{CC} = Min, I_I = −18 mA				−1.5	V
V_{OH}	High Level Output Voltage	V_{CC} = Min, I_{OH} = Max, V_{IH} = Min	DM54	2.5	3.4		V
			DM74	2.7	3.4		
V_{OL}	Low Level Output Voltage	V_{CC} = Min, I_{OL} = Max, V_{IL} = Max	DM54		0.25	0.4	V
			DM74		0.35	0.5	
		I_{OL} = 4 mA, V_{CC} = Min	DM74		0.25	0.4	
I_I	Input Current @ Max Input Voltage	V_{CC} = Max, V_I = 7V				0.1	mA
I_{IH}	High Level Input Current	V_{CC} = Max, V_I = 2.7V				20	μA
I_{IL}	Low Level Input Current	V_{CC} = Max, V_I = 0.4V				−0.36	mA
I_{OS}	Short Circuit Output Current	V_{CC} = Max (Note 2)	DM54	−20		−100	mA
			DM74	−20		−100	
I_{CCH}	Supply Current with Outputs High	V_{CC} = Max			2.4	4.8	mA
I_{CCL}	Supply Current with Outputs Low	V_{CC} = Max			4.4	8.8	mA

Switching Characteristics at V_{CC} = 5V and T_A = 25°C (See Section 1 for Test Waveforms and Output Load)

Symbol	Parameter	R_L = 2 kΩ				Units
		C_L = 15 pF		C_L = 50 pF		
		Min	Max	Min	Max	
t_{PLH}	Propagation Delay Time Low to High Level Output	4	13	6	18	ns
t_{PHL}	Propagation Delay Time High to Low Level Output	3	11	5	18	ns

Note 1: All typicals are at V_{CC} = 5V, T_A = 25°C.

Note 2: Not more than one output should be shorted at a time, and the duration should not exceed one second.

June 1986
Revised March 2000

DM74LS32
Quad 2-Input OR Gate

General Description

This device contains four independent gates each of which performs the logic OR function.

Ordering Code:

Order Number	Package Number	Package Description
DM74LS32M	M14A	14-Lead Small Outline Integrated Circuit (SOIC), JEDEC MS-120, 0.150 Narrow
DM74LS32SJ	M14D	14-Lead Small Outline Package (SOP), EIAJ TYPE II, 5.3mm Wide
DM74LS32N	N14A	14-Lead Plastic Dual-In-Line Package (PDIP), JEDEC MS-001, 0.300 Wide

Devices also available in Tape and Reel. Specify by appending the suffix letter "X" to the ordering code.

Connection Diagram

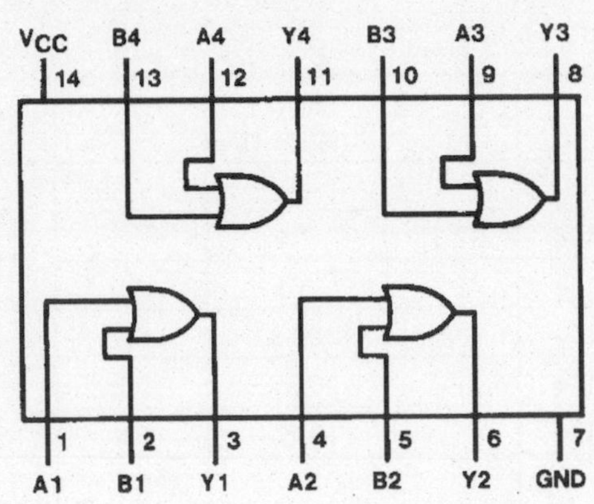

Function Table

$Y = A + B$

Inputs		Output
A	B	Y
L	L	L
L	H	H
H	L	H
H	H	H

H = HIGH Logic Level
L = LOW Logic Level

Absolute Maximum Ratings (Note 1)

Supply Voltage	7V
Input Voltage	7V
Operating Free Air Temperature Range	0°C to +70°C
Storage Temperature Range	−65°C to +150°C

Note 1: The "Absolute Maximum Ratings" are those values beyond which the safety of the device cannot be guaranteed. The device should not be operated at these limits. The parametric values defined in the Electrical Characteristics tables are not guaranteed at the absolute maximum ratings. The "Recommended Operating Conditions" table will define the conditions for actual device operation.

Recommended Operating Conditions

Symbol	Parameter	Min	Nom	Max	Units
V_{CC}	Supply Voltage	4.75	5	5.25	V
V_{IH}	HIGH Level Input Voltage	2			V
V_{IL}	LOW Level Input Voltage			0.8	V
I_{OH}	HIGH Level Output Current			−0.4	mA
I_{OL}	LOW Level Output Current			8	mA
T_A	Free Air Operating Temperature	0		70	°C

Electrical Characteristics

over recommended operating free air temperature range (unless otherwise noted)

Symbol	Parameter	Conditions	Min	Typ (Note 2)	Max	Units
V_I	Input Clamp Voltage	V_{CC} = Min, I_I = −18 mA			−1.5	V
V_{OH}	HIGH Level Output Voltage	V_{CC} = Min, I_{OH} = Max V_{IH} = Min	2.7	3.4		V
V_{OL}	LOW Level Output Voltage	V_{CC} = Min, I_{OL} = Max V_{IL} = Max		0.35	0.5	V
		I_{OL} = 4 mA, V_{CC} = Min		0.25	0.4	
I_I	Input Current @ Max Input Voltage	V_{CC} = Max, V_I = 7V			0.1	mA
I_{IH}	HIGH Level Input Current	V_{CC} = Max, V_I = 2.7V			20	μA
I_{IL}	LOW Level Input Current	V_{CC} = Max, V_I = 0.4V			−0.36	mA
I_{OS}	Short Circuit Output Current	V_{CC} = Max (Note 3)	−20		−100	mA
I_{CCH}	Supply Current with Outputs HIGH	V_{CC} = Max		3.1	6.2	mA
I_{CCL}	Supply Current with Outputs LOW	V_{CC} = Max		4.9	9.8	mA

Note 2: All typicals are at V_{CC} = 5V, T_A = 25°C.

Note 3: Not more than one output should be shorted at a time, and the duration should not exceed one second.

Switching Characteristics

at V_{CC} = 5V and T_A = 25°C

Symbol	Parameter	R_L = 2 kΩ				Units
		C_L = 15 pF		C_L = 50 pF		
		Min	Max	Min	Max	
t_{PLH}	Propagation Delay Time LOW-to-HIGH Level Output	3	11	4	15	ns
t_{PHL}	Propagation Delay Time HIGH-to-LOW Level Output	3	11	4	15	ns

SN5446A, '47A, '48, SN54LS47, 'LS48, 'LS49 SN7446A, '47A, '48, SN74LS47, 'LS48, 'LS49 BCD-TO-SEVEN-SEGMENT DECODERS/DRIVERS

'46A, '47A, 'LS47 feature

- **Open-Collector Outputs Drive Indicators Directly**
- **Lamp-Test Provision**
- **Leading/Trailing Zero Suppression**

'48, 'LS48 feature

- **Internal Pull-Ups Eliminate Need for External Resistors**
- **Lamp-Test Provision**
- **Leading/Trailing Zero Suppression**

'LS49 feature

- **Open-Collector Outputs**
- **Blanking Input**

SN5446A, SN5447A, SN54LS47, SN5448, SN54LS48 . . . J PACKAGE
SN7446A, SN7447A, SN7448 . . . N PACKAGE
SN74LS47, SN74LS48 . . . D OR N PACKAGE
(TOP VIEW)

Signal	Pin	Pin	Signal
B	1	16	V_{CC}
C	2	15	f
$\overline{LT}$	3	14	g
$\overline{BI}/\overline{RBO}$	4	13	a
$\overline{RBI}$	5	12	b
D	6	11	c
A	7	10	d
GND	8	9	e

SN54LS47, SN54LS48 . . . FK PACKAGE
(TOP VIEW)

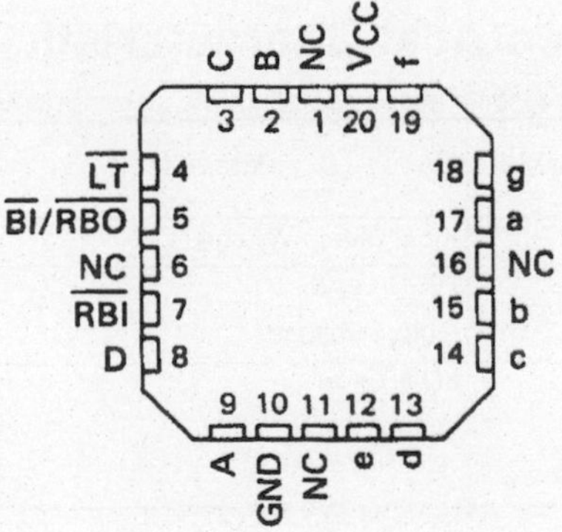

SN54LS49 . . . J OR W PACKAGE
SN74LS49 . . . D OR N PACKAGE
(TOP VIEW)

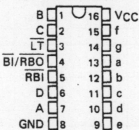

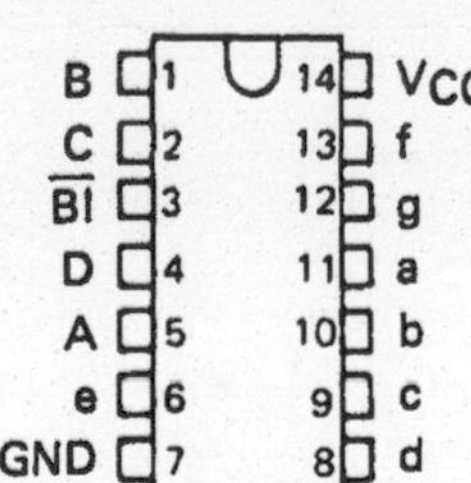

SN54LS49 . . . FK PACKAGE
(TOP VIEW)

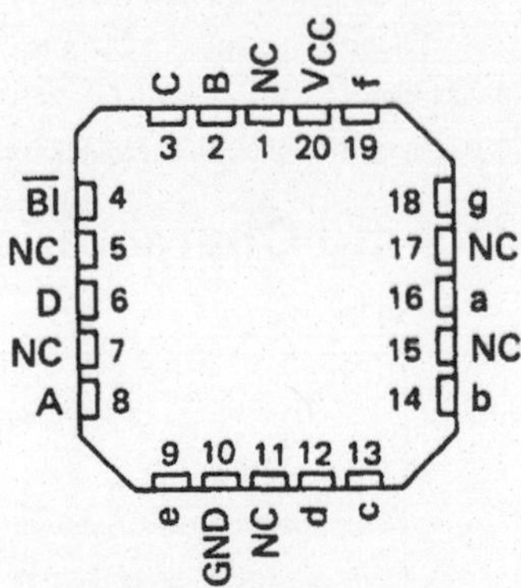

NC – No internal connection

- **All Circuit Types Feature Lamp Intensity Modulation Capability**

TYPE	DRIVER OUTPUTS				TYPICAL POWER DISSIPATION	PACKAGES
	ACTIVE LEVEL	OUTPUT CONFIGURATION	SINK CURRENT	MAX VOLTAGE		
SN5446A	low	open-collector	40 mA	30 V	320 mW	J, W
SN5447A	low	open-collector	40 mA	15 V	320 mW	J, W
SN5448	high	2-kΩ pull-up	6.4 mA	5.5 V	265 mW	J,W
SN54LS47	low	open-collector	12 mA	15 V	35 mW	J, W
SN54LS48	high	2-kΩ pull-up	2 mA	5.5 V	125 mW	J, W
SN54LS49	high	open-collector	4 mA	5.5 V	40 mW	J, W
SN7446A	low	open-collector	40 mA	30 V	320 mW	J, N
SN7447A	low	open-collector	40 mA	15 V	320 mW	J, N
SN7448	high	2-kΩ pull-up	6.4 mA	5.5 V	265 mW	J, N
SN74LS47	low	open-collector	24 mA	15 V	35 mW	J, N
SN74LS48	high	2-kΩ pull-up	6 mA	5.5 V	125 mW	J, N
SN74LS49	high	open-collector	8 mA	5.5 V	40 mW	J, N

logic symbols†

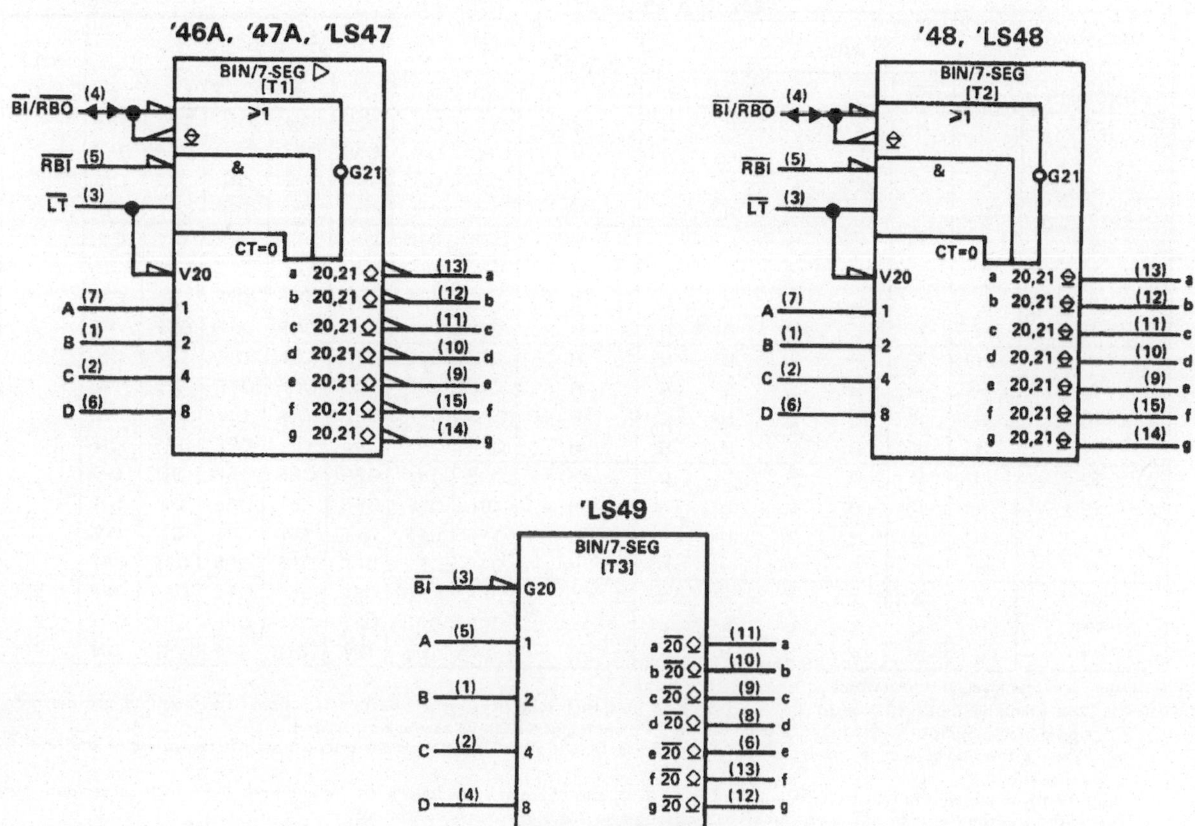

†These symbols are in accordance with ANSI/IEEE Std 91-1984 and IEC Publication 617-12. Pin numbers shown are for D, J, N, and W packages.

description

The '46A, '47A, and 'LS47 feature active-low outputs designed for driving common-anode LEDs or incandescent indicators directly. The '48, 'LS48, and 'LS49 feature active-high outputs for driving lamp buffers or common-cathode LEDs. All of the circuits except 'LS49 have full ripple-blanking input/output controls and a lamp test input. The 'LS49 circuit incorporates a direct blanking input. Segment identification and resultant displays are shown below. Display patterns for BCD input counts above 9 are unique symbols to authenticate input conditions.

The '46A, '47A, '48, 'LS47, and 'LS48 circuits incorporate automatic leading and/or trailing-edge zero-blanking control ($\overline{RBI}$ and $\overline{RBO}$). Lamp test ($\overline{LT}$) of these types may be performed at any time when the $\overline{BI}/\overline{RBO}$ node is at a high level. All types (including the '49 and 'LS49) contain an overriding blanking input ($\overline{BI}$), which can be used to control the lamp intensity by pulsing or to inhibit the outputs. Inputs and outputs are entirely compatible for use with TTL logic outputs.

The SN54246/SN74246 and '247 and the SN54LS247/SN74LS247 and 'LS248 compose the 6 and the 9 with tails and were designed to offer the designer a choice between two indicator fonts.

a
f b
g
e c
d

SEGMENT IDENTIFICATION

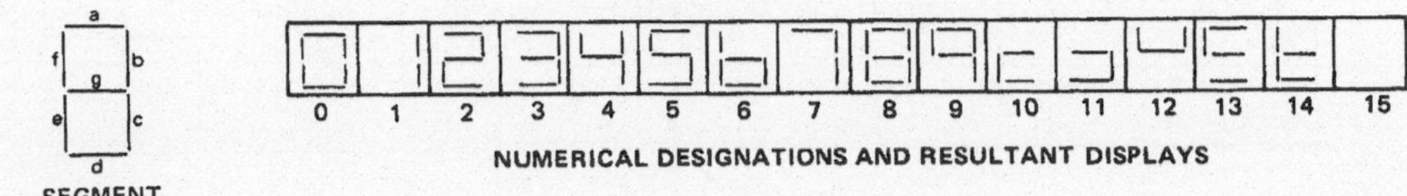

NUMERICAL DESIGNATIONS AND RESULTANT DISPLAYS

'46A, '47A, 'LS47 FUNCTION TABLE (T1)

DECIMAL OR FUNCTION	INPUTS						$\overline{BI}/\overline{RBO}$†	OUTPUTS							NOTE
	$\overline{LT}$	$\overline{RBI}$	D	C	B	A		a	b	c	d	e	f	g	
0	H	H	L	L	L	L	H	ON	ON	ON	ON	ON	ON	OFF	
1	H	X	L	L	L	H	H	OFF	ON	ON	OFF	OFF	OFF	OFF	
2	H	X	L	L	H	L	H	ON	ON	OFF	ON	ON	OFF	ON	
3	H	X	L	L	H	H	H	ON	ON	ON	ON	OFF	OFF	ON	
4	H	X	L	H	L	L	H	OFF	ON	ON	OFF	OFF	ON	ON	
5	H	X	L	H	L	H	H	ON	OFF	ON	ON	OFF	ON	ON	
6	H	X	L	H	H	L	H	OFF	OFF	ON	ON	ON	ON	ON	
7	H	X	L	H	H	H	H	ON	ON	ON	OFF	OFF	OFF	OFF	1
8	H	X	H	L	L	L	H	ON	ON	ON	ON	ON	ON	ON	
9	H	X	H	L	L	H	H	ON	ON	ON	OFF	OFF	ON	ON	
10	H	X	H	L	H	L	H	OFF	OFF	OFF	ON	ON	OFF	ON	
11	H	X	H	L	H	H	H	OFF	OFF	ON	ON	OFF	OFF	ON	
12	H	X	H	H	L	L	H	OFF	ON	OFF	OFF	OFF	ON	ON	
13	H	X	H	H	L	H	H	ON	OFF	OFF	ON	OFF	ON	ON	
14	H	X	H	H	H	L	H	OFF	OFF	OFF	ON	ON	ON	ON	
15	H	X	H	H	H	H	H	OFF	OFF	OFF	OFF	OFF	OFF	OFF	
BI	X	X	X	X	X	X	L	OFF	OFF	OFF	OFF	OFF	OFF	OFF	2
RBI	H	L	L	L	L	L	L	OFF	OFF	OFF	OFF	OFF	OFF	OFF	3
LT	L	X	X	X	X	X	H	ON	ON	ON	ON	ON	ON	ON	4

H = high level, L = low level, X = irrelevant

NOTES:
1. The blanking input ($\overline{BI}$) must be open or held at a high logic level when output functions 0 through 15 are desired. The ripple-blanking input ($\overline{RBI}$) must be open or high if blanking of a decimal zero is not desired.
2. When a low logic level is applied directly to the blanking input ($\overline{BI}$), all segment outputs are off regardless of the level of any other input.
3. When ripple-blanking input ($\overline{RBI}$) and inputs A, B, C, and D are at a low level with the lamp test input high, all segment outputs go off and the ripple-blanking output ($\overline{RBO}$) goes to a low level (response condition).
4. When the blanking input/ripple blanking output ($\overline{BI}/\overline{RBO}$) is open or held high and a low is applied to the lamp-test input, all segment outputs are on.

† $\overline{BI}/\overline{RBO}$ is wire AND logic serving as blanking input ($\overline{BI}$) and/or ripple-blanking output ($\overline{RBO}$).

logic diagrams (positive logic)

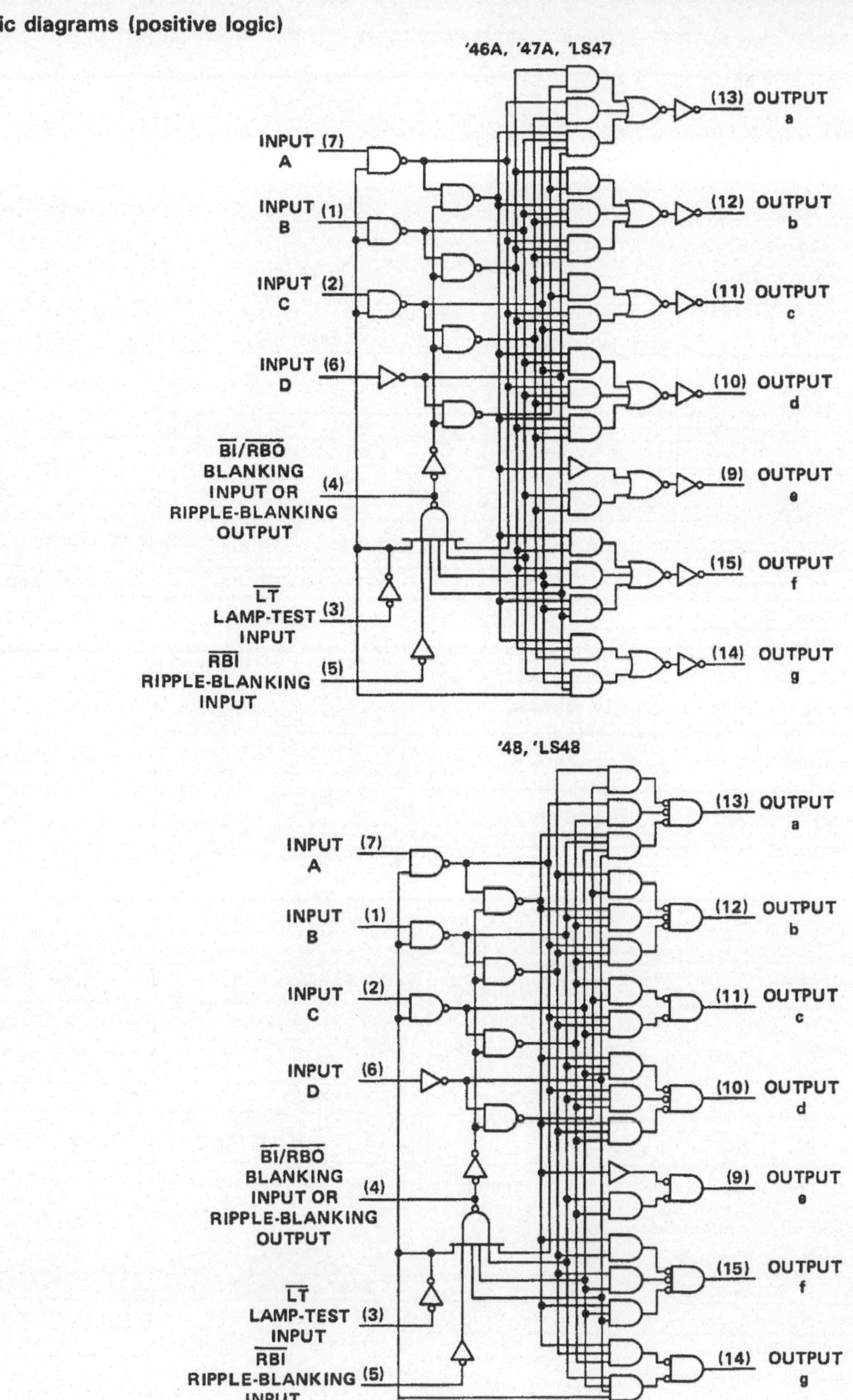

Pin numbers shown are for D, J, N, and W packages.

absolute maximum ratings over operating free-air temperature range (unless otherwise noted)

Supply voltage, V_{CC} (see Note 1) . . . 7 V
Input voltage . . . 5.5 V
Current forced into any output in the off state . . . 1 mA
Operating free-air temperature range: SN5446A, SN5447A . . . –55°C to 125°C
SN7446A, SN7447A . . . 0°C to 70°C
Storage temperature range . . . –65°C to 150°C

NOTE 1: Voltage values are with respect to network ground terminal.

recommended operating conditions

		SN5446A			SN5447A			SN7446A			SN7447A			UNIT
		MIN	NOM	MAX	MIN	NOM	MAX	MIN	NOM	MAX	MIN	NOM	MAX	
Supply voltage, V_{CC}		4.5	5	5.5	4.5	5	5.5	4.75	5	5.25	4.75	5	5.25	V
Off-state output voltage, $V_{O(off)}$	a thru g			30			15			30			15	V
On-state output current, $I_{O(on)}$	a thru g			40			40			40			40	mA
High-level output current, I_{OH}	$\overline{BI}/\overline{RBO}$			–200			–200			–200			–200	μA
Low-level output current, I_{OL}	$\overline{BI}/\overline{RBO}$			8			8			8			8	mA
Operating free-air temperature, T_A		–55		125	–55		125	0		70	0		70	°C

electrical characteristics over recommended operating free-air temperature range (unless otherwise noted)

PARAMETER			TEST CONDITIONS†		MIN	TYP‡	MAX	UNIT
V_{IH}	High-level input voltage				2			V
V_{IL}	Low-level input voltage						0.8	V
V_{IK}	Input clamp voltage		V_{CC} = MIN, I_I = –12 mA				–1.5	V
V_{OH}	High-level output voltage	$\overline{BI}/\overline{RBO}$	V_{CC} = MIN, V_{IH} = 2 V, V_{IL} = 0.8 V, I_{OH} = –200 μA		2.4	3.7		V
V_{OL}	Low-level output voltage	$\overline{BI}/\overline{RBO}$	V_{CC} = MIN, V_{IH} = 2 V, V_{IL} = 0.8 V, I_{OL} = 8 mA			0.27	0.4	V
$I_{O(off)}$	Off-state output current	a thru g	V_{CC} = MAX, V_{IH} = 2 V, V_{IL} = 0.8 V, $V_{O(off)}$ = MAX				250	μA
$V_{O(on)}$	On-state output voltage	a thru g	V_{CC} = MIN, V_{IH} = 2 V, V_{IL} = 0.8 V, $I_{O(on)}$ = 40 mA			0.3	0.4	V
I_I	Input current at maximum input voltage	Any input except $\overline{BI}/\overline{RBO}$	V_{CC} = MAX, V_I = 5.5 V				1	mA
I_{IH}	High-level input current	Any input except $\overline{BI}/\overline{RBO}$	V_{CC} = MAX, V_I = 2.4 V				40	μA
I_{IL}	Low-level input current	Any input except $\overline{BI}/\overline{RBO}$	V_{CC} = MAX, V_I = 0.4 V				–1.6	mA
		$\overline{BI}/\overline{RBO}$					–4	
I_{OS}	Short-circuit output current	$\overline{BI}/\overline{RBO}$	V_{CC} = MAX				–4	mA
I_{CC}	Supply current		V_{CC} = MAX, See Note 2	SN54'		64	85	mA
				SN74'		64	103	

†For conditions shown as MIN or MAX, use the appropriate value specified under recommended operating conditions.
‡All typical values are at V_{CC} = 5 V, T_A = 25°C.
NOTE 2: I_{CC} is measured with all outputs open and all inputs at 4.5 V.

switching characteristics, V_{CC} = 5 V, T_A = 25°C

PARAMETER		TEST CONDITIONS	MIN	TYP	MAX	UNIT
t_{off}	Turn-off time from A input	C_L = 15 pF, R_L = 120 Ω, See Note 3			100	ns
t_{on}	Turn-on time from A input				100	
t_{off}	Turn-off time from $\overline{RBI}$ input				100	ns
t_{on}	Turn-on time from $\overline{RBI}$ input				100	

NOTE 3: Load circuits and voltage waveforms are shown in Section 1.

absolute maximum ratings over operating free-air temperature range (unless otherwise noted)

Supply voltage, V_{CC} (see Note 1) . . . . 7 V
Input voltage . . . . 7 V
Peak output current ($t_w \leqslant 1$ ms, duty cycle $\leqslant$ 10%) . . . . 200 mA
Current forced into any output in the off state . . . . 1 mA
Operating free-air temperature range: SN54LS47 . . . . –55°C to 125°C
SN74LS47 . . . . 0°C to 70°C
Storage temperature range . . . . –65°C to 150°C

NOTE 1: Voltage values are with respect to network ground terminal.

recommended operating conditions

		SN54LS47			SN74LS47			UNIT
		MIN	NOM	MAX	MIN	NOM	MAX	
Supply voltage, V_{CC}		4.5	5	5.5	4.75	5	5.25	V
Off-state output voltage, $V_{O(off)}$	a thru g			15			15	V
On-state output current, $I_{O(on)}$	a thru g			12			24	mA
High-level output current, I_{OH}	$\overline{BI}/\overline{RBO}$			–50			–50	μA
Low-level output current, I_{OL}	$\overline{BI}/\overline{RBO}$			1.6			3.2	mA
Operating free-air temperature, T_A		–55		125	0		70	°C

electrical characteristics over recommended operating free-air temperature range (unless otherwise noted)

PARAMETER			TEST CONDITIONS†		SN54LS47			SN74LS47			UNIT
					MIN	TYP‡	MAX	MIN	TYP‡	MAX	
V_{IH}	High-level input voltage				2			2			V
V_{IL}	Low-level input voltage						0.7			0.8	V
V_{IK}	Input clamp voltage		V_{CC} = MIN,	I_I = –18 mA			–1.5			–1.5	V
V_{OH}	High-level output voltage	$\overline{BI}/\overline{RBO}$	V_{CC} = MIN, V_{IL} = V_{IL} max,	V_{IH} = 2 V, I_{OH} = –50 μA	2.4	4.2		2.4	4.2		V
V_{OL}	Low-level output voltage	$\overline{BI}/\overline{RBO}$	V_{CC} = MIN, V_{IH} = 2 V, V_{IL} = V_{IL} max	I_{OL} = 1.6 mA		0.25	0.4		0.25	0.4	V
				I_{OL} = 3.2 mA					0.35	0.5	
$I_{O(off)}$	Off-state output current	a thru g	V_{CC} = MAX, V_{IL} = V_{IL} max,	V_{IH} = 2 V, $V_{O(off)}$ = 15 V			250			250	μA
$V_{O(on)}$	On-state output voltage	a thru g	V_{CC} = MIN, V_{IH} = 2 V, V_{IL} = V_{IL} max	$I_{O(on)}$ = 12 mA		0.25	0.4		0.25	0.4	V
				$I_{O(on)}$ = 24 mA					0.35	0.5	
I_I	Input current at maximum input voltage		V_{CC} = MAX,	V_I = 7 V			0.1			0.1	mA
I_{IH}	High-level input current		V_{CC} = MAX,	V_I = 2.7 V			20			20	μA
I_{IL}	Low-level input current	Any input except $\overline{BI}/\overline{RBO}$	V_{CC} = MAX,	V_I = 0.4 V			–0.4			–0.4	mA
		$\overline{BI}/\overline{RBO}$					–1.2			–1.2	
I_{OS}	Short-circuit output current	$\overline{BI}/\overline{RBO}$	V_{CC} = MAX		–0.3		–2	–0.3		–2	mA
I_{CC}	Supply current		V_{CC} = MAX,	See Note 2		7	13		7	13	mA

†For conditions shown as MIN or MAX, use the appropriate value specified under recommended operating conditions.
‡All typical values are at V_{CC} = 5 V, T_A = 25°C.
NOTE 2: I_{CC} is measured with all outputs open and all inputs at 4.5 V.

switching characteristics, V_{CC} = 5 V, T_A = 25°C

PARAMETER		TEST CONDITIONS	MIN	TYP	MAX	UNIT
t_{off}	Turn-off time from A input	C_L = 15 pF, R_L = 665 Ω, See Note 3			100	ns
t_{on}	Turn-on time from A input				100	
t_{off}	Turn-off time from $\overline{RBI}$ input, outputs (a-f) only				100	ns
t_{on}	Turn-on time from $\overline{RBI}$ input, outputs (a-f) only				100	

NOTE 3: Load circuits and voltage waveforms are shown in Section 1.

August 1986
Revised March 2000

DM74LS86
Quad 2-Input Exclusive-OR Gate

General Description

This device contains four independent gates each of which performs the logic exclusive-OR function.

Ordering Code:

Order Number	Package Number	Package Description
DM74LS86M	M14A	14-Lead Small Outline Integrated Circuit (SOIC), JEDEC MS-120, 0.150 Narrow
DM74LS86SJ	M14D	14-Lead Small Outline Package (SOP), EIAJ TYPE II, 5.3mm Wide
DM74LS86N	N14A	14-Lead Plastic Dual-In-Line Package (PDIP), JEDEC MS-001, 0.300 Wide

Devices also available in Tape and Reel. Specify by appending the suffix letter "X" to the ordering code.

Connection Diagram

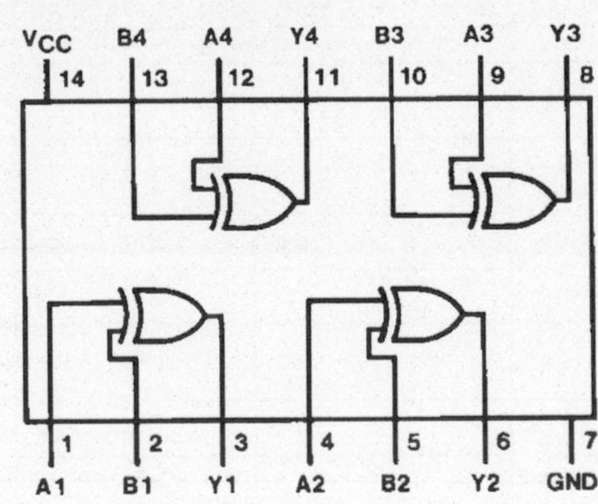

Function Table

$$Y = A \oplus B = \overline{A}\,B + A\overline{B}$$

Inputs		Output
A	B	Y
L	L	L
L	H	H
H	L	H
H	H	L

H = HIGH Logic Level
L = LOW Logic Level

Absolute Maximum Ratings(Note 1)

Supply Voltage	7V
Input Voltage	7V
Operating Free Air Temperature Range	0°C to +70°C
Storage Temperature Range	−65°C to +150°C

Note 1: The "Absolute Maximum Ratings" are those values beyond which the safety of the device cannot be guaranteed. The device should not be operated at these limits. The parametric values defined in the Electrical Characteristics tables are not guaranteed at the absolute maximum ratings. The "Recommended Operating Conditions" table will define the conditions for actual device operation.

Recommended Operating Conditions

Symbol	Parameter	Min	Nom	Max	Units
V_{CC}	Supply Voltage	4.75	5	5.25	V
V_{IH}	HIGH Level Input Voltage	2			V
V_{IL}	LOW Level Input Voltage			0.8	V
I_{OH}	HIGH Level Output Current			−0.4	mA
I_{OL}	LOW Level Output Current			8	mA
T_A	Free Air Operating Temperature	0		70	°C

Electrical Characteristics

over recommended operating free air temperature range (unless otherwise noted)

Symbol	Parameter	Conditions	Min	Typ (Note 2)	Max	Units
V_I	Input Clamp Voltage	V_{CC} = Min, I_I = −18 mA			−1.5	V
V_{OH}	HIGH Level Output Voltage	V_{CC} = Min, I_{OH} = Max, V_{IL} = Max, V_{IH} = Min	2.7	3.4		V
V_{OL}	LOW Level Output Voltage	V_{CC} = Min, I_{OL} = Max, V_{IL} = Max, V_{IH} = Min		0.35	0.5	V
		I_{OL} = 4 mA, V_{CC} = Min		0.25	0.4	
I_I	Input Current @ Max Input Voltage	V_{CC} = Max, V_I = 7V			0.2	mA
I_{IH}	HIGH Level Input Current	V_{CC} = Max, V_I = 2.7V			40	μA
I_{IL}	LOW Level Input Current	V_{CC} = Max, V_I = 0.4V			−0.6	mA
I_{OS}	Short Circuit Output Current	V_{CC} = Max (Note 3)	−20		−100	mA
I_{CCH}	Supply Current with Outputs HIGH	V_{CC} = Max (Note 4)		6.1	10	mA
I_{CCL}	Supply Current with Outputs LOW	V_{CC} = Max (Note 5)		9	15	mA

Note 2: All typicals are at V_{CC} = 5V, T_A = 25°C.

Note 3: Not more than one output should be shorted at a time, and the duration should not exceed one second.

Note 4: I_{CCH} is measured with all outputs OPEN, one input at each gate at 4.5V, and the other inputs grounded.

Note 5: I_{CCL} is measured with all outputs OPEN and all inputs grounded.

Switching Characteristics

at V_{CC} = 5V and T_A = 25°C

Symbol	Parameter	Conditions	R_L = 2 kΩ				Units
			C_L = 15 pF		C_L = 50 pF		
			Min	Max	Min	Max	
t_{PLH}	Propagation Delay Time LOW-to-HIGH Level Output	Other Input Low		18		23	ns
t_{PHL}	Propagation Delay Time HIGH-to-LOW Level Output			17		21	ns
t_{PLH}	Propagation Delay Time LOW-to-HIGH Level Output	Other Input High		10		15	ns
t_{PHL}	Propagation Delay Time HIGH-to-LOW Level Output			12		15	ns

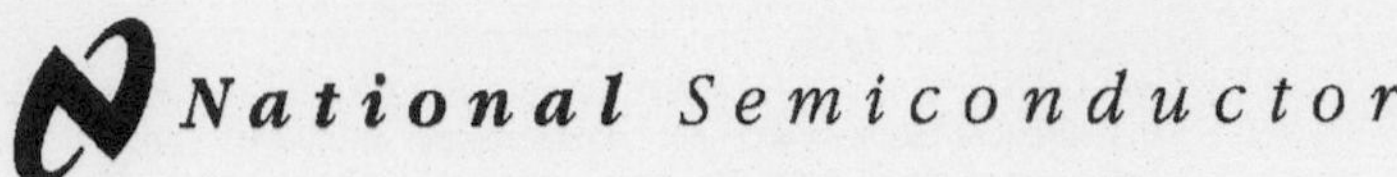

54153/DM54153/DM74153 Dual 4-Line to 1-Line Data Selectors/Multiplexers

General Description

Each of these data selectors/multiplexers contains inverters and drivers to supply fully complementary, on-chip, binary decoding data selection to the AND-OR-invert gates. Separate strobe inputs are provided for each of the two four-line sections.

Features

- Permits multiplexing from N lines to 1 line
- Performs parallel-to-serial conversion
- Strobe (enable) line provided for cascading (N lines to n lines)
- High fan-out, low-impedance, totem-pole outputs
- Typical average propagation delay times

  From data 11 ns
  From strobe 18 ns
  From select 20 ns
- Typical power dissipation 170 mW
- Alternate Military/Aerospace device (54153) is available. Contact a National Semiconductor Sales Office/Distributor for specifications.

Connection Diagram

Dual-In-Line Package

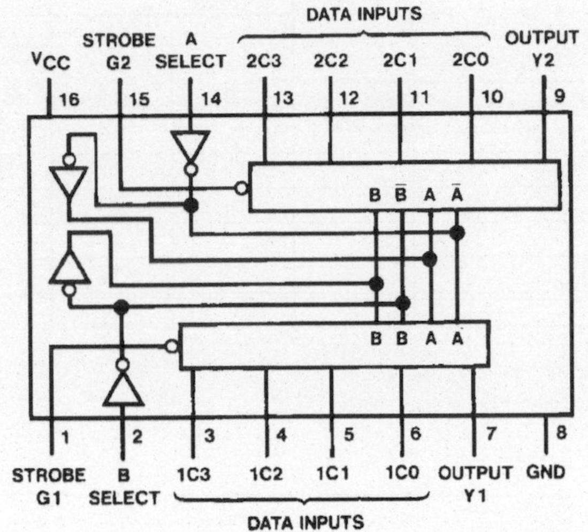

TL/F/6547–1

Order Number 54153DMQB, 54153FMQB, DM54153J, DM54153W or DM74153N
See NS Package Number J16A, N16E or W16A

Function Table

Select Inputs		Data Inputs				Strobe	Output
B	A	C0	C1	C2	C3	G	Y
X	X	X	X	X	X	H	L
L	L	L	X	X	X	L	L
L	L	H	X	X	X	L	H
L	H	X	L	X	X	L	L
L	H	X	H	X	X	L	H
H	L	X	X	L	X	L	L
H	L	X	X	H	X	L	H
H	H	X	X	X	L	L	L
H	H	X	X	X	H	L	H

Select inputs A and B are common to both sections.

H = High Level, L = Low Level, X = Don't Care

RRD-B30M105/Printed in U. S. A.

June 1989

Absolute Maximum Ratings (Note)

If Military/Aerospace specified devices are required, please contact the National Semiconductor Sales Office/Distributors for availability and specifications.

Supply Voltage	7V
Input Voltage	5.5V
Operating Free Air Temperature Range	
DM54 and 54	−55°C to +125°C
DM74	0°C to +70°C
Storage Temperature Range	−65°C to +150°C

Note: *The "Absolute Maximum Ratings" are those values beyond which the safety of the device cannot be guaranteed. The device should not be operated at these limits. The parametric values defined in the "Electrical Characteristics" table are not guaranteed at the absolute maximum ratings. The "Recommended Operating Conditions" table will define the conditions for actual device operation.*

Recommended Operating Conditions

Symbol	Parameter	DM54153			DM74153			Units
		Min	Nom	Max	Min	Nom	Max	
V_{CC}	Supply Voltage	4.5	5	5.5	4.75	5	5.25	V
V_{IH}	High Level Input Voltage	2			2			V
V_{IL}	Low Level Input Voltage			0.8			0.8	V
I_{OH}	High Level Output Current			−0.8			−0.8	mA
I_{OL}	Low Level Output Current			16			16	mA
T_A	Free Air Operating Temperature	−55		125	0		70	°C

Electrical Characteristics over recommended operating free air temperature range (unless otherwise noted)

Symbol	Parameter	Conditions		Min	Typ (Note 1)	Max	Units
V_I	Input Clamp Voltage	V_{CC} = Min, I_I = −12 mA				−1.5	V
V_{OH}	High Level Output Voltage	V_{CC} = Min, I_{OH} = Max V_{IL} = Max, V_{IH} = Min		2.4	3.2		V
V_{OL}	Low Level Output Voltage	V_{CC} = Min, I_{OL} = Max V_{IH} = Min, V_{IL} = Max			0.2	0.4	V
I_I	Input Current @ Max Input Voltage	V_{CC} = Max, V_I = 5.5V				1	mA
I_{IH}	High Level Input Current	V_{CC} = Max, V_I = 2.4V				40	μA
I_{IL}	Low Level Input Current	V_{CC} = Max, V_I = 0.4V				−1.6	mA
I_{OS}	Short Circuit Output Current	V_{CC} = Max (Note 2)	DM54	−20		−55	mA
			DM74	−18		−57	
I_{CC}	Supply Current	V_{CC} = Max (Note 3)	DM54		34	52	mA
			DM74		34	60	

Note 1: All typicals are at V_{CC} = 5V, T_A = 25°C.

Note 2: Not more than one output should be shorted at a time.

Note 3: I_{CC} is measured with the outputs open and all inputs grounded.

Switching Characteristics at V_{CC} = 5V and T_A = 25°C (See Section 1 for Test Waveforms and Output Load)

Symbol	Parameter	From (Input) To (Output)	R_L = 400Ω, C_L = 30 pF		Units
			Min	Max	
t_{PLH}	Propagation Delay Time Low to High Level Output	Data to Y		18	ns
t_{PHL}	Propagation Delay Time High to Low Level Output	Data to Y		23	ns
t_{PLH}	Propagation Delay Time Low to High Level Output	Select to Y		34	ns
t_{PHL}	Propagation Delay Time High to Low Level Output	Select to Y		34	ns
t_{PLH}	Propagation Delay Time Low to High Level Output	Strobe to Y		30	ns
t_{PHL}	Propagation Delay Time High to Low Level Output	Strobe to Y		23	ns

Logic Diagram

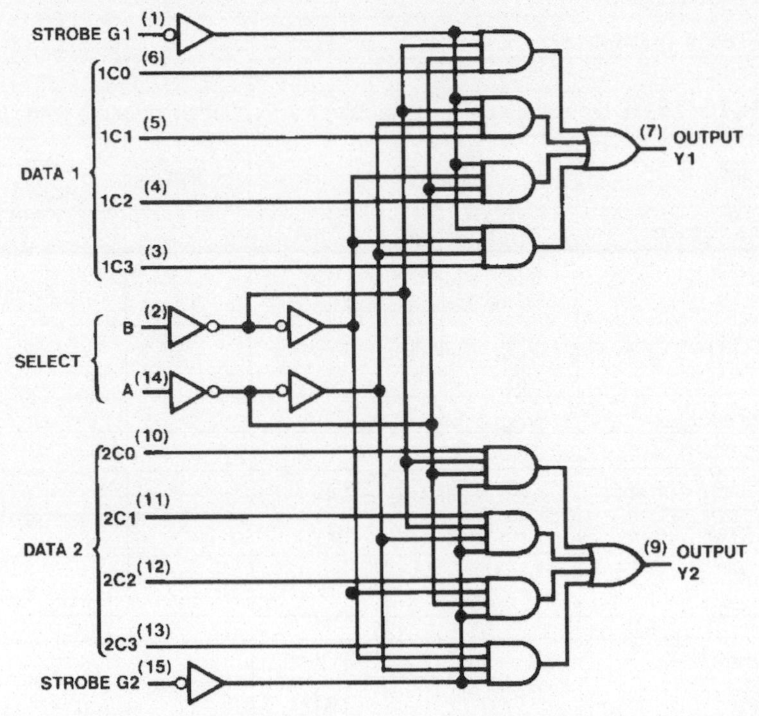

TL/F/6547–2

Physical Dimensions inches (millimeters)

June 1989

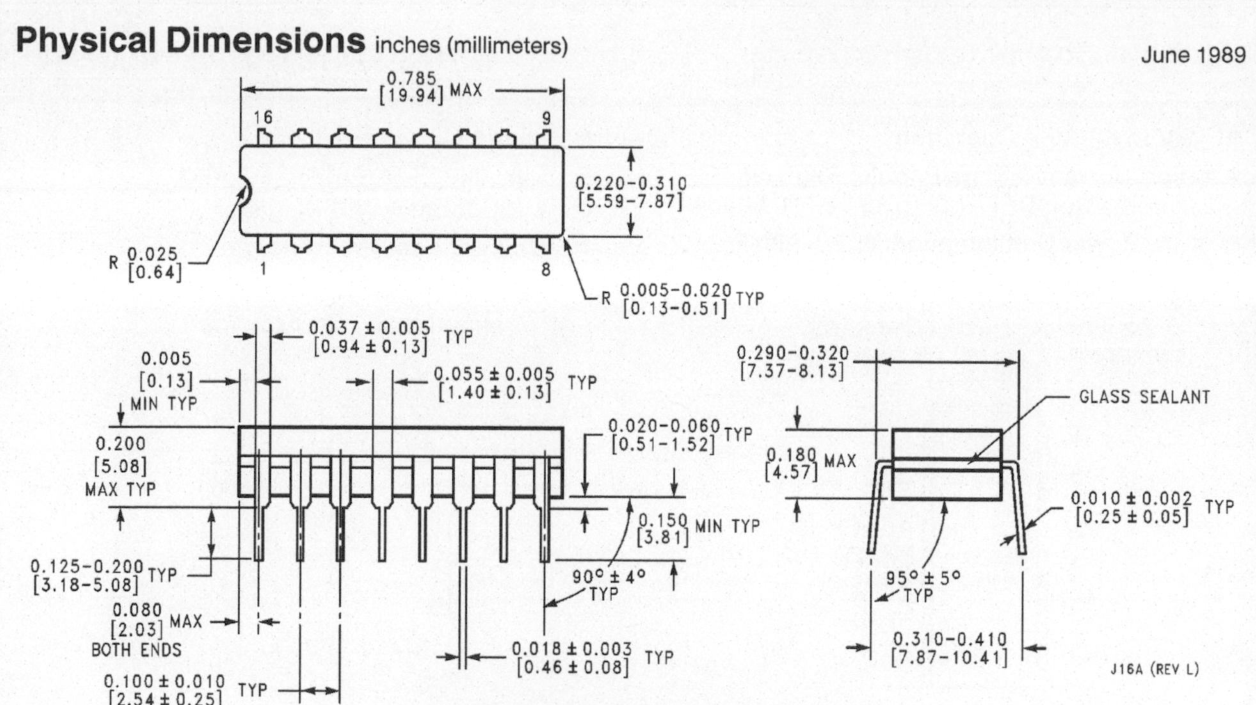

16-Lead Ceramic Dual-In-Line Package (J)
Order Number 54153DMQB or DM54153J
NS Package Number J16A

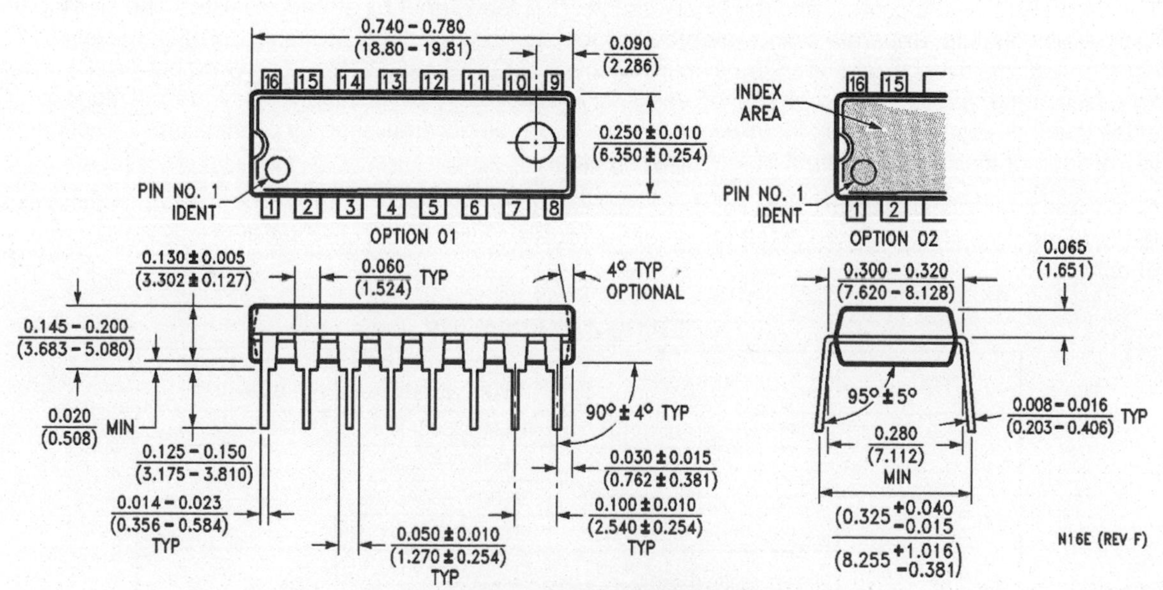

16-Lead Molded Dual-In-Line Package (N)
Order Number DM74153N
NS Package Number N16E

- **2-V to 6-V V_{CC} Operation**
- **High-Current 3-State Parallel Register Outputs Can Drive Up To 15 LSTTL Loads**
- **Low Power Consumption, 80-µA Max I_{CC}**
- **Typical t_{pd} = 14 ns**
- **±6-mA Output Drive at 5 V**
- **Low Input Current of 1 µA Max**
- **8-Bit Counter With Register**
- **Counter Has Direct Clear**

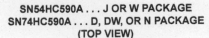

SN54HC590A . . . J OR W PACKAGE
SN74HC590A . . . D, DW, OR N PACKAGE
(TOP VIEW)

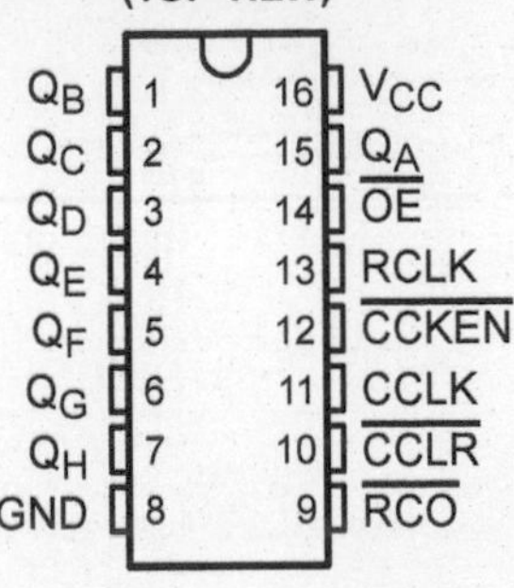

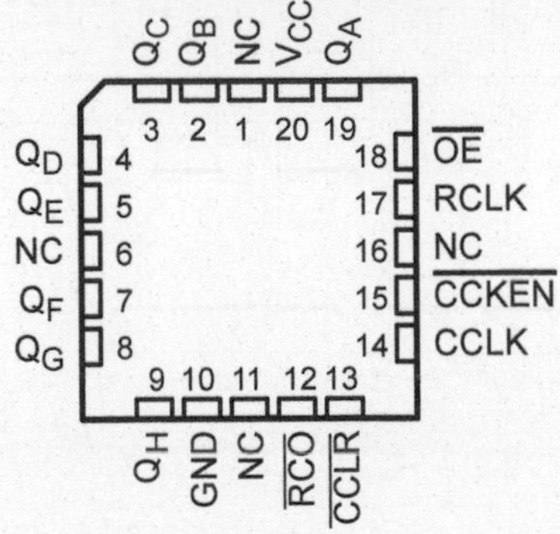

NC – No internal connection

description/ordering information

The ’HC590A devices contain an 8-bit binary counter that feeds an 8-bit storage register. The storage register has parallel outputs. Separate clocks are provided for both the binary counter and storage register. The binary counter features direct clear ($\overline{CCLR}$) and count-enable ($\overline{CCKEN}$) inputs. A ripple-carry output ($\overline{RCO}$) is provided for cascading. Expansion is accomplished easily for two stages by connecting $\overline{RCO}$ of the first stage to $\overline{CCKEN}$ of the second stage. Cascading for larger count chains can be accomplished by connecting $\overline{RCO}$ of each stage to the counter clock (CCLK) input of the following stage.

CCLK and the register clock (RCLK) inputs are positive-edge triggered. If both clocks are connected together, the counter state always is one count ahead of the register. Internal circuitry prevents clocking from the clock enable.

ORDERING INFORMATION

T_A	PACKAGE†		ORDERABLE PART NUMBER	TOP-SIDE MARKING
−40°C to 85°C	PDIP – N	Tube of 25	SN74HC590AN	SN74HC590AN
	SOIC – D	Tube of 40	SN74HC590AD	HC590A
		Reel of 2500	SN74HC590ADR	
		Reel of 250	SN74HC590ADT	
	SOIC – DW	Tube of 40	SN74HC590ADW	HC590A
		Reel of 2000	SN74HC590ADWR	
−55°C to 125°C	CDIP – J	Tube of 25	SNJ54HC590AJ	SNJ54HC590AJ
	CFP – W	Tube of 150	SNJ54HC590AW	SNJ54HC590AW
	LCCC - FK	Tube of 55	SNJ54HC590AFK	SNJ54HC590AFK

† Package drawings, standard packing quantities, thermal data, symbolization, and PCB design guidelines are available at www.ti.com/sc/package.

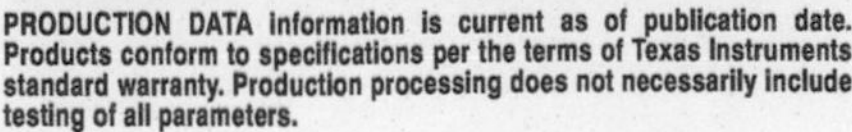

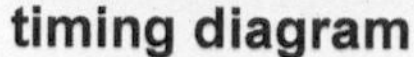

timing diagram

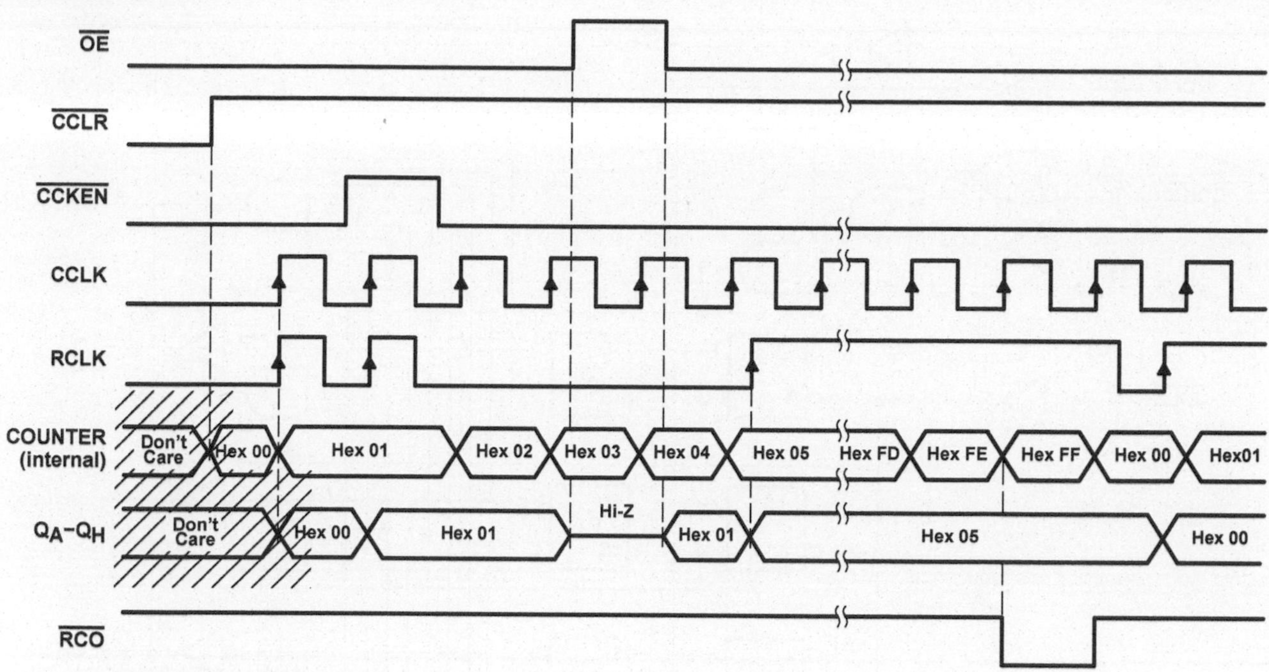

TIMING SEQUENCE

1. Clear Counter (asynchronous).
2. Count up: 0x01. Store 0x00 in register.
3. Inhibit counter clock ($\overline{CCKEN}$ = HIGH). Store 0x01 in register.
4. Count 0x02, 0x03.
5. 3-state the outputs
6. Count up: 0x04
7. Enable outputs.
8. Continue up: 0x05
9. Store 0x05 in register.
10. Continue counting: 0x06...0xFD, 0xFE, 0xFF, 0x00, etc.
11. Store 0x00 in register.

logic diagram (positive logic)

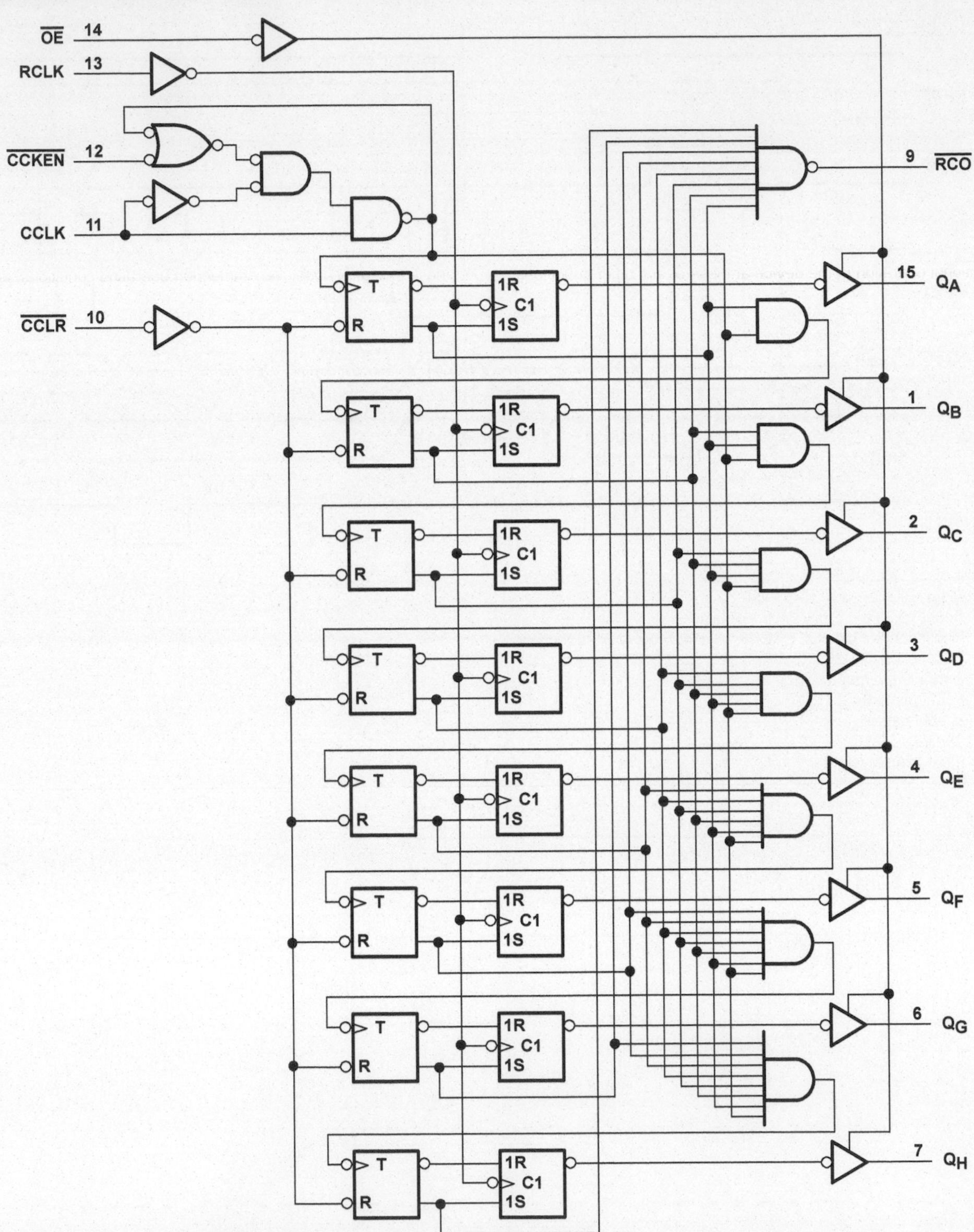

Pin numbers shown are for the D, DW, J, N, and W packages.

absolute maximum ratings over operating free-air temperature range (unless otherwise noted)†

Supply voltage range, V_{CC} .... −0.5 V to 7 V
Input clamp current, I_{IK} ($V_I < 0$ or $V_I > V_{CC}$) (see Note 1) .... ±20 mA
Output clamp current, I_{OK} ($V_O < 0$ or $V_O > V_{CC}$) (see Note 1) .... ±20 mA
Continuous output current, I_O ($V_O = 0$ to V_{CC}) .... ±35 mA
Continuous current through V_{CC} or GND .... ±70 mA
Package thermal impedance, θ_{JA} (see Note 2): D package .... 73°C/W
DW package .... 57°C/W
N package .... 67°C/W
Storage temperature range, T_{stg} .... −65°C to 150°C

† Stresses beyond those listed under "absolute maximum ratings" may cause permanent damage to the device. These are stress ratings only, and functional operation of the device at these or any other conditions beyond those indicated under "recommended operating conditions" is not implied. Exposure to absolute-maximum-rated conditions for extended periods may affect device reliability.

NOTES: 1. The input and output voltage ratings may be exceeded if the input and output current ratings are observed.
2. The package thermal impedance is calculated in accordance with JESD 51-7.

recommended operating conditions (see Note 3)

			SN54HC590A			SN74HC590A			UNIT
			MIN	NOM	MAX	MIN	NOM	MAX	
V_{CC}	Supply voltage		2	5	6	2	5	6	V
V_{IH}	High-level input voltage	V_{CC} = 2 V	1.5			1.5			V
		V_{CC} = 4.5 V	3.15			3.15			
		V_{CC} = 6 V	4.2			4.2			
V_{IL}	Low-level input voltage	V_{CC} = 2 V			0.5			0.5	V
		V_{CC} = 4.5 V			1.35			1.35	
		V_{CC} = 6 V			1.8			1.8	
V_I	Input voltage		0		V_{CC}	0		V_{CC}	V
V_O	Output voltage		0		V_{CC}	0		V_{CC}	V
t_t‡	Input transition (rise and fall) time	V_{CC} = 2 V			1000			1000	ns
		V_{CC} = 4.5 V			500			500	
		V_{CC} = 6 V			400			400	
T_A	Operating free-air temperature		−55		125	−40		85	°C

‡ If this device is used in the threshold region (from $V_{IL}max = 0.5$ V to $V_{IH}min = 1.5$ V), there is a potential to go into the wrong state from induced grounding, causing double clocking. Operating with the inputs at $t_t = 1000$ ns and $V_{CC} = 2$ V does not damage the device; however, functionally, the CCLK and RCLK inputs are not ensured while in the shift, count, or toggle operating modes.

NOTE 3: All unused inputs of the device must be held at V_{CC} or GND to ensure proper device operation. Refer to the TI application report, *Implications of Slow or Floating CMOS Inputs*, literature number SCBA004.

electrical characteristics over recommended operating free-air temperature range (unless otherwise noted)

PARAMETER	TEST CONDITIONS		V_{CC}	T_A = 25°C			SN54HC590A		SN74HC590A		UNIT
				MIN	TYP	MAX	MIN	MAX	MIN	MAX	
V_{OH}	$V_I = V_{IH}$ or V_{IL}	I_{OH} = −20 µA	2 V	1.9	1.998		1.9		1.9		V
			4.5 V	4.4	4.499		4.4		4.4		
			6 V	5.9	5.999		5.9		5.9		
		$\overline{RCO}$, I_{OH} = −4 mA	4.5 V	3.98	4.3		3.7		3.84		
		Q_A–Q_H, I_{OH} = −6 mA		3.98	4.3		3.7		3.84		
		$\overline{RCO}$, I_{OH} = −5.2 mA	6 V	5.48	5.8		5.2		5.34		
		Q_A–Q_H, I_{OH} = −7.8 mA		5.48	5.8		5.2		5.34		
V_{OL}	$V_I = V_{IH}$ or V_{IL}	I_{OL} = 20 µA	2 V		0.002	0.1		0.1		0.1	V
			4.5 V		0.001	0.1		0.1		0.1	
			6 V		0.001	0.1		0.1		0.1	
		$\overline{RCO}$, I_{OL} = 4 mA	4.5 V		0.17	0.26		0.4		0.33	
		Q_A–Q_H, I_{OL} = 6 mA			0.17	0.26		0.4		0.33	
		$\overline{RCO}$, I_{OL} = 5.2 mA	6 V		0.15	0.26		0.4		0.33	
		Q_A–Q_H, I_{OL} = 7.8 mA			0.15	0.26		0.4		0.33	
I_I	$V_I = V_{CC}$ or 0		6 V		±0.1	±100		±1000		±1000	nA
I_{OZ}	$V_O = V_{CC}$ or 0		6 V		±0.01	±0.5		±10		±5	µA
I_{CC}	$V_I = V_{CC}$ or 0,	I_O = 0	6 V			8		160		80	µA
C_i			2 V to 6 V		3	10		10		10	pF

PARAMETER MEASUREMENT INFORMATION

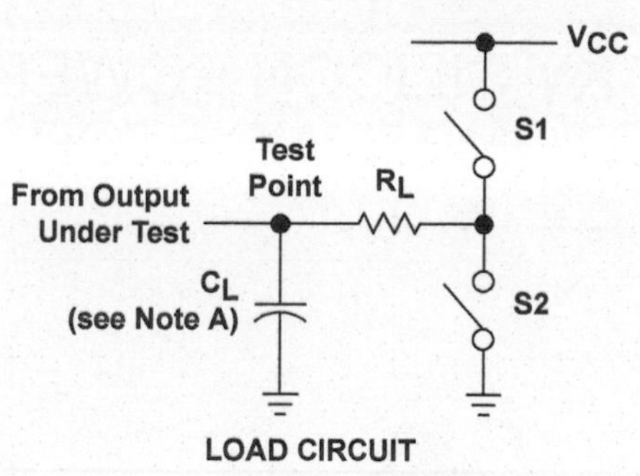

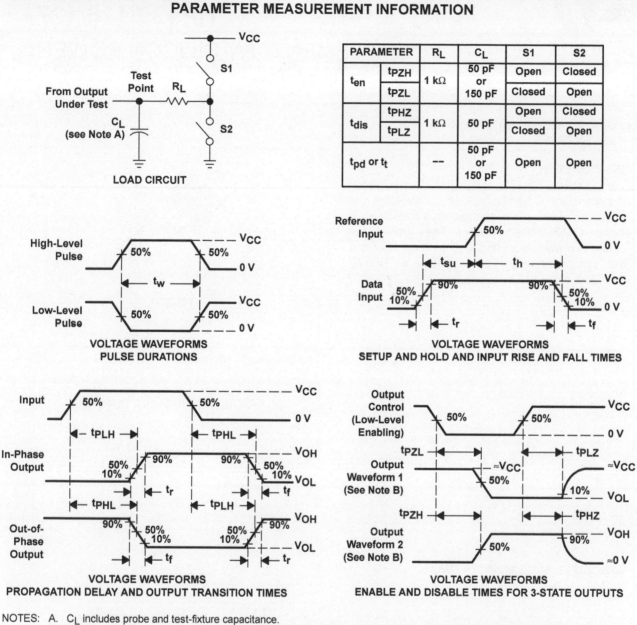

PARAMETER		R_L	C_L	S1	S2
t_{en}	t_{PZH}	1 kΩ	50 pF or 150 pF	Open	Closed
	t_{PZL}			Closed	Open
t_{dis}	t_{PHZ}	1 kΩ	50 pF	Open	Closed
	t_{PLZ}			Closed	Open
t_{pd} or t_t		--	50 pF or 150 pF	Open	Open

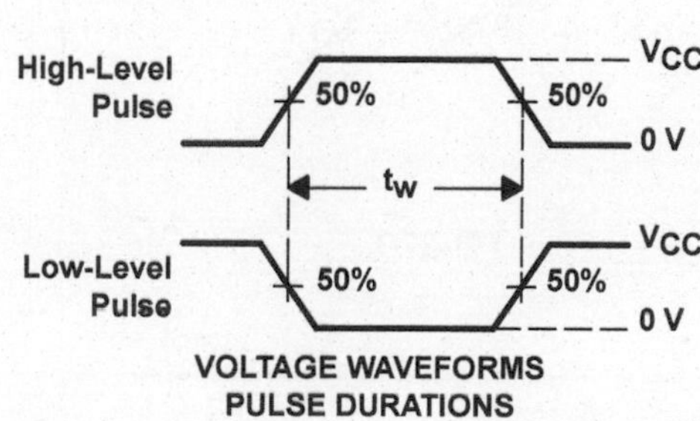

VOLTAGE WAVEFORMS
PULSE DURATIONS

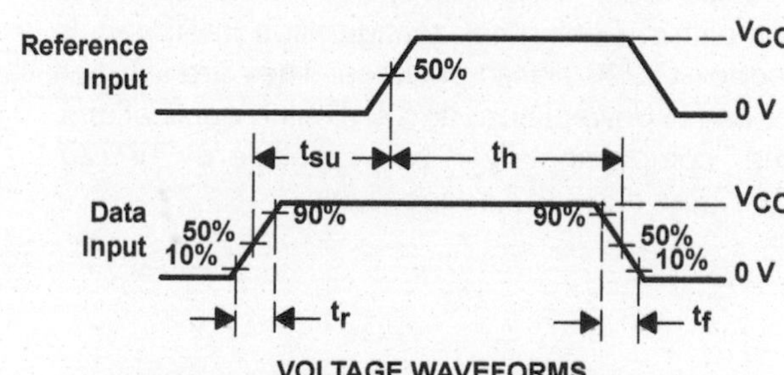

VOLTAGE WAVEFORMS
SETUP AND HOLD AND INPUT RISE AND FALL TIMES

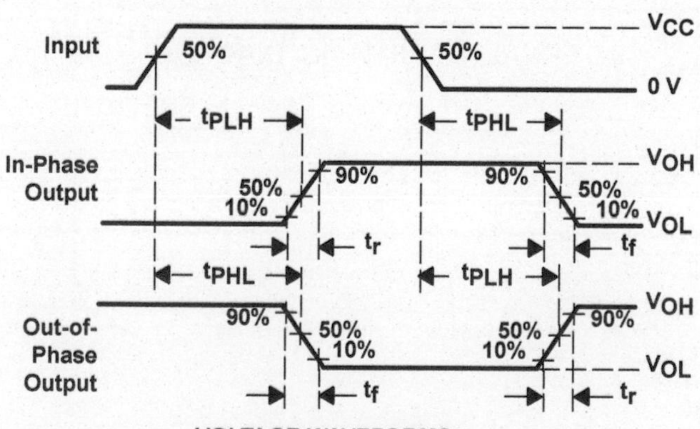

VOLTAGE WAVEFORMS
PROPAGATION DELAY AND OUTPUT TRANSITION TIMES

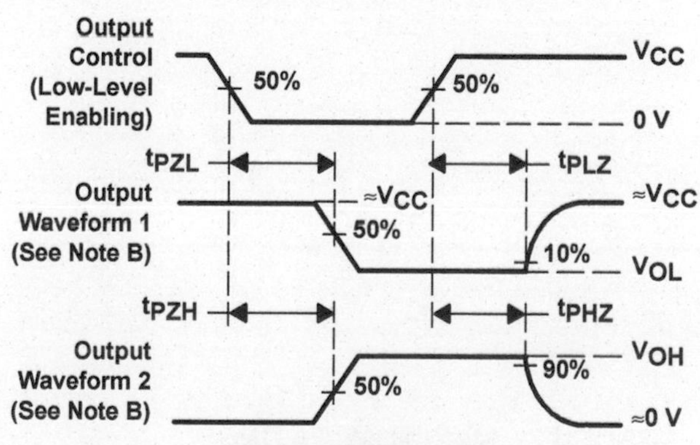

VOLTAGE WAVEFORMS
ENABLE AND DISABLE TIMES FOR 3-STATE OUTPUTS

NOTES: A. C_L includes probe and test-fixture capacitance.
B. Waveform 1 is for an output with internal conditions such that the output is low except when disabled by the output control. Waveform 2 is for an output with internal conditions such that the output is high except when disabled by the output control.
C. Phase relationships between waveforms were chosen arbitrarily. All input pulses are supplied by generators having the following characteristics: PRR ≤ 1 MHz, Z_O = 50 Ω, t_r = 6 ns, t_f = 6 ns.
D. The outputs are measured one at a time with one input transition per measurement.
E. t_{PLZ} and t_{PHZ} are the same as t_{dis}.
F. t_{PZL} and t_{PZH} are the same as t_{en}.
G. t_{PLH} and t_{PHL} are the same as t_{pd}.

Figure 1. Load Circuit and Voltage Waveforms

TIP120/121/122
TIP125/126/127

COMPLEMENTARY SILICON POWER DARLINGTON TRANSISTORS

- STMicroelectronics PREFERRED SALESTYPES

DESCRIPTION

The TIP120, TIP121 and TIP122 are silicon Epitaxial-Base NPN power transistors in monolithic Darlington configuration mounted in Jedec TO-220 plastic package. They are intented for use in power linear and switching applications. The complementary PNP types are TIP125, TIP126 and TIP127, respectively.

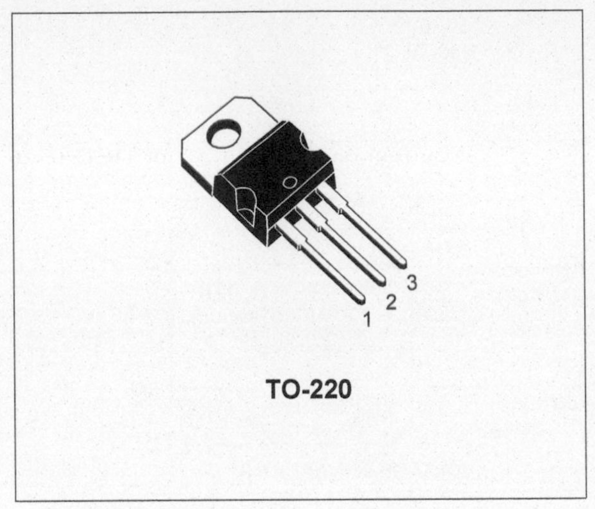

TO-220

INTERNAL SCHEMATIC DIAGRAM

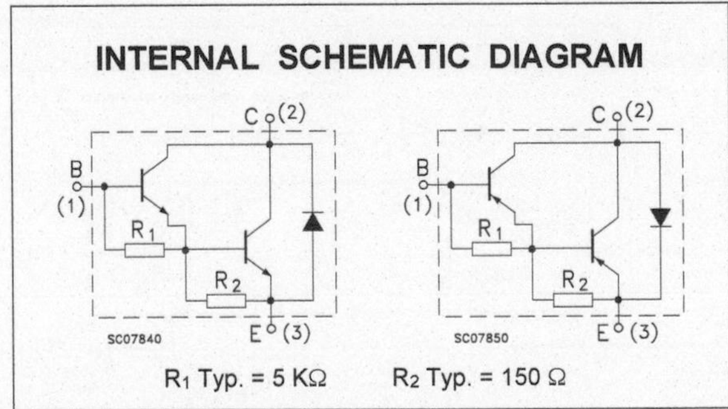

R_1 Typ. = 5 KΩ R_2 Typ. = 150 Ω

ABSOLUTE MAXIMUM RATINGS

Symbol	Parameter		Value			Unit
		NPN	TIP120	TIP121	TIP122	
		PNP	TIP125	TIP126	TIP127	
V_{CBO}	Collector-Base Voltage (I_E = 0)		60	80	100	V
V_{CEO}	Collector-Emitter Voltage (I_B = 0)		60	80	100	V
V_{EBO}	Emitter-Base Voltage (I_C = 0)		5			V
I_C	Collector Current		5			A
I_{CM}	Collector Peak Current		8			A
I_B	Base Current		0.1			A
P_{tot}	Total Dissipation at $T_{case} \leq 25\ ^oC$ $T_{amb} \leq 25\ ^oC$		65 2			W W
T_{stg}	Storage Temperature		-65 to 150			^oC
T_j	Max. Operating Junction Temperature		150			^oC

* For PNP types voltage and current values are negative.

THERMAL DATA

$R_{thj-case}$	Thermal Resistance Junction-case	Max	1.92	°C/W
$R_{thj-amb}$	Thermal Resistance Junction-ambient	Max	62.5	°C/W

ELECTRICAL CHARACTERISTICS (T_{case} = 25 °C unless otherwise specified)

Symbol	Parameter	Test Conditions		Min.	Typ.	Max.	Unit
I_{CEO}	Collector Cut-off Current (I_B = 0)	for **TIP120/125** for **TIP121/126** for **TIP122/127**	V_{CE} = 30 V V_{CE} = 40 V V_{CE} = 50 V			0.5 0.5 0.5	mA mA mA
I_{CBO}	Collector Cut-off Current (I_B = 0)	for **TIP120/125** for **TIP121/126** for **TIP122/127**	V_{CB} = 60 V V_{CB} = 80 V V_{CB} = 100 V			0.2 0.2 0.2	mA mA mA
I_{EBO}	Emitter Cut-off Current (I_C = 0)	V_{EB} = 5 V				2	mA
$V_{CEO(sus)}$*	Collector-Emitter Sustaining Voltage (I_B = 0)	I_C = 30 mA for **TIP120/125** for **TIP121/126** for **TIP122/127**		 60 80 100			 V V V
$V_{CE(sat)}$*	Collector-Emitter Saturation Voltage	I_C = 3 A I_C = 5 A	I_B = 12 mA I_B = 20 mA			2 4	V V
$V_{BE(on)}$*	Base-Emitter Voltage	I_C = 3 A	V_{CE} = 3 V			2.5	V
h_{FE}*	DC Current Gain	I_C = 0.5 A I_C = 3 A	V_{CE} = 3 V V_{CE} = 3 V	1000 1000			

* Pulsed: Pulse duration = 300 μs, duty cycle < 2 %
For PNP types voltage and current values are negative.

3-Axis, ±2 *g*/±4 *g*/±8 *g*/±16 *g* Digital Accelerometer

Data Sheet **ADXL345**

FEATURES

- **Ultralow power: as low as 23 μA in measurement mode and 0.1 μA in standby mode at V_S = 2.5 V (typical)**
- **Power consumption scales automatically with bandwidth**
- **User-selectable resolution**
  - **Fixed 10-bit resolution**
  - **Full resolution, where resolution increases with *g* range, up to 13-bit resolution at ±16 *g* (maintaining 4 m*g*/LSB scale factor in all *g* ranges)**
- **Embedded memory management system with FIFO technology minimizes host processor load**
- **Single tap/double tap detection**
- **Activity/inactivity monitoring**
- **Free-fall detection**
- **Supply voltage range: 2.0 V to 3.6 V**
- **I/O voltage range: 1.7 V to V_S**
- **SPI (3- and 4-wire) and I^2C digital interfaces**
- **Flexible interrupt modes mappable to either interrupt pin**
- **Measurement ranges selectable via serial command**
- **Bandwidth selectable via serial command**
- **Wide temperature range (−40°C to +85°C)**
- **10,000 *g* shock survival**
- **Pb free/RoHS compliant**
- **Small and thin: 3 mm × 5 mm × 1 mm LGA package**

APPLICATIONS

- **Handsets**
- **Medical instrumentation**
- **Gaming and pointing devices**
- **Industrial instrumentation**
- **Personal navigation devices**
- **Hard disk drive (HDD) protection**

GENERAL DESCRIPTION

The ADXL345 is a small, thin, ultralow power, 3-axis accelerometer with high resolution (13-bit) measurement at up to ±16 *g*. Digital output data is formatted as 16-bit twos complement and is accessible through either a SPI (3- or 4-wire) or I^2C digital interface.

The ADXL345 is well suited for mobile device applications. It measures the static acceleration of gravity in tilt-sensing applications, as well as dynamic acceleration resulting from motion or shock. Its high resolution (3.9 m*g*/LSB) enables measurement of inclination changes less than 1.0°.

Several special sensing functions are provided. Activity and inactivity sensing detect the presence or lack of motion by comparing the acceleration on any axis with user-set thresholds. Tap sensing detects single and double taps in any direction. Free-fall sensing detects if the device is falling. These functions can be mapped individually to either of two interrupt output pins. An integrated memory management system with a 32-level first in, first out (FIFO) buffer can be used to store data to minimize host processor activity and lower overall system power consumption.

Low power modes enable intelligent motion-based power management with threshold sensing and active acceleration measurement at extremely low power dissipation.

The ADXL345 is supplied in a small, thin, 3 mm × 5 mm × 1 mm, 14-lead, plastic package.

FUNCTIONAL BLOCK DIAGRAM

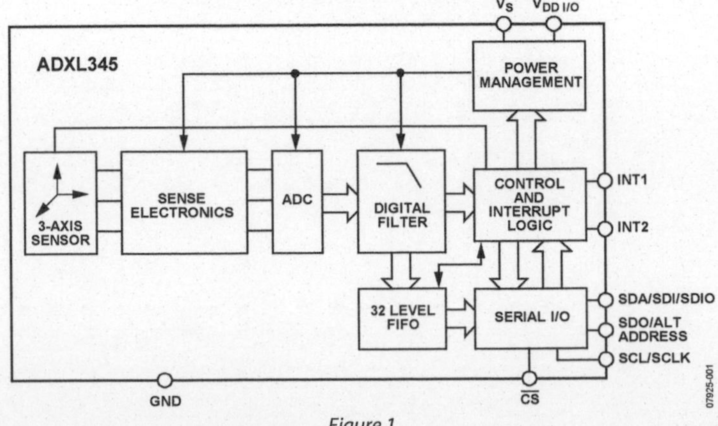

Figure 1.

Rev. E Document Feedback

One Technology Way, P.O. Box 9106, Norwood, MA 02062-9106, U.S.A.
Tel: 781.329.4700
Technical Support **www.analog.com**

SPECIFICATIONS

T_A = 25°C, V_S = 2.5 V, $V_{DD\ I/O}$ = 1.8 V, acceleration = 0 *g*, C_S = 10 µF tantalum, $C_{I/O}$ = 0.1 µF, output data rate (ODR) = 800 Hz, unless otherwise noted. All minimum and maximum specifications are guaranteed. Typical specifications are not guaranteed.

Table 1.

Parameter	Test Conditions	Min	Typ[1]	Max	Unit
SENSOR INPUT	Each axis				
Measurement Range	User selectable		±2, ±4, ±8, ±16		*g*
Nonlinearity	Percentage of full scale		±0.5		%
Inter-Axis Alignment Error			±0.1		Degrees
Cross-Axis Sensitivity[2]			±1		%
OUTPUT RESOLUTION	Each axis				
All *g* Ranges	10-bit resolution		10		Bits
±2 *g* Range	Full resolution		10		Bits
±4 *g* Range	Full resolution		11		Bits
±8 *g* Range	Full resolution		12		Bits
±16 *g* Range	Full resolution		13		Bits
SENSITIVITY	Each axis				
Sensitivity at X_{OUT}, Y_{OUT}, Z_{OUT}	All *g*-ranges, full resolution	230	256	282	LSB/*g*
	±2 *g*, 10-bit resolution	230	256	282	LSB/*g*
	±4 *g*, 10-bit resolution	115	128	141	LSB/*g*
	±8 *g*, 10-bit resolution	57	64	71	LSB/*g*
	±16 *g*, 10-bit resolution	29	32	35	LSB/*g*
Sensitivity Deviation from Ideal	All *g*-ranges		±1.0		%
Scale Factor at X_{OUT}, Y_{OUT}, Z_{OUT}	All *g*-ranges, full resolution	3.5	3.9	4.3	mg/LSB
	±2 *g*, 10-bit resolution	3.5	3.9	4.3	mg/LSB
	±4 *g*, 10-bit resolution	7.1	7.8	8.7	mg/LSB
	±8 *g*, 10-bit resolution	14.1	15.6	17.5	mg/LSB
	±16 *g*, 10-bit resolution	28.6	31.2	34.5	mg/LSB
Sensitivity Change Due to Temperature			±0.01		%/°C
0 *g* OFFSET	Each axis				
0 *g* Output for X_{OUT}, Y_{OUT}		−150	0	+150	mg
0 *g* Output for Z_{OUT}		−250	0	+250	mg
0 *g* Output Deviation from Ideal, X_{OUT}, Y_{OUT}			±35		mg
0 *g* Output Deviation from Ideal, Z_{OUT}			±40		mg
0 *g* Offset vs. Temperature for X-, Y-Axes			±0.4		mg/°C
0 *g* Offset vs. Temperature for Z-Axis			±1.2		mg/°C
NOISE					
X-, Y-Axes	ODR = 100 Hz for ±2 *g*, 10-bit resolution or all *g*-ranges, full resolution		0.75		LSB rms
Z-Axis	ODR = 100 Hz for ±2 *g*, 10-bit resolution or all *g*-ranges, full resolution		1.1		LSB rms
OUTPUT DATA RATE AND BANDWIDTH	User selectable				
Output Data Rate (ODR)[3, 4, 5]		0.1		3200	Hz
SELF-TEST[6]					
Output Change in X-Axis		0.20		2.10	*g*
Output Change in Y-Axis		−2.10		−0.20	*g*
Output Change in Z-Axis		0.30		3.40	*g*
POWER SUPPLY					
Operating Voltage Range (V_S)		2.0	2.5	3.6	V
Interface Voltage Range ($V_{DD\ I/O}$)		1.7	1.8	V_S	V
Supply Current	ODR ≥ 100 Hz		140		µA
	ODR < 10 Hz		30		µA
Standby Mode Leakage Current			0.1		µA
Turn-On and Wake-Up Time[7]	ODR = 3200 Hz		1.4		ms

ABSOLUTE MAXIMUM RATINGS

Table 2.

Parameter	Rating
Acceleration	
Any Axis, Unpowered	10,000 *g*
Any Axis, Powered	10,000 *g*
V_S	−0.3 V to +3.9 V
$V_{DD\ I/O}$	−0.3 V to +3.9 V
Digital Pins	−0.3 V to $V_{DD\ I/O}$ + 0.3 V or 3.9 V, whichever is less
All Other Pins	−0.3 V to +3.9 V
Output Short-Circuit Duration (Any Pin to Ground)	Indefinite
Temperature Range	
Powered	−40°C to +105°C
Storage	−40°C to +105°C

Stresses at or above those listed under Absolute Maximum Ratings may cause permanent damage to the product. This is a stress rating only; functional operation of the product at these or any other conditions above those indicated in the operational section of this specification is not implied. Operation beyond the maximum operating conditions for extended periods may affect product reliability.

THERMAL RESISTANCE

Table 3. Package Characteristics

Package Type	θ_{JA}	θ_{JC}	Device Weight
14-Terminal LGA	150°C/W	85°C/W	30 mg

PACKAGE INFORMATION

The information in Figure 2 and Table 4 provide details about the package branding for the ADXL345. For a complete listing of product availability, see the Ordering Guide section.

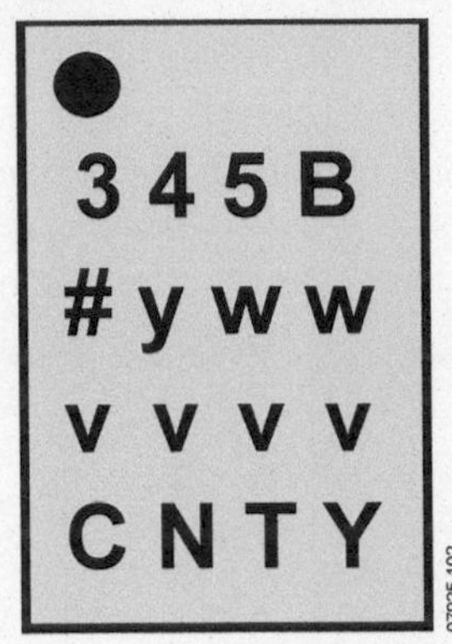

Figure 2. Product Information on Package (Top View)

Table 4. Package Branding Information

Branding Key	Field Description
345B	Part identifier for ADXL345
#	RoHS-compliant designation
yww	Date code
vvvv	Factory lot code
CNTY	Country of origin

ESD CAUTION

ESD (electrostatic discharge) sensitive device. Charged devices and circuit boards can discharge without detection. Although this product features patented or proprietary protection circuitry, damage may occur on devices subjected to high energy ESD. Therefore, proper ESD precautions should be taken to avoid performance degradation or loss of functionality.

THEORY OF OPERATION

The ADXL345 is a complete 3-axis acceleration measurement system with a selectable measurement range of ±2 *g*, ±4 *g*, ±8 *g*, or ±16 *g*. It measures both dynamic acceleration resulting from motion or shock and static acceleration, such as gravity, that allows the device to be used as a tilt sensor.

The sensor is a polysilicon surface-micromachined structure built on top of a silicon wafer. Polysilicon springs suspend the structure over the surface of the wafer and provide a resistance against forces due to applied acceleration.

Deflection of the structure is measured using differential capacitors that consist of independent fixed plates and plates attached to the moving mass. Acceleration deflects the proof mass and unbalances the differential capacitor, resulting in a sensor output whose amplitude is proportional to acceleration. Phase-sensitive demodulation is used to determine the magnitude and polarity of the acceleration.

POWER SEQUENCING

Power can be applied to V_S or $V_{DD\ I/O}$ in any sequence without damaging the ADXL345. All possible power-on modes are summarized in Table 6. The interface voltage level is set with the interface supply voltage, $V_{DD\ I/O}$, which must be present to ensure that the ADXL345 does not create a conflict on the communication bus. For single-supply operation, $V_{DD\ I/O}$ can be the same as the main supply, V_S. In a dual-supply application, however, $V_{DD\ I/O}$ can differ from V_S to accommodate the desired interface voltage, as long as V_S is greater than or equal to $V_{DD\ I/O}$.

After V_S is applied, the device enters standby mode, where power consumption is minimized and the device waits for $V_{DD\ I/O}$ to be applied and for the command to enter measurement mode to be received. (This command can be initiated by setting the measure bit (Bit D3) in the POWER_CTL register (Address 0x2D).) In addition, while the device is in standby mode, any register can be written to or read from to configure the part. It is recommended to configure the device in standby mode and then to enable measurement mode. Clearing the measure bit returns the device to the standby mode.

Table 6. Power Sequencing

Condition	V_S	$V_{DD\ I/O}$	Description
Power Off	Off	Off	The device is completely off, but there is a potential for a communication bus conflict.
Bus Disabled	On	Off	The device is on in standby mode, but communication is unavailable and creates a conflict on the communication bus. The duration of this state should be minimized during power-up to prevent a conflict.
Bus Enabled	Off	On	No functions are available, but the device does not create a conflict on the communication bus.
Standby or Measurement	On	On	At power-up, the device is in standby mode, awaiting a command to enter measurement mode, and all sensor functions are off. After the device is instructed to enter measurement mode, all sensor functions are available.

RoHS Compliant

Sense

Series 206/208

Through-Hole DIP Switch

- Available with SPST, SPDT, DPST, 3PST circuit choices
- Available with low profile, standard, or extended actuator heights. Consult the ordering information for options.
- RoHS compliant
- Optional top tape seal for board spray washing

Description

The terminals are molded into the thermoset base and provide an electrostatic discharge shield rating to 22KV when the OFF side terminals are connected to ground. The optimized contact design incorporating a dimple-to-flat surface wiping interface provides long-term contact corrosion resistance making this the ideal choice for any HVAC, server, or security system.

Ordering Information

Series	Number of Poles	Number of Throws	Number of Switch Positions	Actuator Height	Bottom Epoxy Seal	Top Tape Seal	Actuation Preset
206-/208 -	1	2	1	E	S	T	N

Number of Poles:

Code	No. of poles
Blank	For SPST
1	Single pole
2	Double pole
3	3 poles

Number of Throws:

Code	Spec.
Blank	For SPST
1	Single throw
2	Double throw

Number of Switch Positions:

Code	No. of switch positions
1	1 position
2	2 positions
3	3 positions
4	4 positions
5	5 positions
6	6 positions
7	7 positions
8	8 positions
9	9 positions
10	10 positions
12	12 positions

Actuator Height:

Code	Spec.
Blank	Standard (0.89mm/.035")
E	Extended (3.43mm/.135") (SPST only)
LP	Low profile (Flush) (SPST & SPDT only)

Bottom Epoxy Seal:

Code	Bottom epoxy seal
Blank	No epoxy seal
S	Epoxy seal (Required for 206-1S)

Top Tape Seal:

Code	Top tape seal
Blank	No top tape seal
T	Top tape seal (Not available for extended actuator or 1-position SPST DIP switch)

Actuation Preset:

Code	Spec.
BLANK	Ship at OFF position
N	Ship at ON position (SPST, DPST & 3PST only)

Notes: 1.Contact CTS for other common features not listed.

2. Not available in a Double Pole Double Throw (DPDT) construction

Mechanical Specifications

Figure 1 - SPST

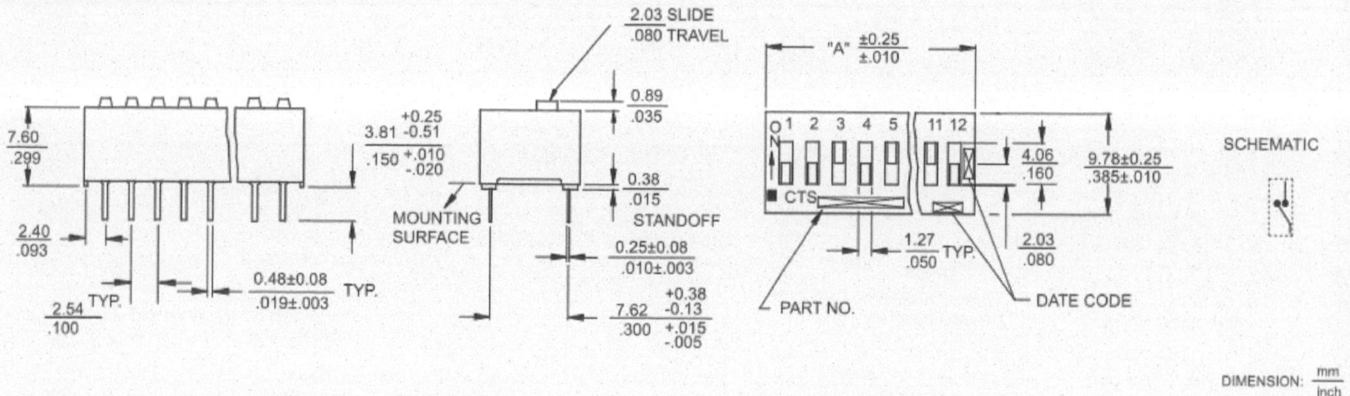

Figure 2 – SPDT

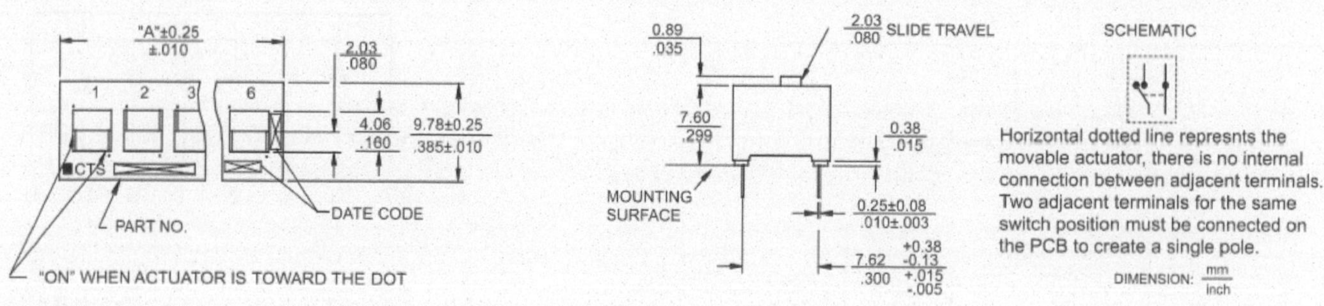

Figure 3 – DPST

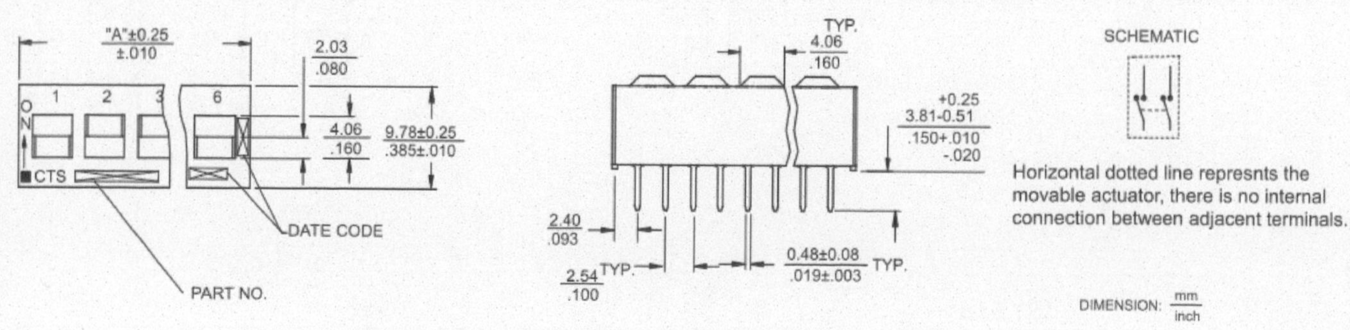

SEVEN SEGMENT DISPLAY INDICATORS
СЕМИСЕГМЕНТНЫЕ ИНДИКАТОРЫ

COMPONENT LABELING
СИСТЕМА ОБОЗНАЧЕНИЙ

Kingbright

S	5161	BS	SR
1	2	3	4

1. TYPE / 1. ТИП

(S) - single digit / один знак
PS - 16 seg. / сег.
D - two digits / два знака
PD - 2x 16 seg. / сег.
B - three digits / три знака
F - ±1
SB - single digit, two colors
один знак, два цвета

2. DIGIT SIZE / 2. РАЗМЕР ЗНАКА

Digit size in inches or fractions of an inch

Размер знака в дюймах или долях дюйма

3. CONNECTION / 3. ПОДКЛЮЧЕНИЕ

A/BS - common anode / общий анод
C - common cathode / общий катод
X - universal / универсальный

4. COLOR AND BRIGHTNESS / 4. ЦВЕТ СВЕЧЕНИЯ И ЯРКОСТЬ

H - red / красный
E - orange / оранжевый
G - green / зеленый
Y - yellow / желтый
SR - superbright red / красный суперяркий
SG - superbright green / зеленый суперяркий

(S) 5161A/BS / 5161C

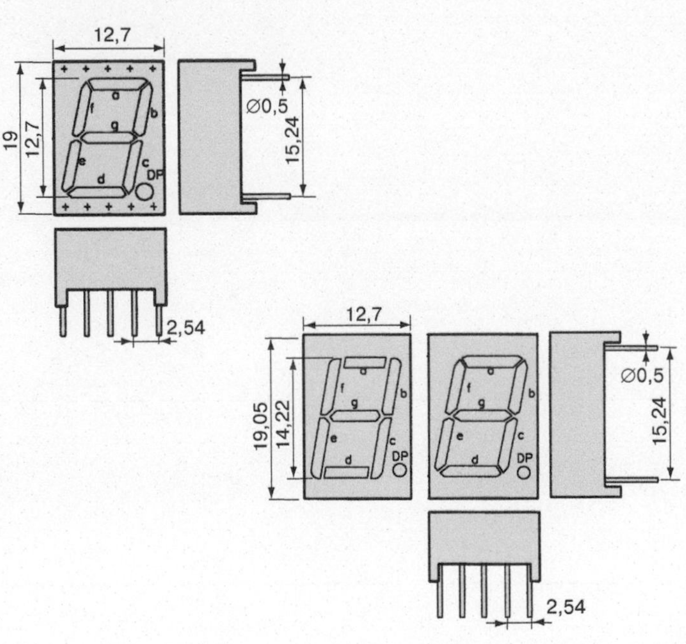

(S) 5161A/BS SCHEMATIC / CXEMA

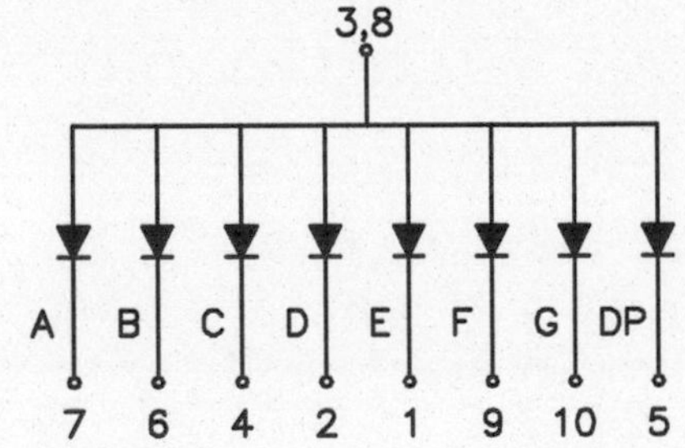

(S) 5161C SCHEMATIC / CXEMA

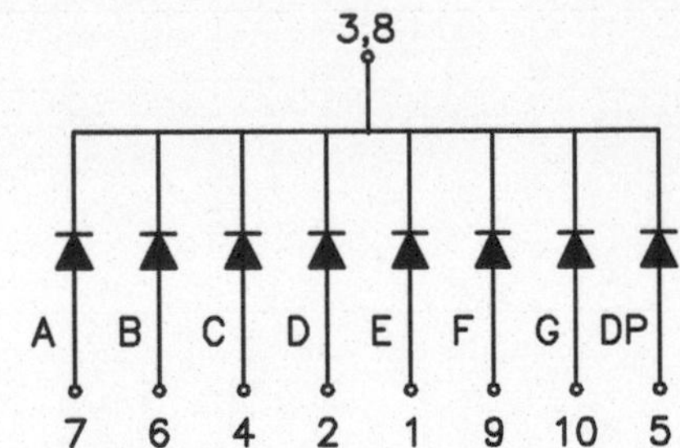

	a	b	c	d	e	f	g	DP	OA/O
(S) 5161	7	6	4	2	1	9	10	5	3,8

	a	b	c	d	e	f	g	DP	OA/O
(S) 5161A/BS	7	6	4	2	1	9	10	5	3,8
(S) 5161C	7	6	4	2	1	9	10	5	3,8

e-mail: sales@chipindustry.ru

Тел.: (095) 973-70-73 (многоканальный)